Kerry Kulkens

Guide to
Love, Sex
and your Stars

DREAMCORP
IMPROVEMENTS

First published in 1999
by Dreamcorp Improvements Pty Ltd
ACN 007 435 609
PO Box 7151,
St Kilda Road,
Melbourne, Victoria, Australia 3004

Produced by
Pacific Client Publishing
ACN 053 814 878
32 Walsh Street,
West Melbourne, Victoria, Australia 3003

National Library of Australia cataloguing-in-publication data:

Kulkens, Kerry.
Kerry Kulkens' guide to love, sex and your stars.

ISBN 0-9586404-0-8
ISBN 0-646-37202-5 (pbk.)

1. Astrology. 2. Occultism. I. Title. II. Title: Guide to love, sex and your stars.

133.5

Edited by Debbie Doyle (Living Proof — Book Editing)
Text and cover designed by Sarn Potter
Page make-up by SPG
Illustrations by Dominique Falla (Small Hours Studio)

Printed by
Canberra Press
ACN 051 748 282

foreword

I first met Kerry at her modest Belgrave shop early in 1979, having booked an appointment for a consultation. In those days I wasn't nearly as well known as I am now. The TV program *Prisoner* had only just started screening, but Kerry assured me I'd be an 'international star' before the year was out. How right she was: within a year, *Prisoner* was Australia's top-rating series, and – more to the point – was being viewed by thirty-nine million people in the United States. A big first for any Australian show!

Kerry went on to tell me I'd remarry (I was divorced at the time), that the wedding would be in a bluestone church, and that the groom would be a younger man. She was right on all three counts. She made many other predictions that have since proved to be accurate, and some I'm still waiting on.

Some people believe that astrology, tarot, numerology, witchcraft and so on are all bunk. I find it interesting to note how few of these people have ever made any sort of study of the practices and beliefs they so easily dismiss.

For those of us who believe there's more to life than what we can see and feel but who aren't involved in strictly observing a religion, people such as Kerry offer a spiritual oasis in an unforgiving world. What sets Kerry apart from many would-be soothsayers – and I believe there are many frauds out there – is her attitude. She has a gift that she uses not just to make a living but to help as many people as possible.

You have to respect Kerry's knowledge: she's a genuine expert in her field, having made a profound and lifelong study of everything to do with the occult. She seldom mixes her words, and she gets right down to business, sometimes to the point of seeming abrupt. Although her gift has brought her neither unbridled joy nor fabulous wealth, it's endured and helped many people, and for Kerry these are reward enough.

I like and trust Kerry, and I hope that reading this book brings you to a greater understanding of her and her craft.

Oh – I've just figured out why I was asked to write this foreword: because Kerry also told me I could sell sand to the Arabs, refrigerators to the Eskimos and humour to the Irish. But I already knew that!

Val Lehman

Contents

there's something about Kerry ...

Not many people know that Kerry is a trained psychiatric nurse as well as the eccentric white witch who provides psychic advice to a host of national and international celebrities and politicians. Her face is well known in Australia, especially in Victoria's picturesque Dandenong mountains, where she's regularly seen, broomstick in tow, running errands for her busy shop. Thousands of people visit her in a bid to find love and happiness. Her words of wisdom and her astrological interpretations have riveted people for more than thirty years because she's able to reveal the past, present and future with accuracy and in great detail.

Because she's dedicated years to practising witchcraft and to hand mixing her own speciality potions, she's a walking encyclopaedia for any subject related to the occult and witchcraft. She's appeared on most of Australia's popular TV shows, and her distinctive voice graces the airwaves for many top-rating talkback-radio programs.

Every year, Kerry releases her eagerly awaited predictions of events and natural disasters, which are widely published in Australia and New Zealand. In 1997, she was the only psychic who predicted that Australia would be plagued by massive food poisonings, which occurred that year, and that our drinking water would be contaminated, as happened in Sydney the following year. She even warned there'd be a tragic mining disaster, which sadly occurred in Newcastle only one week after she had her premonition. On a lighter note, she's also well known for picking the right lottery numbers!

You can purchase many of the ingredients and items mentioned in *Kerry Kulkens' Guide to Love, Sex and Your Stars* through Kerry's catalogue. To obtain a free copy of the *Kerry Kulkens Catalogue*, please send a letter of request, including your postal details, to: The Kerry Kulkens Catalogue
PO Box 78
Belgrave, Victoria, Australia 3160

Introduction

My name is Kerry Kulkens, and I'm a sixth-generation white witch and psychic. I've written this book in order to share with you the wisdom my family has accumulated through the ages. The wisdom is called magic. The magic I speak of is love, and the love is achieved by way of spells and astrology. My magic isn't black and doesn't call forth the dark forces; it enhances and enriches humankind.

It seems just like yesterday that I sat by my grandmother's side, spellbound by her accounts of the rich tapestry of life that was yet to unfold. My grandmother believed that my palm held much promise for success, and her green eyes glowed as she interpreted my tea leaves. I was mesmerised by her gift, and on that day I vowed to follow in her footsteps and to deliver her beliefs.

My grandmother told me of her life with the gypsies – the circle of people who are always on the move – and about their campfires and music. Her voice radiated with excitement as she remembered that whenever her people came to a new town, they'd dispense herbal medicine, read palms and entertain people.

My grandmother wasn't like other people. She spoke to spirits, and I vividly remember one spirit she was especially fond of: a Mrs Watts. Although she and Mrs Watts talked quite often, I witnessed only one conversation, because Gran was a very private lady. I remember seeing her face go pale when Mrs Watts told Gran that Gran would be joining her soon. I couldn't imagine living my life without having this snowy-haired woman of mystic dimensions by my side, guiding me and nurturing my psychic gift and love of witchcraft.

Gran died peacefully two weeks after having her last conversation with Mrs Watts. Among the few possessions she left me were books about magic and witchcraft, and notes about spells that had been handed down from her great-grandmother to her mother.

My father was a circus entertainer. During the Second World War when he was a soldier serving in France, a heavy tree fell on him. He escaped injury only because the ground was soft. Although the villagers said the incident was a miracle, my father simply smiled and said nothing: he knew deep down that a force from beyond was protecting him. He was a very spiritual man who kept to himself.

During the war years, he was often absent from home, and it was through my bond with him and my concern for his wellbeing on the battlefields that my psychic gift was realised. Whenever I thought of him and wished for him to make contact with us, we'd receive a letter from him. He'd often come to me in my dreams and tell me he was still alive.

When my father went to war and for many years after he returned, I was plagued by a recurring vision of a grey-faced man clutching his chest. It wasn't until after my father died of emphysema that I realised who that old man was: my father died clutching his chest.

My mother was a studious person and always seemed to have her head in a book. Just before she died, she told me she had to 'go to Queen Victoria'. At the time, I didn't know what she meant. However, on the day after her funeral, it all made sense: her great-granddaughter was born at Melbourne's Queen Victoria Memorial Hospital. Her great-granddaughter very much resembles my mother, and I believe my mother was born again through her great-granddaughter.

Today, it's hard to believe I'm surrounded by grandchildren who do the same thing with me as I did with my Gran. I only hope my words of wisdom see them through life safely and happily.

A few thankyous

My book has been made possible because of the inspiration and combined efforts of my husband Michael Kulkens, my family and my writing colleague Angie Kotzamichalis, who helped me find the words to communicate my knowledge.

A special thankyou goes to the talented creative-team members who worked tirelessly to create such a wonderful book.

I would especially like to thank you, the reader, for taking some time out of your precious life to read this book.

Blessed Be.

ASTROLOGY

Understanding astrology

Astrology is considered to be the world's oldest celestial science. Since the earliest times, star gazing has been a part of people's life. People marked the seasonal changes according to the longest and shortest day and according to the times when night and day were the same length. They used this method to devise a simple calendar for hunting and planting, and they also noted the position or state of the sun or moon at the time of significant events.

People soon realised that specific sky phenomena coincided with specific earthly events. The parallels eventually came to be viewed as omens, and the members of each tribe embellished their own myths to suit their view of the world. The heavens gradually became replete with fables about gods, demons and heroes, and this complex hierarchy of celestial beings watched, judged and manipulated people's life.

As civilisations evolved and the body of knowledge grew, the earliest astrologers kept meticulous calendars and more-complete records of celestial movements. The most convenient way of studying the stars was to connect their groups into the recognisable patterns we now call constellations. The sky was thereby divided into twelve segments, each of which represented its own constellation. People also noted that the planets often seemed to wander through the sky against this constellation backdrop.

THE PLANETS

The planets eventually acquired their own personality and mythology, and astrologers soon began to affix significance to the planets' position against specific constellations. The night sky was like a grand soap opera in which gods and goddesses played out their dramas and the consequences were manifested on earth by way of droughts, floods and other natural occurrences.

Throughout the centuries, astrologers have charted and interpreted celestial objects' cycles and movements. They deal with the planets, eight of which are Earth's sister planets: Mercury, Venus, Mars, Jupiter, Saturn, Uranus, Neptune and Pluto. Neither of the other two 'planets', the Sun and the Moon, is actually a planet, because a planet circles the sun.

Astrologers are interested in where each planet can be found on the 'track' and where the planets are with reference to each other. They use the twelve signs of the zodiac – the 'star signs' – to describe the planets' positions, and they use the aspects to describe the relationship between the planets. The planets represent the energies that drive our physical, emotional, mental and institutional systems. The energies manifest differently, depending on the planets' position in the signs of the zodiac. Various signs channel the energies into various behaviour patterns, which are then recognised as personality traits.

In the zodiac, the twelve star signs are divided into categories. The first category is the *modes*, and the second is the *elements*.

THE MODES

The three *modes* are *cardinal*, *fixed* and *mutable*. The four *cardinal-mode* star signs are Aries, Cancer, Libra and Capricorn. The four *fixed-mode* star signs are Taurus, Leo, Scorpio and Aquarius. The four *mutable-mode* star signs are Gemini, Virgo, Sagittarius and Pisces. People born under the cardinal mode are motivators and like to get things moving. People born under the fixed mode are immovable, don't like change and are persistent and stubborn. People born under the mutable mode are often changeable, tend to follow a zig-zag course through life and are flexible but inconsistent.

CARDINAL	FIXED	MUTABLE
Aries ♈	Taurus ♉	Virgo ♍
Cancer ♋	Leo ♌	Gemini ♊
Libra ♎	Scorpio ♏	Sagittarius ♐
Capricorn ♑	Aquarius ♒	Pisces ♓

THE ELEMENTS

The four *elements* are *fire*, *earth*, *air* and *water*. The *fire* element controls Aries, Leo and Sagittarius. Fire represents go-getters who literally burn with energy and activity. These people's drawback is that they use other people as their fuel and therefore leave people destroyed behind them.

The *earth* element controls Taurus, Virgo and Capricorn. As the name suggests, earth represents very earthy people who are solid and reliable and whose word is their bond. These people are very practical but sometimes indelicate. Their faults are that they aren't enterprising and they can't see far enough ahead.

The *air* element controls Gemini, Libra and Aquarius. Air represents people who are guided by the air. These people have great ideas, are quite sociable and try to change their environment. Their main fault is that they can talk a lot of hot air.

The *water* element controls Cancer, Scorpio and Pisces. Water represents people who tend to be a bit secretive and mysterious. These people are very respectful of other people's ideas and feelings, are very sensitive and tend to pick up their environment's atmosphere. Their main drawback is that they can be drippy and wishy-washy.

EARTH	FIRE	AIR	WATER
Capricorn ♑	Aries ♈	Libra ♎	Cancer ♋
Taurus ♉	Leo ♌	Aquarius ♒	Scorpio ♏
Virgo ♍	Sagittarius ♐	Gemini ♊	Pisces ♓

Finding love through astrology

When it comes to finding our ideal partner, most of us would like to wave a magic wand and have the lover of our dreams materialise. Because astrology is dedicated to promoting deeper harmony in human affairs, it's the closest thing to a wand you'll get. More often than not, it'll be through astrology that you're given an accurate guide to the partner who'll best suit your needs.

Who do you have in mind? A lover to set your senses reeling? A friend to confide in and respect your revelations? A business partner? A good marriage partner? A good provider? An intellectual or a poet? Finding your partner through astrology is a sensible way of avoiding the pitfalls associated with random choice. Mind you, if pitfalls are what you're looking for, at least you'll know where to find them!

If you want a bit of spice in your love life, an Arien or Gemini will have a lighthearted approach. If it's quantity you're after, a Cancerian will go the distance. If a serious affair is your heart's desire, a Taurean or Cancerian will suit you. If you can handle constantly dishing out flattery and playing a willing slave to a heavy-handed master, go for a Leo lover.

If you want a clean, healthy and efficient lifestyle, plant a Virgoan in your bedroom. A Libran will strive for harmony and companionship in your marriage. If you crave simple eroticism to satisfy your sexual fantasies, a Scorpion might be what you need, and he or she will want a perfect blending of mind and body. A Sagittarian will hunt you down and then not know what to do with you.

All Sagittarians think they invented sex, and they can't wait to flaunt their sexuality.

Your Capricornian will be the master of his or her own art, will take you to the height of ecstasy and won't dim with age. Watch out for Aquarians: they're the sultans of sex. You'll think your Aquarian will try to talk you into something for the good of your soul – then he or she will try and get you into bed. A Piscean will want an artistic environment to match his or her personality and can be very loving with the right mate.

Reading about the divorce rate for each star sign might help you decide whether or not your lover is a good risk. Taureans have the highest divorce rate, followed by Ariens, Geminis and Pisceans. Virgoans and Librans have a lower divorce rate, and the partners for keeping you in the style you yearn for are Cancerians, Scorpions and Pisceans – preferably not all at the same time!

A brief description of each star sign

ARIES   21 March – 20 April

Ariens are impulsive, spur-of-the-moment people. They're always trying to prove they're better than other people and trying to improve on their last performance. They seem to be tireless and tend to be a bit self-centred and egotistical. They easily get fired up about an idea but can also lose interest very quickly. Like the ram, they keep butting in. They aren't very tactful, and they're prone to losing their temper when they're with slow, indecisive people.

TAURUS   21 April – 20 May

Taureans, as their element earth suggests, are down-to-earth, practical people who like the comforts of life. They want to have a solid family life and don't have their head in the clouds. They prefer to have solid, genuine friendships and can be very generous. They have an affinity with the land and are possessive, conservative and dependable. They can sometimes seem to be too pleased with themselves.

GEMINI   21 May – 21 June

Geminis never seem to grow up: they stay young at heart. They're very changeable and restless, are extremely talkative and seem to have a split personality. They can get out of a difficult situation simply by talking. They seem to have a flair for languages and are usually good at journalism or TV compering.

CANCER   22 June – 22 July

Cancerians have a strong imagination and are kind and sensitive. They have a strong 'mother hen' instinct. They're shrewd and good at homemaking, but they can also be overly emotional, overly sensitive, moody and self-pitying. They're also easily flattered and rather untidy.

LEO   23 July – 22 August

Leos are generous, creative, broadminded, ostentatious and good at organising. On the negative side, though, they can be dogmatic, intolerant, tyrannical, self-opinionated and pompous.

VIRGO   23 August – 23 September

Virgoans are discriminating and precise to the point of being obsessed with being exact, neat and tidy. They're modest when successful, and they can be rather finicky and hard to please. They're born to worry.

LIBRA   24 September – 23 October

Librans are charming, romantic, refined and fond of the nice things in life. They can also be a bit too idealistic and tactful. They're also indecisive, and they like to flirt, trifle and see-saw through relationships. Other people influence them very much.

SCORPIO   24 October – 22 November

Scorpions have strong feelings and are rather emotional. They're very imaginative and purposeful. They can be insidious at times and keep greatness in sight. They can also be jealous, stubborn, vengeful, secretive and anything but docile.

SAGITTARIUS   23 November – 20 December

Sagittarians are optimistic, broadmined and tolerant and can at times be philosophical. They're very moralistic, they have sound judgement, and they're sincere and scrupulous. On the negative side, they can be radical, overly optimistic, noisy, irresponsible, careless and tactless.

CAPRICORN   21 December – 19 January

Capricornians are dependable, cautious, ambitious and determined. They have a great sense of humour and are patient and persevering. On the negative side, they see things in only black and white: there are no shades in between. They can also be pessimistic and conservative and a bit of a 'wet blanket' at times.

AQUARIUS   20 January – 19 February

Aquarians are independent and humanitarian people.

They're friendly, loyal, idealistic and progressive and have an inventive mind. On the negative side, they can be moody and contrary. They can be tactless at the worst of times as well as quite perverse.

PISCES   20 February – 20 March

Pisceans are modest, compassionate, tolerant and understanding and can be quite impressionable and easily influenced. They can also be vague, secretive and scatterbrained, and at times they border on the impractical.

What your birthday says about you

The day of the month on which you were born can tell you a lot about your personality. A person born on the first, for example, will differ very much from a person born on the second or the thirty-first. Find which day you, your partner and your friends were born on and see whether the description rings true.

THE FIRST

Love is important for you: you love to be in love. However, you don't always choose wisely, and you won't stop looking for the most satisfying love. Sex and romance play an important part when you're selecting a love partner. If you don't find a partner who's on your level spiritually, you go for the next-best person. If you do find your perfect match, you're inclined to hang on a bit too much.

THE SECOND

It's sometimes very hard for people to get you to talk and express your thoughts, and your loved ones are sometimes at a loss when they don't know what you want. For you, love isn't thunder and lightning; it's passive and serene. You also have a tendency to be suspicious of your mate and to therefore ruin a good thing. You love to dress up and look nice for the person you've chosen, and you expect him or her to do the same.

THE THIRD

Although you're very interested in sexual love, you seem to have a shy streak and find it hard to communicate your feelings to your lover. He or she mightn't appreciate it when you have a confidential discussion with your best friend. The person you choose is quiet, and you like to keep your lovemaking and life the same, because privacy is often important for you in order to keep the flame burning.

THE FOURTH

You're a practical and naturally cautious person, so you should look for a special person to be your lover. Your deep sexual passion could sometimes lead you to go for someone who has nothing in common with you. Although in a sombre moment you're ambitious and you look for quality, when passion blinds you, you can't seem to see straight.

THE FIFTH

Your sexuality isn't very obvious. You and your colleagues born on the fifth are very complex and come in many disguises. You're very jealous of other people's possessions, and you want to keep your loved one close to you. However, this doesn't rule out a bit of infidelity if the opportunity arises. This quality could be called selfishness: taking all and giving nothing.

THE SIXTH

You're independent and demanding, and you want to make your own rules about love and sex. You're also romantic one moment and very sensual the next. People usually find you to be interesting and worth chasing. Although you love to be loved, you shy away from someone who's planning to hem you in. You don't like too much drama in your love life, because you believe that true feelings can be shown in a dignified way.

THE SEVENTH

Although you like life and people and you love to have fun, very few people meet your high standards: friends, yes; lovers, no. You're very demanding of the lover you really want: he or she has to be on your intellectual level, pursue your artistic interests and be able to converse brilliantly with you about subjects that interest you.

THE EIGHTH

You believe in knights in shining armour and beautiful maidens in chastity belts.

For you, love is romance and dreams, and if sex comes, it has to be pure and clean. However, your feelings are as strong as most people's, and in this very sexually 'upfront' age, you find you're confused. Oddly, you find you get very tired of your 'pure poet' lover and that you wish for a more earthy person with whom to share your bed.

THE NINTH

People born on the ninth love to 'flaunt it': the females have a penchant for wearing clothes that reveal various bodily parts, and the males love to wear open-neck shirts that reveal their macho chest. You're openly sexual, and you love getting a lot of attention. If you aren't happy in a relationship, you move on. You prefer having many lovers to being loyal to one person, and you have a tendency to hurt people because of your very casual and selfish attitude.

THE TENTH

You're very romantic, 'full of love' and the original 'mother hen' type. You care about and want your loved ones around you, and you rue the day your children go out into the world. You work hard at your own life and usually end up being very happily married. You usually have a big family and love every moment of family life. You're also a great organiser.

THE ELEVENTH

You're well versed in rules and regulations, and you expect your friends to be the same; you find it quite distasteful if they aren't. Your love life also has to follow the rules: boy meets girl, boy woos girl, and so on. Nothing shakes you in maintaining your ideals. Love and sex are very serious matters for you, and you wouldn't dream of making fun of them.

THE TWELFTH

This is the day of shipboard romances, little flirtations, and fun and games. However, when you do find the right person, you're usually very faithful. Marriage won't stop you from gathering admirers, and you're very happy to have a few, but they don't usually make you stray. Love and sex are important for you, and you look carefully for the right partner.

THE THIRTEENTH

You have a very practical mind but usually bend under pressure. Although you even look like a person whose last thought is sex, you think about sex quite often. Because you have a sound mind, you usually choose a good partner and stay with him or her for a long time, even if your marriage doesn't meet your expectations. You usually compromise and stay with it, though.

THE FOURTEENTH

If you didn't worry as much, you'd really enjoy your love life. A regular commitment doesn't interest you, and if you ever do think about marriage, it's usually as being something that happens for other people. You aren't obsessed with sex and can go for long periods without thinking about it. You're prone to suffer from day-to-day worrying about the practical things in life.

THE FIFTEENTH

You change your mind so often that getting your own way becomes second nature to you. Although you like love and sex, you can never decide who's the right person for you. Because you love parties and entertainment, you hate settling into a humdrum life, either at work or in marriage. You don't believe in fidelity and therefore don't make a very good marriage prospect.

THE SIXTEENTH

You're vague and moody, so you often confuse people: they don't know whether to interpret you as being sensual, romantic or serious. You also aren't that interested in sex – only at times. You often hurt your friends and lovers, because they take your moods personally.

THE SEVENTEENTH

Your love-and-sex life is very strong, and your personality usually conveys the fact. Although you love to entertain and to have a good time, you aren't very discreet about your lovers. You could find yourself left out of some fun times because of your non-caring attitude and your very often acid tongue.

THE EIGHTEENTH

Because you're a very private person and a bit shy, you don't like people to know about your love life, even though there's usually nothing to hide. You're a very perceptive person, you often choose your partner for life, and you remain very happily faithful. You're also interested in your lover's working life and prospects.

THE NINETEENTH

You're sensible in knowing you have to have time to look around before settling, so you don't commit yourself when you first meet someone you fancy. You're very demanding in love and marriage, and only the very best partner satisfies you. Sex is important and should always be available for you, because you don't like to have to wait to be noticed.

THE TWENTIETH

Because you aren't very easily understood, you encounter some problems when communicating your wishes to your lover. You're also very slowly aroused, and you miss opportunities as a result of being hesitant. What you really wish to have is a friend and lover in one, and when you find him or her, you're a gentle and considerate lover.

THE TWENTY-FIRST

You trust your luck much too often: use your head a bit more, and don't fall for the obvious traps that thrillseekers set. You're an incurable romantic who believes that a beautiful mind lies behind only a beautiful face. Because you also like to engage in light, flirty talk and frothy conversation, don't be surprised when people take you for a lightweight.

THE TWENTY-SECOND

Because you're a very ambitious person, you make sure you have security before starting to look for love. You often find your lover at your workplace: perhaps it's your boss or a budding politician. If you're a male, you could marry the boss's daughter and end up owning the business. You accept nothing but the best, and you trust that sex and love will come to you in good time.

THE TWENTY-THIRD

You're an interesting and fun person, so you get a bit bored when you're with dull, boring people. You usually leave a relationship in which you're not getting your fair share of fun. You're able to love and leave a person as often as you see fit. People you really care for might think of you as being unreliable, which is something you don't want to be.

THE TWENTY-FOURTH

You have a tendency to take all and give nothing, because you're either scared of being hurt or simply selfish. However, really loving someone requires give and take. You and your colleagues born on the twenty-fourth are often beautiful people, have lots of friends and cultivate specific attitudes towards the opposite sex; sincerity isn't one of them.

THE TWENTY-FIFTH

Although you're mysterious and hard to understand, you're very sure of yourself, so you usually get what you want. When you're a teenager you usually get into trouble with your parents, but when you're mature you settle down happily. You and your colleagues born on the twenty-fifth either marry or have children late; otherwise, you stay happily single and without children. Because your sex life develops slowly, you could remain alone.

THE TWENTY-SIXTH

You aren't very reliable in relationships, and you love to have fun and entertain. Because you have very strong but shortlived sexual encounters, you're often left alone for long periods. You love to play the field and are probably very untrustworthy as a marriage partner.

THE TWENTY-SEVENTH

When you're very young and in your teens you have many admirers and friends, and you often find it hard to pick the wolf from the sheep. You do use people, though, especially for entertainment and fun. You find it too hard to cultivate any really strong feeling about someone special. The one redeeming thing about your emotional life is that as you grow older you become more reliable.

THE TWENTY-EIGHTH

You love to be the star of the show and usually get yourself into some kind of limelight. You don't mind breaking a few hearts on your way to stardom, and you have very strong ideas about the one and only who'll eventually replace all your fans. Because you're good looking, it's a bit hard for people to find the real you underneath all that glamour.

THE TWENTY-NINTH

You're one of the most undomesticated people of all, and you actually hate the idea of settling down. You're often very hard on your lover, and when somebody else is on the horizon, you discard the original person for usually trivial reasons. Your wish to be secure might be your only motivation for ever marrying, and you remain single at heart forever.

THE THIRTIETH

You usually realise that anything good is worth working for, so when you marry you usually take the situation seriously and make it work. Although your sex life isn't very strong, you expect a relationship to be pleasant and longlasting. Because you're a bit stubborn, your partner might sometimes find you hard to please.

THE THIRTY-FIRST

You have too much hesitation in your life, so go on and let yourself enjoy life. If you're the marrying type, don't pretend you're Bachelor of the Year: someone always meets your expectations. You're a hard worker, so make sure you get enough rest and also have some fun. For you, sex is usually what you wish to make of it.

10

THE WITCHES' DAYS OF THE WEEK

Monday's witch has evil eyes;

Tuesday's witch attracts the flies;

Wednesday's witch is foul of mouth;

Thursday's witch is full of louse;

Friday's witch is big of nose;

Saturday's witch has fourteen toes;

But the witch born on Sunday

Has a horrible smell, So keep well away!

If you're born on the cusp

At your time of birth, the position of the eight planets other than Earth, and of the Sun and the Moon, has a lot to do with the way in which you'll live your life. However, I advise people born on the 'cusp' – the border of two sun signs – to have their natal chart drawn up in order to enable them to make use of the good points they can expect to inherit from their two cusp signs.

I believe each sign has a seven-day cusp that commences on the nineteenth and finishes on the twenty-fifth day of each month. All people born on the cusp are more flexible and talented, and a wider range of opportunities is open to them. Let's find out how your nature is affected if you're born on one of the twelve cusps.

THE ARIES-TAURUS CUSP
19–25 April

You plan well, work intensely and are able to speedily use inspiration when it arises. Although you like to be at the top, you work towards your goals slowly. You also have great confidence in yourself, real sparkle in your character and a lot of energy.

You have many loyal friends who very much enjoy your companionship. You love to entertain and are very generous. You sort out what you want from what you don't want, and you keep all detrimental influences out of your life.

THE TAURUS-GEMINI CUSP
19–25 May

You're creative, you have active energies and you're very sociable. Your mind is always busy. You're also very talented in the arts. You're very down to earth and always looking ahead. When a critical set of circumstances demands it, you can be very energetic.

You like to associate with only intelligent friends and family members, and you delight in entertaining. You never let anyone talk you into anything, because you insist on studying a matter well before you make a decision. People are always asking you for advice because they know they can trust you.

THE GEMINI-CANCER CUSP
19–25 June

You're a fascinating person, because you're both intellectual and emotional. You're inclined to be interchangeable in liking both an active and a domestic life.

Although you develop your talents very well and are good at anything you attempt, if something doesn't go as planned you lose interest fast.

You might be extremely lucky at having big-money wins. You enjoy talking, and you love to be the centre of attention. You're noted for your hospitality and your unique ideas for parties. You seem to adjust well to circumstances but might have some emotional strife in your life.

THE CANCER-LEO CUSP
19–25 July

Although you're very organised when it comes to family and home matters, you also love to have an easygoing outdoor life. You have to learn how to show your emotions a bit more, because bottling up your dreams and wishes isn't good for your health.

You're loyal to the end, and you might be much too generous for your own good. Join active and lively groups, especially drama or dance ones. You're pure hearted but inclined to take people at face value.

THE LEO-VIRGO CUSP
19–25 August

You submit everything to reason and logic and plan your life very well. In your romantic life you love a clean environment, and you don't marry until you're sure you've found the partner who'll give you a stable home and fulfil your ideals of intellectual companionship.

You might have an amazing career, and you can be very generous with money when your sympathies are aroused. You tend to choose your friends from among solid and constructive people.

THE VIRGO–LIBRA CUSP
19–25 September

You tend to be a perfectionist, so much so that you antagonise people and fail to win their affection. You have a highly developed creative talent that you might use in an unusual and successful career. You demand too much of both yourself and other people.

You have to have a very active social life in order to satisfy the Libran side of your nature. Your quest for the perfect marriage can cause you inner troubles. You like to be consulted about both major and minor problems. Although you give good advice, you can't accept good advice.

THE LIBRA–SCORPIO CUSP
19–25 October

You're a deeply emotional and very complex person whose charm makes you magnetic to other people. You're very artistic, especially when it comes to persuading people about your beliefs. You're very careful with money, and you don't like to spend it.

Socially, you're very much in demand. You avoid whatever is unpleasant and unattractive and seek the best in everything, including people. You can be snobbish and swift to discard people you believe don't come up to the standard you've set.

THE SCORPIO–SAGITTARIUS CUSP
19–25 November

Daily life can be very demanding for you because your emotions and enthusiasm run strong. Your imagination might be responsible for losing you a love affair, because you always seem to imagine the worst. Learn to keep your emotions under control.

You love to travel, and you crave philosophical and spiritual wisdom. Only your emotions can tear you down, which makes romantic involvement a bit too easy for you. You have good fortune and can swiftly recoup any loss or failure. You're highly intelligent and able to gain profit from trouble.

THE SAGITTARIUS–CAPRICORN CUSP
19–25 December

You work tirelessly towards your aims and get real pleasure from steering towards big success. You're interested in people and events, and you have a bit of bad luck in romance because you have high ambitions and don't change yourself for anyone. You can do anything you set your mind to.

Getting rich quick appeals to you very much, so you like taking risks. You enjoy having a good social life as well as attending big gatherings, eating fine dinners and going to lively dances. You therefore balance your work schedule with your heavy schedule based on seeking pleasure and maintaining many friendships.

THE CAPRICORN–AQUARIUS CUSP
19–25 January

Your nature is very difficult for you and other people to cope with: you're constantly at war with yourself over matters to do with your big ambitions. Because you need to have a secure life and you're deeply emotional, you're lured into a marriage that's likely to last.

You have a very independent attitude towards life and people and are too generous with your money. However, when you go broke you bounce back quickly. You like to have many friends, to have a good social life and to give service in many directions. You might use your good sense to contribute much to your community by way of undertaking good works in order to improve it.

THE AQUARIUS–PISCES CUSP
19–25 February

You're a very bright and happy person. You usually aren't emotional and tend to turn away whenever emotions threaten to take over. You're a dreamer rather than a realist. Avoid being by yourself too much: get out more and have a fuller social life.

You probably get very involved with the occult. Although spiritual matters attract you very much, you have to balance the spiritual with the logical. Never let yourself become skewed in one direction. You very likely lead a dedicated life in which serving people is the highest aim.

THE PISCES–ARIES CUSP
19–25 March

You're an aggressive dreamer: you tend to put your inspired ideas to use and to make way for yourself in the world. You're peace loving, and you like to have the newest thing in appliances and cars. You're a very impatient person, and your impatience can defeat you if you aren't willing to work towards your goals a bit more steadily.

You have a great personality, if only you'd show it off. You want to have a wonderful marriage and home so you can believe you've attained ideal love. You also expect too much from your loved ones and children.

Living with each star sign

It's said that you don't truly know someone until you live with him or her. Unfortunately, so many people find living together to be so unbearable that they no longer speak to each other, let alone stay married. In public, however, most of us try to remain on our best behaviour because we want to impress everyone who sees and knows us.

What are we really like at home, though? There might be contrasts between the household members. Even people who claim they never change notice marked differences when they live with someone. Before you take the plunge, read the following description about what to expect from each star sign.

ARIES

Ariens love to get up before sunrise: they believe that 'Early to bed; early to rise' is the best way to go. They like to leave early and to get to their destination before anybody else does, and they can't tolerate waiting or standing in a queue. If you enjoy having peace and quiet, don't live with an Arien: you haven't experienced noise until you've heard an Arien cooking in the kitchen. You won't get to use the bathroom first – or anything else, for that matter.

Get used to hearing your Arien housemate gargling and blowing his or her nose every morning and often during the day. He or she will also tell you what the rules are and will insist you obey them. However, Ariens have a marvellous knack of excluding themselves from observing any regulations that might limit them when they don't want to be limited. They might be fanatical about exercise and will want you to join them in maintaining good health.

TAURUS

A Taurean is the person for you if you like to have a relaxed home life. Taureans are very difficult to wake in the morning because they love their sleep. You'll no doubt get used to cleaning up their mess and picking up after them. Where your Taurean housemate has been, you might find food and partly finished drinks lying around. You'll have to be very patient with him or her, because he or she isn't all that easy to live with.

If you're lucky, you won't be totally responsible for doing all the laundry and cleaning for you and your Taurean.

If you bring home anything special to eat, devour it right away or you won't even get to taste it. Taureans are always late, and there's no point complaining: they won't change their ways. They won't change one habit for love, money or anything else. However, if they have money they're generous with it.

GEMINI

If you enjoy telephones ringing, radios and stereos blaring and non-stop chattering, you'll love living with a Gemini. There's never a dull moment with Geminis. You'd better not be nervous, because they have abundant nervous energy for both you and them. They move around constantly and don't keep still for very long.

Geminis love to travel anywhere. If they don't have transport and you do, you'll soon find you have to ask them for permission to use your own car. They always have something to say and have lots of unfinished projects lying around.

CANCER

If you like to have breakfast in bed and to have everything done for you, you'll love living with a Cancerian. However, I don't mean to mislead you: Cancerians aren't always great to live with. They love to be appreciated, so if you like to cook and are good at cooking, keep them happy by occasionally returning the favour and bringing them a meal in bed. Get used to their funny little habits, because you might find yourself adopting their ways.

You'll either like or grow to like their family members, who are always welcome to stay as long as they wish, so you might have to get used to bedding down on the floor. If you're a good housekeeper, you'll rate highly with your Cancerian housemate. You also have to be careful what you say to Cancerians, because they're easily hurt. Get used to their low moods that can cause them to become despondent.

LEO

Leos are proud of both their home and the people in it. If you don't or can't conduct yourself in a way so as to deserve their approval, you'll be made to feel uncomfortable every moment you live with them. Either be prepared to live up to their expectations or don't bother living together. Your Leo housemate will expect you to be well dressed and well groomed before you can go out with him or her. Leos also don't like it if you mope around the house poorly dressed.

If you know neither how to compliment nor how to brag, you'd do well to get in some practice: Leos have to be continually reassured by the people closest to them. Get used to their tall stories that make them look good, because you'll hear the stories very frequently. Leos will also expect you to entertain elegantly at times.

VIRGO

You have to be almost perfect in order to live with a Virgoan. It'll be easier if you don't smoke, but if you do, you'll have to promptly empty and clean your ashtray. Clean your feet before entering the home, put your dirty clothes in the laundry basket, hang your clothes up and wash each dirty dish or knife after use – and whatever you do, don't put something back in the wrong spot. Clean the bathroom after each use and make your own bed as soon as you get out of it.

Although these small requirements will keep your Virgoan housemate happy for a while, other little chores will be required of you the longer you live together. Be prepared to have your faults pointed out, along with how to correct them. Remember that you mightn't have to do a lot of housework, though, because your Virgoan will clean constantly.

LIBRA

In order to live with Librans, you have to either learn to appreciate what they call art or be willing to try. Be prepared to listen to music, especially classical pieces, around the clock. Although Librans aren't really hung up on cleanliness, they want everything to be neat and tidy. Make sure your bedspread hangs over the mattress neatly all round and that the towels are neatly placed on their rack. Never rearrange a room without obtaining your Libran house-mates' approval, and never redecorate their room or apartment, because they fancy themselves as being the redecorating expert.

Their taste might be anything but good, and don't become irritated when they alternate from one side of an issue to the other. One day they'll be all for something, the next day against it. Just remember that their yes can also mean no and that their no can also mean yes. Learn to give them both time and the benefit of the doubt. If you're tactful, your opinion might be of some use to them – although they'll never admit it.

SCORPIO

Scorpions aren't well known for either their neat home or their neat appearance.

Therefore, if you're used to living in a messy home or you don't really care about neatness, a Scorpion will be your sort of housemate. Scorpions' surroundings usually have a thrown-together look. They don't believe in maintaining spic-and-span cleanliness: rough enough is good enough. To make your living together easier, simply pile what you need where you can find it. Once or twice a year, though, be prepared for a complete house clean-out, because when Scorpions do clean they mean clean.

Scorpions also like to be totally comfortable at home, so you'd better not be overly modest: when you come home, you might find them either completely or partly nude in front of the TV. Be prepared to share everything with them, including your underwear. You can have some good times with them, however, because they like to do almost anything that feels good.

SAGITTARIUS

If you plan to live with a Sagittarian, you'll soon know it's necessary for him or her to have space, both literally and figuratively. Don't feel you can get away with cluttering up the home environment. Never bother your Sagittarian housemate with petty details: you have to be either willing or able to take care of paying the rent, buying the groceries and preparing the meals. This doesn't mean you'll have any money, though, and you won't be encouraged to talk about everyday things such as the weather and Mrs Rafferty up the road. However, if you wish to debate or discuss religious or philosophical issues, your Sagittarian will be a willing conversation partner.

Because Sagittarians also like long-distance travel, you'll have to be willing to travel with them: nothing pleases them more than getting away. Be prepared for the travel stories, slides and photos they like to share, and be ready to go out on the town at a minute's notice. Get used to being home alone, because Sagittarians lose track of the time and you'll be left at home wondering where they are. Remember that you won't get away with fencing them in.

CAPRICORN

If you want to live with a Capricornian, be warned that he or she has only one real love: his or her career and business. Capricornians will constantly ask for your support in their reaching the top of the career ladder. Be prepared to socialise in the best of company, whether or not the company appeals to you. Your Capricornian housemate will probably want you to dress up and put on a good show, mainly in order to benefit him or her professionally. Furthermore, when it might also benefit him or her socially, be prepared for being out of the limelight: he or she will want to take the leading role.

Capricornians don't appreciate foolishness and can have no sense of humour. If you don't like constant picking at your clothes, appearance or hair, don't live with a Capricornian. Be prepared for his or her dark moods, which can come at any time and last for days. Capricornians prefer being at work to being at home. Forget about socialising unless either it's good for business or it can boost their worldly image.

AQUARIUS

If you intend to live with an Aquarian, be prepared to have a strange relationship. You have to be inclined to give them moral support while they're working. If you don't relish the thought of having a number of visitors frequently in your home, don't live with an Aquarian. He or she will think nothing of inviting several people around on the spur of the moment, including people who seem to have nothing in common with him or her.

Aquarians can be quite stubborn. If you like to be with someone you know will be willing to do what you want to do, don't live with an Aquarian. Although it might seem to you that you and your Aquarian housemate get up in different worlds, if you stick around long enough you'll find there's a definite theme of constancy. You'll find neither a truer nor a more loyal friend than an Aquarian.

PISCES

Because Pisceans are very sloppy, be prepared for sloppiness if you're planning to live with one. Nothing has a special place, and nothing is in its logical place, so don't be surprised if you find the milk and sugar in either the bathroom or the bedroom. Be prepared to bump into easels, to stand on open tubes of paint or to trip over musical instruments if you're not especially careful. If you wish to have a clean and orderly environment, either make it that way yourself or don't live with a Piscean. He or she will leave the lid off the toothpaste and never tighten the lid on containers.

Although Pisceans are careful about their personal hygiene, their interest doesn't extend beyond themselves. They like to dance and they love to listen to music, which they'll have playing constantly. They don't like to be bothered with either bills or mundane details of any kind, so you'll probably have to mail their cheques for them. They're basically sweet-natured people.

The children of each star sign

Children can reach for the stars,
Be they ruled by Jupiter or Mars.
Launch them gently towards heavenly constellations;
Sustain them by infinite vision and dedication.

Wouldn't it be nice if you were a mind reader – as I am – when it came to the unenviable task of understanding your children? Young Michael sulks in his room after undergoing the least provocation. Baby Kerry has to be the centre of attention, and if she isn't all hell breaks loose. You can never hold little Angie's attention for longer than two minutes before she starts rushing about on her own errands.

What do these three children have in common? It's that they aren't understood properly, because the zodiac's influence on children is mostly ignored. When you understand that Michael is a Cancerian, you'll realise he's very sensitive and easily hurt. When you have this knowledge confidently up your sleeve, you have a framework through which to handle Michael's sensitivity.

In order to interact successfully with your children, you have to have a lot of love and understanding, as any harassed parent knows. By understanding your children's character – broadly speaking, because the sun sign gives only a general view – you can see what makes both their strong and their weak points.

When you support and strengthen these points, you go a long way towards transforming your children into well-adjusted adults who are able to cope in a stress-torn world. I have Cancerian and Aquarian children. Had I not been forearmed with astrology, I would have floundered along doing my best on their behalf. It would have been a hit-or-miss situation.

Children and their adult counterparts don't always reveal what they don't wish other people to see. I found astrology to be invaluable for plumbing the depths of their being. I could 'plant' their future using the stars as my guide. I knew my Cancerian would be a homebody devoted to family life; this proved to be the case. I also knew my Aquarian would pursue intellectual interests outside the home and be career oriented; this also proved to be the case.

Naturally, I was able to chart their horoscope in order to produce a specific analysis. However, if you're unable to have your children's horoscope charted, an assessment based solely on their zodiac sign will be sufficient for the purposes of this section of the book.

My grandchildren range from Capricornians and Leos to Librans and Sagittarians, and their personality reflects the zodiac system's diversity. Included in my group of grandchildren is an apprentice witch who'll follow in her grandmother's broom prints.

Have a look through the following list: I'm sure you'll find a familiar child lurking in there somewhere.

ARIES

The symbol for Mars-ruled Ariens is the ram. The ram is a very appropriate symbol, because your Arien child is always butting head first into potentially dangerous situations. The word caution is virtually unknown to impatient Arien children, so you have to teach it to them. They want things done by yesterday and use their considerable energy to explode into a violent outburst if they're thwarted. Although little rams are very bright and full of ideas, you have to encourage them to follow through because they won't work through their ideas slowly in order to realise them.

Two qualities you have to encourage in Arien children are consistency and tact. Ariens can be exasperating but don't mean to be. They're always on the go: a natural legacy of Mars stamina and energy. They aren't ill very often. Your Arien child's optimism and confidence will bring a bright light into your life.

TAURUS

Taurean children are patient plodders. Although their slow, methodical pace will have you climbing walls, if you push them you'll only turn them into raging bulls. Once their energy is spent, they'll calmly go back to their usual habits and finish tasks that their quicker brothers and sisters lack the endurance to complete. The key to handling little bulls is to let them do things in their own time. They can be very intractable and stubborn and can't be led around by a nose ring. Suggest things to them and cajole them, because these two methods will work wonders for getting them to co-operate.

Taureans love all the comforts a good home can bestow, but make sure they don't over-eat, because over-eating is one of their failings. They also don't like strenuous activity, so you have to encourage them to exercise moderately in order to prevent them from becoming obese. Venus-ruled Taurean children are charming and have a loving nature, and they bestow charm and love on their parents in great abundance.

GEMINI

Gemini children are mercurial livewires. They don't like to stay in the same spot for long, and you'll have difficulty keeping them indoors, because they hate to be cooped up. If you want to temporarily anchor them, try giving the younger ones some interesting puzzles and the older ones video games – anything that will keep them intellectually stimulated. They love a good verbal battle and will have you reaching for the aspirin as a result of their mental gymnastics.

Gemini is symbolised by the twins, and Geminis indeed seem to be in two minds most of the time. They plead with you to buy them something and you buy it, only to find, to your dismay, that they're no longer interested. Your Mercury-quick Gemini child will have you exasperated at the best of times. The most effective way to handle them is to stimulate their curiosity and to issue challenges, not orders; in this way you'll get them to put their little thinking caps on. Being controlled by the element of air, Gemini children are very friendly and outgoing and will want you to be a friend as well as a parent. Try it: these kids can bring you a lot of fun and pleasure.

CANCER

Cancerian children are very sensitive and touchy, just like their symbol the crab. Although they can be happy and outgoing, when faced with stress they'll retreat into their little shell and brood. The retreat could take some time, because their confidence is easily shaken.

You have to handle Moon-ruled Cancerians carefully and with sensitivity. Encourage your Cancerian child to be involved in activities outside the home, and organise activities that will help draw him or her outward towards other people. Cancerian children will always play the child, and their home and family come first. You'll reap many rewards from developing your own kind of devotion to your quiet crab.

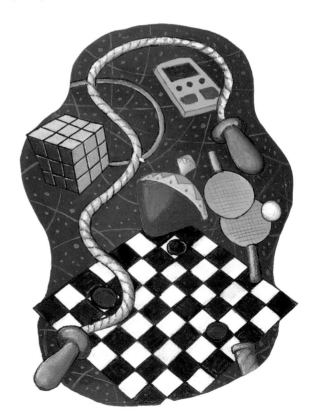

LEO

You'll discover very early on that your Leo child doesn't take orders; he or she will co-operate only when you use inducements, cajolery and – especially – flattery. Sun-ruled Leos are boundlessly enthusiastic and optimistic and place their trust in untrustworthy people. Caution your Leo child against being too trusting, otherwise he or she will be badly hurt as a result of being betrayed. Although your little lion's wounds will heal, he or she won't forgive the offender.

Leos like to be the centre of attention, and you'll usually find your Leo child at the centre of things, be it taking charge of a game or instructing family members. Leos don't like to be on the outer, and when they are they find the situation intolerable. Because your Leo child will be generous to a fault, try to caution him or her not to give something valuable away when the mood strikes. Flattery will get you everywhere and will be your best strategy in the continual struggle for dominance with your charming, effervescent and regal Leo child.

VIRGO

Virgoan children are methodical and orderly. They'll keep their room tidy and neat, because they like to have their belongings in the correct place. Mercury-ruled Virgoans take a practical approach to all their activities. You have to encourage Virgoans of all ages to play and relax more: they can become rundown if they're allowed to function at a compulsive level. Virgoan children always want to know why and won't be fobbed off with stock answers. They're nervous little souls, and they have to have their proper rest. Make sure their wish to serve people isn't

abused, because if it is they'll plunge into deep despair.

Virgoan children tend to be serious, so lighten up their activities and encourage them to see the brighter side of life. Being symbolised by the virgin and therefore associated with purity, Virgoans worry about their health, so try to incorporate health foods and healthy eating in your child's daily regimen. You'll find it disconcerting when your Virgoan child analyses you and informs you of more efficient ways to do things. Be patient: all Virgoans have to believe they're useful and that they have a role in achieving objectives.

LIBRA

Libran children have charm in abundance and know how to use it. Being charming is usually the tack they take in order to avoid confrontation. Venus-ruled Librans are great procrastinators: they take a lot of time to come to a decision – if they come to one at all. This 'weighing up' aspect of their personality is the result of their symbol, the scales.

You'll have to encourage your Libran child to adopt a course of action by constantly reassuring him or her; reassurance is something he or she will continually seek from you. Librans avoid open warfare at all costs because they prefer not to hurt people. Libran children have to learn not to give in to other people for the sake of peace – well, at least not all the time. You might have to encourage them frequently in order to build up their self-esteem. Librans need to know they're loved, and they have a lot of love to give in return.

SCORPIO

Your Scorpion child will have a way of staring you out, so when you're accusing him or her of something make sure it's based on fact. Scorpions are almost psychic in their perceptions, and your Scorpion child will sometimes be able to anticipate your thoughts and actions. Scorpions closet themselves away when a dark mood strikes, and when this happens it's best to leave them alone. Your Pluto-ruled Scorpion child will want to have both your undivided attention and your wholehearted approval, although he or she will probably never tell you. You'll mostly have to rely on cues in order to get your message across.

Scorpion children can have a demanding and aggressive attitude towards other people, and even when you resort to detective work you'll never uncover the secrets they hold dear. The symbol for Scorpio is the scorpion, the creature known for its lethal tail sting. If your Scorpion child is thwarted, watch out for the passionate sting he or she emits on your unsuspecting self. However, most problems will be minimised if you use the kind-but-firm approach. Scorpion children love deeply and intensely, and never mind if they aren't demonstrative: the feelings are there.

SAGITTARIUS

Sagittarian children are adventurous and boisterous and are unfailingly optimistic, so they dare themselves to undertake ventures that are downright dangerous. Your little archer will have a lot of Jupiterian luck on his or her side, so disaster will be circumvented usually but not always. Sagittarian children will gamble on their luck too much. They want an answer to everything, and you'll be continually wracking your brains to come up with one. Always be honest with them, because they tend to live in a fantasy world and have to be brought down to earth, at least occasionally.

Sagittarian children are fun loving and very friendly. They respond to a logical approach to their behaviour. Their temper outbursts don't last long and are usually treatable. When these Jupiter-ruled children are choosing playmates, they aren't discerning: the whole street will be their friend. Although they can be downright trivial and very blunt, they have many compensations, including their loving nature. You'll find your life is much enriched as a result of their joy in life.

CAPRICORN

Capricornian children like to play it safe: they neither gamble nor seek adventure. Because they're very methodical, you won't have to exhort them to be neat: they'll be tidy as a matter of course. Baby Capricornians will have their possessions in the right place and expect them to be kept that way. You'll have to encourage your Saturn-ruled child to be more flexible in his or her approach to other people. Because they have a reserved nature, Capricornian children don't make friends easily. You'll have to organise group activities in which your child can participate. Although your little goat seems to be solemn and remote, behind this misleading exterior is a warm interior that requires warm support in order to bring it out. Capricornians of all ages need affection but won't ask for it. In a loving environment, Capricornian children achieve wonders. Remember to show them that fun is also a part of life.

AQUARIUS

Aquarian children literally do their own thing. You won't find a more independent person than an Aquarian – which

doesn't help you much when you're wanting your child to conform to family living. Unfortunately, he or she will be neither dictated to nor regimented in any way. Aquarian children confound their parents with their reasonings for why they shouldn't do something. These Uranus-ruled children have quick intelligence and should be helped to strengthen this gift. Mental stimulus is an important element in their development. Give them a logical reason for what you want done and if they can't overturn it they'll do it. The emotional approach carries no weight with them.

Aloof Aquarian children need time to be alone in order to recharge their batteries, and at these times you shouldn't hinder them. These little water bearers are very humane and compassionate and are a bright light in a dark world. Although tolerance and helping people in need won't always be translated on a personal level, your little crusader will express these traits whether or not you approach him or her. Aquarian children need lots of support and affection, even if they don't seem to.

PISCES

Piscean children are given to daydreaming, are kind and sensitive and wilt under pressure. These Neptune-ruled children don't take the lead and require a strong hand to direct them. They also need help in developing a more positive outlook and in learning not to lean on people who might lead them astray. Pisceans of any age have low vitality and usually don't enjoy robust health, so make sure your child has plenty of sleep and a good diet. Don't let these little fish avoid either making decisions or taking responsibility for themselves, because they'll avoid both if they can. Let them use their imagination for positive projects such as performing in school plays or writing poems. Giving these little charmers endless love and affection is the only way to get them to function at their best. Remember to be firm and to gently coax them into strengthening their character: they can't spend their life sitting on your knee.

How you age according to your star sign

Read on and discover how your physical appearance and way of thinking are likely to change from infancy to adolescence and from your mid-twenties to middle and older age.

ARIES

From infancy onwards you're a rather loud-mouthed person. Everything has to be done in a hurry, and you lose your temper when things don't move fast enough. In your mid-twenties you start to be able to control your temper a bit better and to take advantage of your natural sex appeal. You hate to look your age, and this probably explains why you like to fall in love with people much younger than you. Also, you don't stop making plans for the future.

TAURUS

It's probably during infancy that you start indulging in good food and drink and getting plenty of sleep. Later on, you enjoy playing house. You hate doing things in a hurry, prefer to move at a rather steady and plodding pace and don't like taking risks. There's no stopping and starting with you: you simply go for it. You're set in your ways, and people have to take you exactly the way you are. You aren't particularly worried about growing old. You might become a bit on the plump side, like a contented and cuddly old pussy cat.

GEMINI

Although as an infant you're a bit of a cry-baby, you're able to talk and walk early. In your opinion, your teenage years are and were the best years of your life. You don't like to get past the age of about thirty; middle and old age simply don't suit you. This is why you like to mix with younger people and usually don't look your age. Nevertheless, you enjoy your second childhood.

CANCER

As an infant, you love to be mothered and fussed over. You're a bit on the timid side, and the big, bad world overwhelms you. In your mid-twenties, your motherly nature comes to the fore. The mid-twenties male finds it a bit hard to let go of his mother's apron strings. Although you don't like middle age, you grow old very gracefully. Ideally, you spend your elder years surrounded by beautiful antiques in an old, mansion-style house.

LEO

As an infant, you certainly want and demand all the attention you believe is your due; you love it when people drool and coo over you. At school, you want to be *numero uno*, and as a teenager you want to be the universal heart-throb. In your mid-twenties, it's hard for you to accept the fact that in order to reach the top you have to start at the bottom. In middle age, you become either pompous and self-satisfied or grouchy and niggly. Sex remains very important for you.

VIRGO

As an infant you're rather skinny, and you suffer minor illnesses more than most children do. At an early age, you become good at doing things with your hands. In your teens, you become introverted. In your mid-twenties and your thirties, you simply go your own way and don't hesitate to try everything that takes your fancy. In your middle and older years, younger people can learn a lot from your experiences, and you seem to be content and at peace. You grow old in a nice 'n' easy way.

LIBRA

At any age, you truly miss having been a lovable baby. At school, you certainly don't go for the rough stuff and are probably teacher's pet. You're artistic, and you tend to let people push you around. This attitude lasts until you approach middle age. However, at about that time you get involved in social activities and your life is made difficult because you let people push you around. You therefore learn to fight back. In your old age, though, you again become a bit of a pushover, especially for your children and grandchildren.

SCORPIO

As an infant, you're a cute 'n' cuddly little bundle one minute and a crying, tantrum-throwing brat the next. From an early age, you want to do things yourself and in your own way and are a bit secretive. In your mid-twenties, you like to wield power either in your job or at home. By middle age, you're content because you've reached a position in which you have power and authority. However, if you haven't reached that position, you become embittered. In your old age, you might become obsessed with the life hereafter.

SAGITTARIUS

You're a rather restless child who runs around all over the place. You talk at an early age and also start getting into mischief. At school, you can't help taking advantage of the opposite sex. In your mid-twenties, although you know you should settle down in a steady job, you're a bit too restless. At that age, you have great ambition and can rise to the top reasonably quickly if you try hard. You don't like growing old at all, because you believe you lose your good looks and physique. In your old age, you might get interested in something completely new, merely for the challenge.

CAPRICORN

As an infant, you're a bit slow. You're a late developer, and at school you sometimes feel like a fish out of water. As a child, you feel inadequate, and because of that you're rather shy. You're always afraid of making a fool of yourself. In your mid-twenties, you might become interested in either law or politics, mainly because you strongly believe in justice and fair play. You don't mind getting old at all, because you believe the extra experience you've gained is its own reward. However, you might regret the fact you didn't reach your goal in life. In your old age you want to be respected, and Capricornians usually reach a ripe old age.

AQUARIUS

As an infant, you're well behaved and interested in what's going on around you, and these two traits will remain with you all your life. In your mid-twenties, you're actively involved in community affairs and you aren't very ambitious. In middle age, you're quite easygoing except for the fact you hold some opinions sacred. In old age, although you're at peace, you remain keenly interested in anything new.

PISCES

As an infant, you're quiet and peaceful unless you become frightened. When you do become frightened, it takes hours for your parents to calm you down. At school, you're considered to be a bit of a sissy, mainly because you're rather sensitive. In your mid-twenties, you want to push the world up the right garden path, and because you're an idealist, you have plenty of disappointments. In your middle and old age, you find that younger people listen to you more easily and readily, mainly because you're neither as sour nor as cynical as most older people are.

KERRY KULKENS' GUIDE TO LOVE, SEX AND YOUR STARS

Shopping according to the star signs

If you're at all interested in human nature, you'll find it interesting to learn how the people born under each star sign approach the pleasant or painful task of shopping.

ARIES

Ariens shop as if they're in a race: they rush to the shop, grab what they want and run away when they've got it. They're the type of people who buy the latest fashion item on the spur of the moment then leave it in the wardrobe and never wear it.

TAURUS

Taureans have a great eye for colour and contrast. They make sure the quality of the item they're buying is only the best and that the item isn't too expensive. They're never in a hurry when it comes to shopping, and before they make a special purchase it's not unusual for them to call back several times. Because they consider style to be more important than price, they use everything they buy over and over.

GEMINI

Geminis consider shopping to be a novelty rather than something that has to be done. They usually purchase whatever catches their eye. If a Gemini woman has gone past a dress shop before she's gone to the supermarket, her dependants might go hungry for a week because she's bought a couple of dresses.

CANCER

Cancerians plan their shopping day well in advance. If you go shopping with them, they'll probably have filled their bag with all the newspaper articles about the specials so they're ready to check the specials out. They love to start their shopping early in the morning in order to avoid the stores' peak-hour rush. They usually opt for bargains and go from store to store comparing prices.

LEO

Leos buy the more expensive items because they believe you have to pay for good quality: if you want the best, you have to pay the top price. They seldom consider whether they can afford an item and whether they really need it. They also like to use a credit card rather than pay cash — especially if their partner is wealthy.

VIRGO

If you want to shop for shoes, take a Virgoan with you: he or she probably has a fascination for them. Virgoans can't stand having anything shabby and worn out, so they usually update their wardrobe before anything gets either worn out or dirty. They approach shopping for beauty and health products as a real adventure, because they have to know exactly how each product works and what's in it.

LIBRA

Libran males love to buy belts, so their shopping excursion might include a belt or two. Libran females love hats and costly jewellery as well as belts and will choose the most beautifully designed items available. They also love to show off their waistline, and they buy clothes that do just that.

SCORPIO

Scorpions hate going shopping and would simply love to get someone else to do it for them. They usually have to be forced to go out and buy anything — even to the supermarket to buy groceries. When they do go out and buy something, they usually don't show you until a long time has passed. Then, when you ask them whether the item is new, they tell you it's been around for years.

SAGITTARIUS

Sagittarians expect quality if they pay a good price. They love items that show off their legs, and the females usually buy stockings, jeans or pants that are tight all the way down to the ankles. They like to buy their clothes from expensive boutiques.

CAPRICORN

Capricornians love to shop in the best places in town. They usually spend hours trying on clothes until they're sure they've chosen the right item for themselves and the one that shows off their figure to its best advantage. They don't bother shopping for bargains, and whatever they purchase has to carry a guarantee or be able to be exchanged.

AQUARIUS

Aquarians want you to go shopping with them, because they want to buy something that appeals to someone else: they rarely trust their own decision making when it comes to shopping for important items such as clothes and personal accessories. They'd rather go shopping for someone other than themselves.

PISCES

Pisceans are fun to go shopping with. They love the little things such as household items and bric-a-brac. They don't particularly like shopping for groceries or clothes for a family member unless it's themselves and unless the item is brightly coloured and beautiful.

THREE GIFTS TO BUY THE PEOPLE OF EACH STAR SIGN

STAR SIGN	GIFTS
Aries	Fishing equipment; diamonds; a bow and arrow
Taurus	The latest cookbook; gourmet food; a good milking cow
Gemini	A book about gossip; gadgets; a mobile phone
Cancer	A dog; home decorations; a motorbike
Leo	Gold jewellery; designer clothes; Moet and Chandon champagne
Virgo	Bed linen; an expensive and understated painting; health products
Libra	New Age jewellery and clothes; group therapy; a belt and hat
Scorpio	Leather clothes and accessories; a motorbike; a convertible car for curb crawling
Sagittarius	Camping gear; a ticket to an unspoilt destination; a boat
Capricorn	Horticultural products; books about famous paintings; a genuine painting
Aquarius	A book about psychology; a collection tin; two extra rooms for homeless people
Pisces	A sugar daddy or mummy; a water bed; a set of silver candlesticks

KERRY KULKENS' GUIDE TO LOVE, SEX AND YOUR STARS

Feeling moody?
Maybe it's the Moon

It's beyond question that many of our moods are brought on by the Moon. Some of us are more susceptible to these moods than other people are. Of the people of the twelve star signs, the ones most susceptible to moods are Geminis, Cancerians, Virgoans and Sagittarians.

Each month as the Moon passes through each star sign, watch yourself and other people for the types of mood that can arise. The Moon affects all of us according to the nature of the star sign it's traversing. You can find out which sign the Moon is in by purchasing a moon table either separate to or included in a current astrology book.

The Moon remains in each of the twelve signs for two or three days. It also leaves its signature on your personality when you're born. If, for example, you're a Capricornian whose moon is in Aries, your emotional side will be very different from that of a Capricornian whose Moon is in Cancer.

Our moods can be more or less severe according to the planets that are placed in a specific sign at the same time as the Moon is. When the Moon and Saturn come into conjunction, a bad mood indeed is brought on and it seems to affect us all. On the other hand, a joyful mood is brought on when the Moon occults a beneficial planet, whereby we feel optimistic and uplifted for no reason we're aware of. This joyful mood is inspired by a benevolent and helpful aspect, so this is the time to act on impulse and further your heart's desire if you feel so inclined.

Now let's note exactly which moods can affect us during the Moon's transit of the twelve signs.

MOON IN ARIES

When the Moon is in Aries, we're rash, impulsive and inclined to have a headache, and 'migraineurs' might suffer a migraine. Our mood is based on our inability to get our own way.

MOON IN TAURUS

When the Moon is in Taurus, inanimate things such as our shabby old furniture and lack of money bother us. Our mood is based on our wanting something we don't have.

MOON IN GEMINI

When the Moon is in Gemini, we can't settle down. We feel nervous and restless, and we can worry about an unreceived letter. Our mood is caused by our not knowing enough about a situation.

MOON IN CANCER

When the Moon is in Cancer, people and family affairs can really get on our nerves.

We also get too involved in other people's problems. Our mood is caused by our inability to let people sort out their problems before we sort out our own.

MOON IN LEO

When the Moon is in Leo, our mood can be caused by something to do with our personal standing or reputation as well as our inability to live life on the scale we'd like to. We simply feel like we're not important enough.

MOON IN VIRGO

When the Moon is in Virgo, all kinds of petty detail get on top of us. We're irritated by having to do minor things we don't feel like doing. Our mood is based on our believing we've neglected lesser duties such as housework.

MOON IN LIBRA

When the Moon is in Libra, our mood is caused by the fact we believe we're a victim of a real or fantasised injustice, especially an injustice caused by a loved one. Something to do with a love affair can especially cause this feeling. We simply feel like we aren't appreciated.

MOON IN SCORPIO

When the Moon is in Scorpio, our mood is caused by our brooding or our desire to do something that doesn't eventuate. The mood is based on feelings of frustration or lack of freedom.

MOON IN SAGITTARIUS

When the Moon is in Sagittarius, our mood can be caused by our being somewhere we don't want to be, because we don't like feeling as though we're fenced in. We're simply angry because we have to fit in.

MOON IN CAPRICORN

When the Moon is in Capricorn, our mood is caused by either our fearing economic difficulties or our being prevented from working as we wish. We simply feel like we're a square peg in a round hole.

MOON IN AQUARIUS

When the Moon is in Aquarius, our mood is caused by our feeling as though either other people are restricting us or our personal freedom is being curtailed. The mood is based on our fearing either suffering want or being under duress.

MOON IN PISCES

When the Moon is in Pisces, we worry about either a love affair or our not feeling appreciated enough. Our mood is based on our feeling personally inadequate.

Career choices according to your star sign

When you're deciding on a career, you might make the mistake of basing your decision on salary or on your wish to follow in one of your parents' footsteps. Is that how you should make an important decision such as this? Wouldn't it be wiser to make your career complement your star sign – the *real* you? That way, you'd ensure you have a happy and harmonious working life rather than a miserable one simply because the money's good. From Ariens down to Pisceans, all twelve people of the zodiac deserve the chance to have a brilliant career!

ARIES

As an Arien, you love to make your mark on the world and to be noticed. Although you have to be pushed in order to get started, when you start there's no stopping you. Your head is full of ideas, many of which are original. When you have a new idea, you usually start it rolling then let someone else finish it, because you're about to unleash another idea. Your creative urge would show through best if you were teaching, writing, painting or creating new musical sounds.

TAURUS

As a Taurean, you love beauty and exotic foods.

You usually collect old and beautiful things. You'd love to start an antique business, but because of your love for beautiful things you'd never allow yourself to part with anything. Your best talents would come to the fore if you opened a club or coffee lounge in which you served exotic foods or cakes.

GEMINI

As a Gemini, you have a rather restless nature. You know what you want and give it a go because you believe therein lies the road to happiness and success. I bet you wake up in the morning and have your whole day planned but that when the day ends you've accomplished nothing. Put your thoughts on paper: write either short stories or nice little sayings that bring people happiness. You'd also make a great social worker.

CANCER

As a Cancerian, you have a tendency to 'gather in' both people and ideas. You'd be great as a writer of thrilling short stories. You'd be very satisfied and successful if you used your hands to make crafts or paint pictures or if you helped someone else in the area of handicrafts.

LEO

As a Leo, you won't be happy until you let your creative urge out. Stay away from gambling. For any type of work, going off on your own is the only way your creative urge will show through. You have a natural talent for expressing yourself and would make a great TV or radio personality. The choice is yours, though: either express your creative urge or stick with the crowd.

VIRGO

As a Virgoan, you worry too much about what other people think, and you fear failure. Try to maintain your self-respect without being afraid of what other people think. Paint pictures, write a diary or short story, compose music, write lyrics or even experiment with flower arranging. Be willing to make mistakes, but don't stop doing, trying, creating and experimenting.

LIBRA

As a Libran, you have a longing to save the world. A study of your creative urge reveals you have to present the new and the unusual. You have a remarkable gift for changing people's mind. You'd be great at designing unusual fashions, creating unusual hairstyles or doing make-up artistry. Stick with your first idea, because you tend to talk yourself out of anything you want to do.

SCORPIO

As a Scorpion, you need to express yourself, and the best way for you to do it is through writing. You'd make a great journalist or story writer. You have to learn to give expression to your impulses. Don't waste your emotions, urges or inspirations: learn to analyse them and to live by and with them. This is the basis of your creative urge.

SAGITTARIUS

As a Sagittarian, you sympathise too much with the underdog and therefore tend to be taken advantage of. Be willing to be wrong once in a while if necessary, but don't hold back for fear of making a mistake. You're gifted with intellectual tenacity and quite able to hang on to your beliefs regardless of how unpopular they might be. Your aspirations are great, and you can see them through.

CAPRICORN

As a Capricornian, you have to slow down – even crawl if necessary – because only then do you absorb or digest the life experiences that are tossed your way. Remember that it's your way to be yourself in either world affairs or the arts. If you decide to paint or do pottery, be selective about which pieces you keep, otherwise you'll have a tendency to keep every piece.

AQUARIUS

As an Aquarian, you lack self-confidence. However, once you gain it, the impossible or unknown is a challenge you enjoy. Remember that your hopes and wishes can be made real if you have confidence. Free yourself of preconceived notions, accept the new and remain free to experiment regardless of how ludicrous a plan might at first seem to you. This is your key and your secret for success.

PISCES

As a Piscean, you have a creative urge that has to be expressed.

However, you have two sides: the bubbly, full-of-life person and the worrier who sinks into a state of self-pity and sorrow and who believes he or she is no good. Learn to let your bubbly side out and to keep your brooding side in, and you'll succeed in anything you decide to do. Always remember that you have much to give and much to receive.

Investments according to your star sign

Should you keep your money in the bank, invest in real estate, buy shares or start your own business? Discover how best to invest your hard-earned cash, whether you're a canny Cancerian, a see-sawing Libran or an inventive Aquarian.

ARIES

You're looked on as being impatient and as being compulsively drawn towards speculative types of investment. If you resist gambling or borrowing against future earnings, you might lead yourself to beneficial investments. Beware of get-rich-quick schemes, because you're easily tempted. You'd be better off curbing your impulsiveness and seeking professional advice about slow-growing stocks and dividends. You also have to keep calm if your funds get low, because you tend to panic at the first sign of bad luck.

Use either loan services or cash stocks rather than withdraw funds from the bank. Although your best investment will probably be in hard metals, you'll rarely be lucky if you invest in a goldmine. Other good investments are iron and steel shares; building materials such as slate, sand and cement; and road- and bridge-building projects.

TAURUS

You're one of the most fortunate star signs because you respect money and realise it's a necessary item. Because of this trait, you're prudent in handling money. You aren't likely to be tempted by get-rich-quick schemes. The only time you buy anything impulsively is when you aren't under pressure to make money.

You think about how you can live on your income before you try to expand it. Having many bond issues

satisfies your desire to dabble in the stockmarket, and you'll be satisfied enough with making a steady 7 per cent on your outlay. You're likely to make as much money investing in real estate as you are on the stockmarket. Other good investments are cattle producing; copper; banks; leather goods; finance; and tobacco shares.

GEMINI

Once you realise that great things start off small, you stand a chance of becoming fortunate in your investments. You're very conscious of the fact that money is your means of getting many of the luxuries you enjoy, but don't jeopardise the luxuries you already have. Even before you invest, study your income and budget; if there's a gap between them, forget investing until you've managed to save even a small amount.

When you're investing large sums, get an expert to advise you. For small sums, it's better to follow your intuition. The best type of investment for you is electronics. Another sound investment is anything to do with paper products, such as stationery or publishing. Other good investments are railway shares; duplicating machines; and wordprocessing computers.

CANCER

If anyone is capable of withdrawing from the brink of financial disaster it's you. Your good-fortune streak also works in another way: you're quite likely to blindly invest in something then surprise the professionals by making a financial coup. Although this gift isn't something you can rely on, if you combine using your intuition with studying the stockmarket and also time your investments wisely, your income wil steadily increase. However, you tend to procrastinate and can be easily diverted from your original ideas.

You can obtain good returns from oil, the wine and spirit industry or any investments to do with the ocean. Other good investments are farming properties and real estate; building societies; water-board shares; catering; and the milk board.

LEO

You're always so impressed by the way other people live life that if you mix with people who persistently make investments, some of their enthusiasm rubs off on you. Unfortunately, though, these investors rarely tell you about the mistakes they've made, so try to invest on your own rather than go by what other people say. You're easily tempted into buying into get-rich-quick schemes.

If you're fortunate enough to have a good income you're likely to prosper through your investments, but if you already have financial worries your good judgement can become impaired. You'd be better off seeking professional advice before investing. Real estate and stocks to do with all types of automation are your best form of financial investment.

Other good investments are platinum; the entertainment industry; and the motor-vehicle industry.

VIRGO

You're one of the zodiac's most careful people. You're happiest when you feel financially secure. You might take a long time to make up your mind and therefore miss out on acting on the best market trends. It's as much a mistake to be overly cautious as it is to be reckless. You can make your fortune through making judicious investments, and opportunities can open up for you to use money in many exciting ways without posing a threat to your need for security.

Long-term investments such as planning a personal business venture are likely to appeal to you, whereby you can put your stocks and shares into the background. This strategy could prove to be profitable, especially for personal business ventures to do with paper. Other good investments are pharmaceutical products; food; cereals; health foods; the garment industry; and all industrial shares.

LIBRA

For you, money has a see-saw effect: your financial situation is forever going up and down. When it comes to making investments, you have to learn to be more self-sufficient whereby you rely on your own good sense rather than on friends' advice. Save and invest whatever you can, but limit yourself to businesses to do with either beauty or art.

In the long run, areas such as hairdressing, design or personal creativity are more advantageous for you than stockmarket speculation – so leave Wall Street to the financiers, who are more used to it. Other good investments are luxury items such as diamonds, furs and artworks; TV and radio shares; the music industry; and the entertainment industry.

SCORPIO

You're somewhat fearful of adventuring into financial affairs. You hate failure of any kind, and for you the stock exchange doesn't seem as tantalising and glamorous as it does for many other people. You're likely to always maintain one or two modest investments that offer small but regular dividends and to be content with a dramatic plunge every few years. Although investments in household equipment mightn't sound exciting, you can do very well in these types of financial venture whereby because you're obtaining steady returns you're left free to find adventure in other spheres. Other good investments are brewing; spirits; wines; dyes; drugs; laundering; chemical investments; and surgical investments.

SAGITTARIUS

If you have a bit more money available, it becomes easier for you to let your gambling instincts carry you along in a modest way. Spending money without wondering where the next few dollars will come from is a form of freedom you haven't experienced that can be added to your book of life. Be prudent enough to make sure you have some money in your savings account. Perhaps spend half this money at once on your investments and don't touch the rest until you're making money on the investments.

You'd do best to invest in a travel agency, especially if you have a personal interest in it.

Although all types of transport stock interest you, it's best if you stay away from airline shares. Other good investments are tin; copper; oil; mining; insurance; and petroleum-corporation stock.

CAPRICORN

Your chances of success depend on how well you can survive difficulties and turn bad events into good ones. Only you can release yourself from your inner fears by remaining optimistic. If it's emotionally difficult for you to withdraw your savings, leave your money in a savings account rather than speculate.

Your best type of investment is a partnership, because having someone else's help gives you confidence. Stocks and shares to do with transport, engineering and communications such as a telephone system usually cause you less pain than other investments do. Other good investments are government stocks and bonds; coal mines; cement bricks; building supplies; and real-estate insurance.

AQUARIUS

As each year ends, you find yourself wondering why you've worked so hard but you have so little in the bank to show for it. You aren't the most fortunate of investors, because you can be carried away by spending money on the products of your own inventive mind. It's a sad fact that many Aquarians make the world's greatest inventions but that other people make money from the inventions.

The only beneficial type of land investment for you is usually your own house, because owning it makes you feel independent. This type of investment is a major source of happiness for you. If you can, you might buy two houses: one to live in and one to rent. Although this strategy appeals to you because it's logical, in practice it's rarely a success and it can often produce more hardship. Small investments in electronics can be beneficial for you. Other good investments are aviation; electricity; TV and radio; computers; health food; and government stocks.

PISCES

When you're forced to realise that money is necessary even for a creative person such as you, you pass the turning point and can begin to study matters such as investment. You'll probably work by intuition in the world of stocks and shares, and you might even buy a stock for no better reason than that you like its name. The experts are always amazed when you score a bull's-eye.

Having several small ventures is more likely to appeal to you than making one grand splash on the stockmarket, unless you have a very good income. Stocks to do with travel or liquids often yield the best money for you. Other good investments are footwear; cooking oils; fabric manufacture; cosmetics; and the entertainment industry.

Wealth and success according to your star sign

Most of us have to work for a living, so we might as well be successful and prosperous and enjoy life at the same time. Following are some special tips for promoting success and riches according to your sign.

ARIES

You can get very excited at the start of an endeavour but before it's accomplished you've invariably become fascinated by some other task that pulls you away from it. If you're a successful ideas person, you can delegate your projects' finishing stages. However, if you have to be both the conceiver and the finisher of the work, you'll climb up the next rung of the ladder and simply have to love your work enough to be devoted to it to the very end.

At any point in your life, visualising your goals, dreams and objectives can be enormously helpful for you in defining and attracting them. Visualise yourself enjoying the success and money you long for.

TAURUS

The profit motive is strong for you. As long as money is steadily flowing in, you aren't disturbed by the fact that progress is slow. In these times of instant gratification, it isn't always necessary to make gains the long-term way.

Although you can certainly have long-term deals cooking, don't overlook the quick return; simply think in these terms and you'll soon find this type of opportunity coming your way for you to investigate. To get the big pay-off, you always have to have some extra 'get up and go'.

GEMINI

Concentration and 'one focussing' are high on the list of priorities for you to be successful. I might add that wealth isn't very well represented among Geminis. You can acquire tremendous power by knowing your objective and refusing to be distracted from it by matters that aren't central to your purpose.

One of your best points is your ability to see through a mountain of detail and to quickly and perceptively extract the important pieces of information from it. Becoming aware of this gift and elaborating on it can give you the confidence you require in any competitive business situation that might arise.

CANCER

Feelings of achievement and satisfaction are strong motivators for you to make your mark on your work. Another plus on your side is that you're a hard worker.

Although you might grumble and complain about what you have to give up in order to work hard, underneath you enjoy every minute of your work. Because Cancer is one of the money-and-success signs, you have many things going for you.

LEO

Your creative talents are plentiful and are greatly aided by your Leo cheerfulness, optimism and enthusiasm.

You're probably very popular, and you need loving and to be surrounded by loving and encouraging people. However, you have to accept the fact that you can't be loved by everyone, especially in the business world.

Don't be afraid to push forward and assert yourself, and don't expect to have the red carpet rolled out for you. Polish your talents and make sure you're totally ready, willing and able when opportunities come your way. Don't demand of people what they're unable to give. You'll gain in strength and power in all areas of your life if you become the best of what you can be.

VIRGO

You have an inbuilt ambition to achieve and succeed. There's nothing wrong with your near-compulsion to both achieve and be proud of your work's intrinsic truth value. However, why not combine your brilliance of mind and work ability to create greater success and prosperity, which can open new avenues of creativity for you?

Money is freedom: freedom to create even greater excellence. Simply set the goal of having more money, and your mind will automatically direct you to where and how this can be made possible.

LIBRA

Your lack of staying power sometimes stems from a deep-seated fear of accepting responsibility for your decisions. It takes courage and self-assurance to make choices that can affect people's life and hip-pocket. However, the more you can do this, the more you'll rise like a shining star.

Then again, success means more than taking situations into your own hands: it also means accepting responsibility for your own happiness. As a Libran, your thinking tends towards giving the people closest to you the power to create your contentment and destiny. However, successful and prosperous living is predicated on your ability to take over your own life and work and especially your own destiny.

SCORPIO

You have a powerful need to create success and prosperity. As a Scorpion, you have a natural gift for success. Even failure won't daunt you for very long; in fact, setbacks of any kind can make you angry enough to press forward in order to find new ways around obstacles.

Although you don't like to be kept down by anyone or anything, your downfall be your emotional sensitivity. You're inclined to devote too much time and energy to the negative things that are said about you and done to you. When this happens, you can waste time trying to get even with the very people you should be forgetting. Revenge is a sickness of the soul but somehow also finds its way to your hip-pocket.

SAGITTARIUS

You'd have to do an awful lot of wrong in life not to succeed. Your natural cheerfulness and enthusiasm carry you far towards achieving your goals and towards positioning you in the most advantageous environment. You're gifted with the ability to speak articulately and to communicate your ideas with ease, charm and intelligence.

In any business endeavour, you need freedom to make decisions and to come and go accordingly. If you aren't given this freedom, you can shrivel up and lose your drive overnight. In order to acquire true success and wealth, you require education almost constantly as well as freedom of choice.

CAPRICORN

You're a capable worker, and you have ambition that will take you to great heights. Challenges of any kind bring out the best in you: you seem to grow, strengthen and rejoice in a challenging situation. The only faults that limit your ability to make a big fortune are that you don't aim high enough and you don't take enough risks.

Lift your sights — only smallminded people will fault you for aiming too high.

Don't hold back because of fear; dare to take what to you might seem to be the most outlandish of chances. When you're rewarded with exciting returns, you'll probably find they weren't so outlandish after all.

AQUARIUS

Your greatest gift is perhaps your ability to pull down into practical, concrete reality all the visions that are way off in the heights when you first have them. Also, you can count on your nervous energy to take you where you have to go. Combine this energy with an almost constant stream of bright, workable ideas and a stubborn streak that keeps you going, and you have a pretty good formula for success.

However, in the past you've realised that some of your ideas and schemes are way ahead of their time. Although people who have an inventive mind always have to have the courage to lead, they also have to have the patience that goes with leadership. Nevertheless, if some people are keeping you from success, open up new areas in which you can present and increase your talents and abilities.

PISCES

Once you've packaged your ideas and abilities in a presentable form, it takes durable ambition and lots of energy before you can make it to the top. In your personality, either or both traits can be missing. Although as a Piscean you aren't outgoing, Pisces is one of the money-and-success signs, so if you don't achieve your goal of having greater success and wealth, you can bet you aren't working with your stars and planets.

It helps you greatly when you know exactly what your ambitions and objectives are. Name them to yourself. If you want lots more money and recognition, tell yourself about it.

Find the perfect employee according to his or her star sign

How about using astrology to find the perfect employee for you and your business? Whether it's a babysitter, a pest exterminator, a housekeeper, a garbage collector or even a politician we need, we all have to find hired help sooner or later. When you employ someone, you naturally want a person who's loyal, who's a good worker and who gives you your money's worth. Finding the right person through astrology enables you to delve into his or her personality and determine whether he or she has what it takes before you make your selection.

ARIES

Ariens are self-starters and aren't afraid to get the work done in the least time possible. They love to open a new office and lay out the ground work for getting things under way. They have to be offered work that presents them with a challenge, otherwise they get bored. Some of them are especially good at handling metals and sharp objects and won't mind working at a great height or doing things that could endanger their life.

Ariens don't like to be watched while they're working and will probably work a lot better if left alone. Put any orders to them as a suggestion or even as a dare. If you have tough tasks to tackle, tell them you doubt anyone could do it, because they'll love to prove you wrong.

TAURUS

Taureans are level headed, practical and down to earth. They understand that everyone has to benefit from an employer–employee arrangement. They're reliable and profitable workers who are methodical in everything they do. They're best suited to a job in which the routine has already been established. Unlike most people of the other star signs, they can tolerate repetition. They're very concerned about how much money they're making, and they'll work hard to make that little bit more.

Taureans are good at selling luxury or high-profit items and are especially good in jobs in which they can earn a commission. They like to work with things of the earth. Although they don't respond well to being either put under pressure or ordered around, they appreciate being given suggestions or helpful hints. They might require a bit more training time than other people do, but once they know how things run they seldom fail or disappoint.

GEMINI

Geminis are versatile and adaptable and are so capable they can handle several things at the same time. They mustn't run out of things to do or they'll lose interest in their work and get involved in a non-work activity such as reading, talking on the phone or simply fooling around. During their work hours, they have to be busy both physically and mentally.

The best job for Geminis is one that involves phone work, paging, announcing, writing, typing, printing and/or duplicating: anything that involves communication. If you want to get any work done, try not to have too many Geminis together in the one office.

CANCER

Cancerians are sensitive to people's needs. They don't like to work either on the frontline or in an exposed position, so think twice before you put them at the front desk. Make sure their job involves change, but not too much change, because they excel in a job in which they aren't doing the same thing every day of the week.

If you're thinking of employing a Cancerian for work that involves retirement benefits, profit sharing or insurance, you'll have a long-term employee.

Cancerians aren't fond of taking a lot of directions and don't mind taking orders from qualified people.

When you're giving them an order or offering them a suggestion, remember that they're sensitive and that their feelings can easily be hurt.

LEO

Leos are known for their showmanship. They believe the whole world is a stage, and they'll play any part in order to become popular, including at work. Try to place them in a position that enables them to have a bit of levity now and again. If you can apply a bit of humour or lightheartedness while you're training them, and especially when you're reprimanding them, the results will prove to be a lot better than if you show no humour at all.

The best jobs for Leos are ones that involve persuading customers, patrons or clients to buy, to believe or to do something else. They can tolerate repetition as long as a bit of fun is involved, and they're very big on loyalty.

VIRGO

Virgoans aren't afraid of work, are thorough, and don't work very quickly because they're absolute sticklers for detail. They don't work well in a place that's noisy or unclean. If you assign them a specific place they'll work to organise everything, but if they can't do this they'll be unable to cope with their responsibilities. They'll also follow every step as outlined or required.

Virgoans are efficiency experts and should be allowed to make suggestions, and their good suggestions should be followed. Most of them make good employees. They're seldom very colourful or exciting types, so they shouldn't be employed in positions that involve public contact, creative selling, showmanship or public relations.

LIBRA

Librans are very artistic, or at least have an appreciation for artistic things. They have a highly developed feeling for balance and fairness. They don't like work that involves getting either themselves or their clothes dirty. They like to look neat and tidy at all times. Almost all of them are talented in anything that involves balancing, forming or organising. They make good managers, especially if the position involves the fairness principle when jobs and responsibilities are being assigned.

If the job you want done requires quick decision making, don't get a Libran for it: he or she doesn't like having to make decisions quickly. You'll have to follow the book with reference to pay, hours, overtime, days off, breaks, and adequate and safe working conditions; if you don't, Librans are the type of people who'll put up a good fight.

SCORPIO

Scorpions never give up on anything. They can keep matters confidential, and they have intense feelings. However, you can't expect them to open up to you about their past and their personal life, because they respect their secrets the same as you respect yours. Also, don't count on their socialising with you or their fellow workers. They work best either on their own or in private; they don't even mind working in a basement if it means being left alone to work.

They make excellent investigators and love to find errors, missing persons or missing items.

In time, you might be unpleasantly surprised if your Scorpion employees lose their temper and show how nasty they can be when pushed too far. They aren't the type of employee you'd want to have as an enemy, because even though they're subtle about it they'll get even at your expense. However, if you treat them nicely and are honest with them, you could have a strong ally and a secret supporter.

SAGITTARIUS

Sagittarians are concerned about the big picture rather than with small matters. They have a good sense of humour and are willing to travel for their work. They aren't very interested in details and can become quite bored with repetition. Don't place them in a position in which they have to do the same thing over and over again, otherwise they'll be unable to stand the pressure and they'll goof up and quit.

They work best outside, so if you put them in a small cubicle, they'll crack. They get on well with people because they have an easygoing nature.

If the job you want done requires a lot of travel, living out of a suitcase or dealing with foreigners, a Sagittarian is your best choice. Most Sagittarians have above-average intelligence and are very studious when it comes to advanced education. They'll think highly of you and respect you if you let your sense of humour show.

CAPRICORN

Capricornians are hard workers and serious minded. Because being the best at everything means all to them, they're willing to go the extra mile at work if it means they'll be promoted. Many of them are willing to toil after hours at the expense of family life. Don't allow them to overdo it, because they don't know when to stop. Give them a title that sounds important: rather than call them a cleaner, call them a janitor, and rather than call them a secretary, call them a marketing assistant. This not only makes them feel important; it makes them feel trusted.

Don't be concerned if at times they briefly seem to be either negative or down, because moodiness is in their nature. They get better at their work as they get older. They believe that the older they get, the more experienced they become.

AQUARIUS

Aquarians are intelligent, inventive, friendly and liberal in their thinking. They like to be employed in a place in which they can both make use of their brain and voice their opinions. They don't mind doing the same thing for long periods of time, as long as the job varies a bit every so often. However, because they don't know how to handle difficult, stubborn people, rather than try to handle them they usually lose their cool and show the bad side of their nature.

The best job for Aquarians is one that involves computers or electronic or electrical devices. Although you might think they go about things in an unusual way, don't worry: you'll be pleased with the end result. If the job involves public contact, they'll definitely please you.

PISCES

Pisceans are artistically inclined, sensitive and willing to work as a follower rather than as a leader. Almost all of them have some artistic talent, even if they don't display it. Try not to place them in a situation in which a lot of brawn is called for. Also, they don't mind working in disarray but don't work well in positions for which either a lot of concentration or strict attention to detail is required.

Pisceans need variety and can't work in a job in which there's no change. You have to praise them constantly, because without praise they feel unwanted and become uninterested. You also have to constantly supervise them in order to make sure they're functioning well. Discipline them gently, because it's near-impossible for them to take any abusive treatment. Most of them are easygoing and get along with other people very well.

How to manipulate
each star sign and win

The people of all twelve star signs are manipulated every day of their life. If you don't believe me, think about it for a moment: every time you watch TV and read a magazine or paper, attitudes and opinions are thrown at you. Even when you're speaking with someone, you're being manipulated in a subliminal way because you're listening to what he or she is saying. Why not use this fact for your benefit in order to get what you want from your employees, boss or friends?

ARIES

You'll never succeed in manipulating an Arien if you're too obvious about it. Ariens usually play by their own rules and don't want to have them challenged. Although they can't be either pushed or forced, you can lead them when you're attempting to get what you want. Be subtle, or you won't get to first base. Use the tactic of suggestion but don't give them a direct order; allow them to think they're doing whatever they want.

TAURUS

Taureans are disinclined to do anything in a hurry, so don't try and rush them. The trick to manipulating them is to move slowly: they don't like change unless it makes down-to-earth good sense and offers some sort of benefit. You can bribe them into doing anything but you can't push them. Basically, money talks for them. Always be ready to answer their 'Why?' questions. They will, however, respond to mushy stuff.

GEMINI

You have to be clever and cunning to manipulate Geminis. They're very cunning and very likely to catch you at your own game then turn it around to their benefit. They love a challenge and are fascinated by words and innovative ideas. They're likely to go along with what you want as long as it looks good on paper. You don't have to actually prove it's a good idea; just make it look good.

CANCER

Cancerians are extremely sensitive, and you have to be very careful that while you're manipulating them you aren't hurting their feelings. If you do hurt their feelings, they'll take a long time to come back out of their shell. They'll work towards having basic security, so manipulate them towards it. You have to appeal to their emotions in order to get what you want from them.

LEO

The only way to manipulate Leos is to compliment them first. Persuade them that what you're asking them to do will cause them to be highly regarded. Don't apply too much pressure all at once. Whatever you want to do, make sure you're sickly sweet towards them. They aren't turned on by anything that doesn't benefit them.

VIRGO

Most Virgoans are pretty sharp, so when you're trying to manipulate them, neither trip up nor lie. Remember that they're very logical and that they won't act on anything that doesn't make sense. Spend your time persuading them that what you're trying to get them to do is practical and down to earth. If you have neither the time nor the patience to answer their questions, your efforts will all be for nothing.

LIBRA

You have to be both patient and persistent with Librans: they usually can't make a decision, because they're likely to weigh and measure before they act. They don't like other people to show a level of strength. The best way to get what you want from them is to adopt a smooth and pleasant approach. They'll usually fight to the end if you convince them your idea is for a good cause.

SCORPIO

Scorpions are very suspicious, and you'll have a hard time convincing them you aren't trying to either deceive them or take advantage of them. Don't be too pushy with your suggestions, or you'll get nowhere. Remember that they neither forgive nor forget a betrayal of trust. They're very good at being left to do the job themselves, so give them the idea and they'll act it out for you.

SAGITTARIUS

Sagittarians like the unusual; the more way out, the better.

Remember that whatever you want them to do has to be put to them in a way that makes it sound impossible. If you have a very good sense of humour, they'll be in your control. Similar to Scorpions, they're very good at being left to do the job themselves, so give them the idea and they'll act it out for you.

CAPRICORN

Never forget that Capricornians want to rise to the top no matter what. All your proposals and suggestions will have to make sense, and whatever you do, don't push them. If they believe they're being pushed, they'll probably tell you where to go. They appreciate humour and are open to doing anything whereby virtue might be placed in question.

AQUARIUS

In your attempts to manipulate an Aquarian, your ideas have to be outrageous and out of the ordinary. Communicate your ideas, and don't use pressure. Aquarians value friendship and will be interested in any cause that benefits the underdog. Be prepared for surprises: although you might think you didn't succeed in manipulating them, a few weeks down the track they'll do what you ask. As supporters they're strong and loyal.

PISCES

Whatever you want Pisceans to do has to be ethical and straight down the line: no hanky-panky. Realise that if you abuse their willingness to help, you'll lose their trust and confidence. They respond to the gentle and loving approach. You can trust them, but don't betray their trust.

HOW TO MANIPULATE EACH STAR SIGN AND WIN

39

How to influence other people according to your star sign

We all have our way of persuading people to do something and of convincing them that our intentions are genuine. Are you an assertive Arien, a subtle Scorpion, a confident Capricornian or a passive Piscean?

ARIES

Eagerness and enthusiasm are your trademarks. You use verve and assurance in approaching the task of gaining people's confidence. Your basic style is friendly persuasion, and when it's complemented by sincerity and good judgement, few people can resist your overtures.

You firmly believe anything's possible, and you inevitably back up your belief by earning a long list of achievements. Nevertheless, because your thoughts are usually followed with action and you have an inbuilt rapid response to challenges, you often have remarkable success in new and untried fields.

TAURUS

Your powers of persuasion are invariably based on your appealing to the security consciousness of your targetted buyer, seller, client or customer. Two other factors in your being able to gain people's confidence are your persistence and determination. Despite obstacles, delays, distractions and the fact you occasionally fail to get an enthusiastic response, you stay right in there, persevering to the end – which is usually just how you planned it.

Naturally, there are times when a bit of flexibility and openmindedness to contrasting viewpoints might enhance your persuasiveness even more. However, the certainty and self-assurance you're so plentifully endowed with generate confidence in you. Your professional colleagues, who tend to depend on and trust your judgement, know it's a well-placed trust that pays off.

GEMINI

You have a remarkable flair for communication that covers the spectrum from gentle persuasion to elaborate double talk, so you're usually able to lead almost anyone down your unique garden path. You're never at a loss for words. For you, gaining people's confidence on a permanent basis might be more of a challenge than letting your persuasiveness have an impact on them.

CANCER

You have to overcome your shyness before your powers of persuasion can fully emerge.

When you've taken the plunge into your chosen career or profession, you develop a most persuasive manner in gaining people's confidence. People get the feeling you'll be there when you're needed. You have a unique ability to provide for people's often subconscious yearning to be soothed, pampered, reassured and most of all understood. Your mothering instinct is an effective tool for persuading people and for ensuring your wishes are successfully and profitably expressed in your business and career activities.

LEO

Entertainment is invariably an important factor in your career and financial success. If people can't be persuaded by your way of thinking after they've been wined, dined and seduced, when can they? However, it isn't only your personal style that attracts people and helps you gain their confidence; it's your innate integrity and inner strength. People seem to sense you're someone they can put their trust in.

VIRGO

You place a lot of faith in logic, and relying on logic is your first priority when you attempt to persuade people and gain their confidence. You carefully and painstakingly check all details, cover all bases and go over a plan with a fine-tooth comb before you introduce it to someone. You're articulate and blessed with being able to present your thoughts in an orderly sequence. Because people can detect no overhanging and unexplained loose ends, they usually get an accurate picture of whatever it is you're promoting.

LIBRA

One of your greatest tools in the art of persuasion is your ability to listen.

The fact remains that you ask the right question at the right time, and you never cut in on a punchline. This is a fine art that many of the world's most successful people practise. You're able to focus all your assets and most attractive qualities in one magnetic package that's totally suited to the occasion, and this is why so many Librans go far in life.

SCORPIO

In many of your plans, you focus on the art of subtle but effective persuasion. Your incredible memory and total recall are helpful in fashioning your game plan, on which you bring to bear your intense powers of concentration and insight. You gain people's confidence through your mixture of sincerity, strength of purpose, concentrated effort and sheer magic.

Whether you're operating in business or on a personal level, the intensity and total dedication to the quest of the moment that you direct towards the person you're persuading can be ever so subtle and ever so irresistible. You also expect and usually gain not only people's confidence but their loyalty.

SAGITTARIUS

Friendship is a Sagittarian keyword, and establishing a good rapport with people you wish to persuade and influence comes naturally for you. You rarely have any problems in either persuading people to see things your way or gaining people's confidence.

There's one area you might have to tighten up a bit if you wish to continue your persuasive influence: although you don't mean to make promises you can't keep, you've been known to do so. Your sense of responsibility sometimes wanes when your enthusiasm does, and your prompt helpfulness becomes tardy indifference.

CAPRICORN

Although you respond to challenges quickly, before you act on your responses you tend to study the situation, research it, get all the facts and statistics then make your move. This is how you approach a project in which being persuasive and gaining people's confidence are called for.

Impressive entertainment at elegant places might be a part of your program, but you're quite sincere and earnest in your desire to put your best foot forward. Your integrity and solid practicality come through loud and clear. Sometimes you might find you have to prove yourself before you gain people's confidence.

AQUARIUS

The element of surprise often plays a part in your approach. Whether you wish to catch your competitors offguard or to open possibilities to the people you wish to persuade, or whether it's simply your urge to reveal your individualism, unplanned and unpredictable happenings can often make or break you in your persuasive efforts.

You can be extremely persuasive with people whose thoughts and values run along lines that are totally different from yours. However, these are the people who tend to come up with second thoughts, fears and soundly practical reasons as to why they can't go along with whatever commitment they've made while you had them under your spell.

PISCES

You have a great gift for selling dreams and fantasies. You intuitively pick up on people's desires and needs then concentrate on providing the answers to their wishes. You naturally gravitate towards a career or profession you'll find personally fulfilling, so you're able to promote your ideas sincerely and to gain people's confidence.

Because you're generously endowed with intuition, you can be a veritable fountain of information, facts and stories. Your brand of persuasiveness is that you have a flair for elegance and beauty that enables you to create an environment in which you're at your best.

Your compatibility with the other star signs

The following character descriptions mainly include people's positive and negative traits. However, there are many shades in between, depending on the time, date and place of your birth. Each star sign is addressed from the point of view of the reader. For example, if you're an Arien male, I tell about your relationship with the females of the twelve star signs: as her friend, lover and spouse. Similarly, if you're a Taurean female, read the guide from the viewpoint of the males of the twelve star signs: as his friend, lover and spouse. Go to it and make a success of your relationships!

ARIEN MALE

Arien male with Arien female
Friend: It can be great – it's a very stirring and fast-moving relationship. Lover: There are lots of fireworks and spontaneous loving, but be prepared for eruptions. Spouse: The marriage is never dull, and there's respect on both sides.

Arien male with Taurean female
Friend: It isn't very good – you don't have much in common, you want to dominate her and she becomes obstinate. Lover: Although she has a big sex drive at first, it quickly burns itself out. Spouse: It can work, but she wants security and you want plenty of fun.

Arien male with Gemini female
Friend: Although it isn't longlasting, it's beautiful while it lasts. Lover: It's like a sunburst – short but intense. Spouse: You seem to keep each other's interest alive.

Arien male with Cancerian female
Friend: There are too many clashes – she wants to stay indoors, and you're the outdoor type. Lover: She wants more than just a little fling. Spouse: If you treat her right she's a good mother to your children and very affectionate.

Arien male with Leo female
Friend: You have lots of shared interests and the same joyfulness. Lover: It's good, but you have to go slowly and avoid rushing. Spouse: She's the best partner for you.

Arien male with Virgoan female
Friend: It's no good – she nags you to death. Lover: You have to take the initiative and put some effort into it. Spouse: There are quite a few clashes, because you act on impulse and she wants to change you.

Arien male with Libran female
Friend: You're very different. Lover: Although there's strong physical desire, you want to be master – try to be a bit more gentle and kind. Spouse: You have to take the reins, but be careful you don't trample her underfoot.

Arien male with Scorpion female
Friend: She tends to bottle it up when things go wrong whereas you blow up and forget about it. Lover: You go great guns – you won't get rid of her in a hurry. Spouse: Unless it's a faithful and loyal partnership, it won't last long.

Arien male with Sagittarian female
Friend: You become friends easily and remain so. Lover: Both of you like to have a superficial romance. Spouse: Both of you need to be outgoing outside the relationship – if either or both of you stay at home too much, forget it.

Arien male with Capricornian female
Friend: It's beneficial in the areas of hobbies and business but nothing else. Lover: Although she seems to be a cold fish at first, watch out – she can really bowl you over with her passion. Spouse: She wants to pursue her own career.

Arien male with Aquarian female
Friend: You're compatible, because you have a similar outlook on life – both of you want to be free and independent. Lover: Although it's very tempting at first, it isn't longlasting – she's more interested in companionship. Spouse: She wants to have both an equal share and an equal say in things.

Arien male with Piscean female
Friend: It doesn't last very long – she gets on your nerves unless it goes further than friendship. Lover: She's after love and kindness, and you want excitement. Spouse: She likes to dominate you for fear of losing her own personality.

ARIEN FEMALE

Arien female with Arien male
Friend: Both of you are the outdoor type, so you can have some great times together. Lover: Although it's a very fiery relationship, it isn't a deep one. Spouse: You prefer a strong type, but he doesn't like your attitude.

Arien female with Taurean male
Friend: He's practical but a bit boring, and your interests differ. Lover: Although it's up to you to make the first move, once you have his interest he takes some shifting. Spouse: Although you have a very good family man and he keeps house well, he becomes set in his ways.

Arien female with Gemini male
Friend: Outdoor activities might get you together, and he's active but reliable. Lover: It isn't very lively at first, and his interest soon fades. Spouse: It isn't an ideal match – you start to take the lead, and he sometimes seems to be too childish.

Arien female with Cancerian male
Friend: He wants to run your life and likes being indoors. Lover: It can be a longlasting, tender and loving affair. Spouse: He wants you to fuss over him, which is hard for you to do.

Arien female with Leo male
Friend: It's extremely difficult to keep it on a friendship basis only – there's too much sexual electricity. Lover: The sparks really fly, and he's more faithful than you thought he'd be. Spouse: He wants you to show him you love him, and if you do he's devoted to you.

Arien female with Virgoan male
Friend: Although you love to win him over, you soon lose interest in him. Lover: You find him a bit of a miser – you take the initiative and are disappointed. Spouse: He's too neat and tidy, and he wants you to be the same.

Arien female with Libran male
Friend: Although he's a bit of a drip, you can lord it over him. Lover: He's simply no match for your sexual appetite. Spouse: You have to supervise him all the way – if you want a little lap dog, he's all yours.

Arien female with Scorpion male
Friend: Although both of you like adventure, you want to turn the friendship into a love affair. Lover: It's fireworks at its best – although he's what you imagine a man should be like, he can be too earthy and crude at times. Spouse: He's a bit hard to fathom, and you don't stand for much nonsense from him.

Arien female with Sagittarian male
Friend: Both of you like the great outdoors and sports and want to be on the move all the time. Lover: Although he's quite imaginative, he has a roving eye. Spouse: You aren't a couple who should have children – both of you are too outgoing.

Arien female with Capricornian male
Friend: You can learn a lot from him – if you give it a go, it can be a lasting friendship. Lover: Not much sexual activity goes on – he sometimes feels too old for it. Spouse: He's the oldfashioned type who believes he's the only breadwinner in the family, and it's hard for you to pursue your own career.

Arien female with Aquarian male
Friend: He has plenty of friends and acquaintances and is good company. Lover: Although he isn't very enthusiastic, he's attentive. Spouse: It's an 'Easy come, easy go' sort of marriage.

Arien female with Piscean male
Friend: You have opposing views, so there's too much trouble. Lover: He's suave, and he wants to act out being a romantic-novel character. Spouse: He wants to have a little homemaker, so you aren't his type – unless you want to live with a disciplinarian.

TAUREAN MALE

Taurean male with Arien female
Friend: Although you aren't the outdoor type, you enjoy some outdoor activity with your Arien friend. Lover: You're pretty well matched, although she likes to take the initiative. Spouse: She wants to play the leading role and isn't the homemaker type, so you don't like it.

Taurean male with Taurean female
Friend: You have the same hobbies and the same earthy attitude towards life. Lover: It's an idyllic love affair, and it matures all the time. Spouse: It's a good marriage, and you enjoy each other all the way – but be careful your waistline doesn't spread.

Taurean male with Gemini female
Friend: She's a bit whimsical, like a butterfly. Lover: She has a good imagination, but she doesn't have it for very long. Spouse: She's always on the go – if you can't keep up with her, you lose her.

Taurean male with Cancerian female
Friend: Earth and water aren't a bad combination – they make mud. Lover: Your friendship can grow into some hot loving, and both of you can let your hair down. Spouse: It's a happy marriage – you complement each other very well, and you're faithful to each other because you're a happy homemaking couple.

Taurean male with Leo female

Friend: She does a bit too much talking. Lover: It's a bit onesided. Spouse: It works if you can satisfy her every whim – if you can't, forget it.

Taurean male with Virgoan female

Friend: The friendship is more like a business transaction. Lover: She's too much trouble to handle – almost neurotic. Spouse: As is the case with the friendship, it's more a business venture – everything is nicely organised and in its right place.

Taurean male with Libran female

Friend: She likes your reliability, and both of you like the beautiful things in life. Lover: You're in the box seat – do the right thing and she's great. Spouse: As long as you do the right thing, the marriage shines.

Taurean male with Scorpion female

Friend: Although it takes a bit of time to get started, it's a very solid friendship. Lover: Both of you like to indulge. Spouse: You go together like bread and butter and stick together no matter what.

Taurean male with Sagittarian female

Friend: You have different views and too many arguments. Lover: Although it's good while it lasts, you aren't imaginative enough for her. Spouse: She keeps at you all the time, and if she thinks you've let her down you've had it.

Taurean male with Capricornian female

Friend: It's great – both of you are very loyal and conservative, and it's longlasting. Lover: Although she takes a bit of coaxing, the rewards are worth it. Spouse: It's a tremendous marriage – both of you keep building it up and up and improving all the time.

Taurean male with Aquarian female

Friend: She's too unreliable, and you have too many hassles. Lover: It's hopeless – you're too earthy for her liking. Spouse: It's a bad match – forget it.

Taurean male with Piscean female

Friend: Although you don't seem to have much in common, it's a reasonable friendship. Lover: She likes a bit of romance, but you manage. Spouse: She's no homemaker – actually, she's rather sloppy, so she isn't your cup of tea.

TAUREAN FEMALE

Taurean female with Arien male

Friend: You don't have much to talk about. Lover: He might scorch you a bit, so be ready for some wild action. Spouse: Although he likes a real woman, there are lots of clashes because both of you like to have the leading role.

Taurean female with Taurean male

Friend: There isn't much of a future, because he isn't lively enough for you. Lover: He isn't the real lover you want, and the affair becomes boring. Spouse: He's a good husband, reliable and a good family man.

Taurean female with Gemini male

Friend: He's too fickle, and too many other friends are on the scene. Lover: He's a bit too airy-fairy, and you don't know where you are with him. Spouse: He has too much of a roving eye, and he can be fun but immature.

Taurean female with Cancerian male

Friend: It doesn't remain just friendship for long. Lover: He wants you to take the lead and to fuss over him. Spouse: He can be all right once he's grown up and matured.

Taurean female with Leo male

Friend: It isn't the ideal situation. Lover: It's okay as long as you keep it interesting for him. Spouse: The marriage survives only if you live up to his expectations.

Taurean female with Virgoan male

Friend: For you, he's rather the intellectual type. Lover: He could well be Casanova. Spouse: You have to do quite a bit of giving – can you?

Taurean female with Libran male

Friend: He seems to be right for you. Lover: He's the polite and considerate type, but physical excitement is another thing. Spouse: You have to keep a tight rein on him, and things go smoothly.

Taurean female with Scorpion male

Friend: He might be a bit difficult at times – you almost have to prove you're worthy. Lover: He fascinates you because of his mystique. Spouse: This is a hard one – if you deliver the goods all is well, but if you can't he says it's been nice knowing you.

Taurean female with Sagittarian male

Friend: He's too demanding, and he wants too much of your time and attention. Lover: He wants to be the one who's conquered you. Spouse: He likes you to stay home and make your abode lovely for him for when he gets back from his little escapades.

Taurean female with Capricornian male

Friend: He likes you to be feminine and treats you accordingly. Lover: He's conservative, so you have to be patient. Spouse: Both of you are an earth sign, so you're very compatible.

Taurean female with Aquarian male

Friend: He's too much up in the air. Lover: He isn't as interested in sex as you are. Spouse: Well, you're earth and he's air – need I say more?

Taurean female with Piscean male

Friend: He's too changeable. Lover: He isn't a macho lover. Spouse: He needs a lot of prodding – be the boss and take advantage of him.

GEMINI MALE

Gemini male with Arien female

Friend: It can be quite humorous. Lover: She's ready for action. Spouse: She pushes you all the way.

Gemini male with Taurean female

Friend: Although she isn't good to argue with, you get enjoyment from going to musicals and other forms of entertainment together. Lover: Once you get her interested, watch out. Spouse: She's the perfect homemaker.

Gemini male with Gemini female

Friend: The relationship is airy-fairy. Lover: You talk a lot about sex but don't actually have it. Spouse: It isn't a good match – there's too much indecision.

Gemini male with Cancerian female

Friend: You have trouble trying to work her out. Lover: There might be trouble, and she can be neurotic. Spouse: She smothers you to death.

Gemini male with Leo female

Friend: She's pretty good – your air fans her fire. Lover: There's a lot of showing off. Spouse: It's better not to have children – they'd spoil the fun.

Gemini male with Virgoan female

Friend: It works on an intellectual level only. Lover: The affair is shortlived. Spouse: Both of you get a bit restless.

Gemini male with Libran female

Friend: The friendship is ideal, provided you stick to being friends only. Lover: Your affair is quite idyllic. Spouse: Although you're very well suited, you require a permanent babysitter because you're out together so often.

Gemini male with Scorpion female

Friend: You have too many opposing views. Lover: She isn't interested in having a light affair. Spouse: It isn't a good match – you aren't serious enough for her.

Gemini male with Sagittarian female

Friend: It's a very good friendship. Lover: The affair can be very entertaining. Spouse: It's quite good, and there aren't many problems.

Gemini male with Capricornian female

Friend: You don't see each other very often. Lover: She wants a steady man. Spouse: She might be too ambitious for you.

Gemini male with Aquarian female

Friend: The friendship is okay – just don't let it turn to sex. Lover: Although it's great at first, it fades quickly. Spouse: Both of you are very outgoing, but it's a good match.

Gemini male with Piscean female

Friend: Well, it doesn't stay as just a friendship for long. Lover: Your affair is just the start of something big. Spouse: The only downfall is that she hasn't got both feet on the ground.

GEMINI FEMALE

Gemini female with Arien male

Friend: He might be a bit too impulsive for you. Lover: He might be a bit too fiery for you. Spouse: He's too much the outdoor type.

Gemini female with Taurean male

Friend: He wants most things to be routine. Lover: Although he's quite sexy, he can be selfish. Spouse: Although he's a good provider, he's a bit bossy.

Gemini female with Gemini male

Friend: He's too fickle. Lover: There's a bit of enjoyment at first. Spouse: It isn't a loving union.

Gemini female with Cancerian male

Friend: He's immature. Lover: There's a lot of feeling at first. Spouse: He wants you to be the homemaker only.

Gemini female with Leo male

Friend: He's good fun, and he has plenty of travel in store for you. Lover: He likes to show his expertise. Spouse: The more financial success he has, the better the bond.

Gemini female with Virgoan male

Friend: He might be a bit too practical and keeps to himself too much. Lover: Forget it. Spouse: You aren't serious enough for him.

Gemini female with Libran male

Friend: You like him, and both of you have plenty to talk about. Lover: He tells you what you want to hear. Spouse: Although he can at times be a bit undecided, you can be as well.

Gemini female with Scorpion male

Friend: He's good company, although a bit moody. Lover: He wants to capture you and enslave you. Spouse: He's much too serious for you, and he stifles you.

Gemini female with Sagittarian male

Friend: You have complementary qualities. Lover: He's good for you. Spouse: You're a very good match – all the way.

Gemini female with Capricornian male

Friend: He's great – he treats you like a princess! Lover: When he thinks having an affair is the right thing to do, he's tops. Spouse: He's more like a father than a husband.

Gemini female with Aquarian male

Friend: He's too much of an individual for you. Lover: He wants more and more. Spouse: You have plenty of freedom.

Gemini female with Piscean male

Friend: He's a good friend – nothing more. Lover: No, not really – your liaisons are too infrequent and short. Spouse: You have enough love but no leadership.

CANCERIAN MALE

Cancerian male with Arien female

Friend: She's too aggressive or pushy for your liking. Lover: It never works. Spouse: She pushes you all the time – maybe over the edge.

Cancerian male with Taurean female

Friend: Both of you like the good things in life and to enjoy yourselves. Lover: Although you can really enjoy it, you'd better make it permanent. Spouse: You're a good combination – you become more and more like the one person.

Cancerian male with Gemini female

Friend: She's too fickle and inconsistent for you. Lover: She knows quite a few tricks but is too changeable for you. Spouse: You want someone to really look after you, and she won't.

Cancerian male with Cancerian female

Friend: You have the same ideas and feelings. Lover: You don't enjoy sex with her as you do with people of the other star signs. Spouse: You share the chores equally and have a very good home life.

Cancerian male with Leo female

Friend: She's possibly too ostentatious for you. Lover: If you flatter her she makes you feel on top of the world. Spouse: She isn't the little homemaker you want.

Cancerian male with Virgoan female

Friend: She might be too intellectual for you. Lover: You enjoy sex. Spouse: The marriage is perfect – both of you love your home.

Cancerian male with Libran female

Friend: The relationship doesn't stay platonic for very long. Lover: She gives plenty – and more. Spouse: She prefers partying to homemaking.

Cancerian male with Scorpion female

Friend: Although you're attracted to each other, it doesn't work. Lover: If you're open and frank, you enjoy the affair.

Spouse: You have quite a lot of variety, rows and making up.

Cancerian male with Sagittarian female

Friend: There's too much fire. Lover: When fire and water get together, plenty of steam is made. Spouse: If you're the stay-at-home type, it doesn't work.

Cancerian male with Capricornian female

Friend: You have many qualities in common. Lover: It's great – a real battle of the sexes. Spouse: Well, you have a great homemaker in her.

Cancerian male with Aquarian female

Friend: It's a good friendship. Lover: Although the affair is quite exciting, it might be a bit onesided. Spouse: It mightn't be a good match.

Cancerian male with Piscean female

Friend: If you're honest, the friendship is okay. Lover: She's the right type for you. Spouse: The marriage is really great as long as you do the right thing.

CANCERIAN FEMALE

Cancerian female with Arien male

Friend: No way – he's too demanding. Lover: Don't get involved. Spouse: He's forceful – the marriage is okay if you're content to be a traditional wife.

Cancerian female with Taurean male

Friend: He likes you to ask him to dinner at your place. Lover: Although the affair is okay at first, he takes you for granted. Spouse: Both of you like having children and a nice home life.

Cancerian female with Gemini male

Friend: He keeps you entertained. Lover: He's better than you thought he'd be. Spouse: Although he likes children, he isn't a family man.

Cancerian female with Cancerian male

Friend: It's a close friendship. Lover: It's a good combination. Spouse: You're similar – he likes to run the house too.

Cancerian female with Leo male

Friend: He wants a fun companion. Lover: He's good, even if he does want you to tell him how terrific he is. Spouse: If you want to stay home and be the little mother, the marriage is beaut.

Cancerian female with Virgoan male

Friend: You have to keep it platonic. Lover: Although you find it hard to follow what he's doing, he can be quite good. Spouse: It can be an ideal marriage.

Cancerian female with Libran male

Friend: He gives you plenty of attention. Lover: You have to take the lead. Spouse: He's very kind – if you keep him happy, you have a nice marriage.

Cancerian female with Scorpion male
Friend: He's a bit puzzling for you. Lover: He's either the most lovable or the most disgusting man. Spouse: He expects the world from you.

Cancerian female with Sagittarian male
Friend: You're like ships that pass in the night. Lover: He likes you to be his trophy. Spouse: If you let him be boss, the marriage works okay.

Cancerian female with Capricornian male
Friend: He might be too much to handle for you. Lover: If you break the first barrier, he's great. Spouse: He has conservative ideas, and he's a good father who demands respect.

Cancerian female with Aquarian male
Friend: You don't have much in common. Lover: With him it's 50–50. Spouse: Although you don't lack material things, you miss out on an emotional level.

Cancerian female with Piscean male
Friend: Although the friendship is quite good, you have to try to be open. Lover: He puts you on a pedestal, so you have to come down from there and show him you're made of flesh and blood. Spouse: Because he's a bit weak, you have to make plenty of decisions.

LEO MALE

Leo male with Arien female
Friend: Expect to be involved in plenty of outdoor activities. Lover: If you're sincere, the sex is wonderful. Spouse: You have to work hard to make it work properly.

Leo male with Taurean female
Friend: The friendship becomes routine and very dull. Lover: The affair will be much deeper than a mere fling. Spouse: She's a good match for you – almost exactly what you want.

Leo male with Gemini female
Friend: It's a happy-go-lucky friendship. Lover: You like to outdo each other – you have an outrageously nice time. Spouse: You keep each other young and lively.

Leo male with Cancerian female
Friend: You're a really perfect combination. Lover: You have a lasting bond rather than a true love affair. Spouse: It might be one of the zodiac's best partnerships.

Leo male with Leo female
Friend: There's too much rivalry between you. Lover: The relationship is too artificial. Spouse: There are too many clashes for you to really enjoy the marriage.

Leo male with Virgoan female
Friend: Although you like her at first, you get fed up with her nagging. Lover: You want to really let your hair down, and she doesn't let hers down. Spouse: She's the stay-at-home type – cosy and sweet.

Leo male with Libran female
Friend: You really enjoy each other's company. Lover: You really want to protect her from the big, bad world. Spouse: Although outwardly you seem to be very well matched, are you?

Leo male with Scorpion female
Friend: You find her rather intriguing. Lover: It can be either heaven or hell. Spouse: The marriage is very solid.

Leo male with Sagittarian female
Friend: It's a good friendship – full of fun and glamour. Lover: The affair is quite sensational. Spouse: Although it's a happy marriage, you have to watch your expenses.

Leo male with Capricornian female
Friend: She expects you to treat her like a real lady. Lover: Although you have to put a lot of hard work into the affair, the rewards are worth your while. Spouse: She really takes charge and doesn't fool around.

Leo male with Aquarian female
Friend: It's a good, true, platonic relationship. Lover: She prefers to remain friends only. Spouse: The marriage works well – you respect each other.

Leo male with Piscean female
Friend: The friendship is a bit like *Alice in Wonderland*. Lover: She's a real sex kitten. Spouse: She really looks after the children and the home.

LEO FEMALE

Leo female with Arien male
Friend: You respect him, and you seem to be well suited. Lover: He's a fiery customer, and you might clash a bit too much. Spouse: He wants a good wife and mother.

Leo female with Taurean male
Friend: He might be too earthy for you. Lover: He sweeps you off your feet then drops you. Spouse: He's a solid homemaker.

Leo female with Gemini male
Friend: It's an 'On again, off again' sort of affair. Lover: He has too much of a roving eye. Spouse: He isn't a one-woman man.

Leo female with Cancerian male
Friend: He's attentive but rather moody. Lover: The affair has lots of show but nothing more. Spouse: He wants to do everything and run your life as well.

Leo female with Leo male
Friend: You have a lot in common. Lover: It's a shortlived romance. Spouse: It works if one of you is the boss, otherwise it's a hell of a clash.

Leo female with Virgoan male
Friend: You believe you can learn a lot from him. Lover: He's a bit of an adventurer. Spouse: He overawes you.

Leo female with Libran male
Friend: He treats you like a lady. Lover: He's a real lover boy. Spouse: He's better as a lover for you – and you have to make the decisions.

Leo female with Scorpion male
Friend: Although he interests you, there's no common ground. Lover: He fascinates you but disappoints when it counts. Spouse: There are mental duels, and he wins out.

Leo female with Sagittarian male
Friend: He's good company but very frank. Lover: There's plenty of loving, but he wants to remain free. Spouse: If you keep him interested, he's perfect.

Leo female with Capricornian male
Friend: He treats you to a lot of things. Lover: He wants to make you his private toy. Spouse: He keeps you wondering about the real him.

Leo female with Aquarian male
Friend: He can open your eyes. Lover: The sex is superb. Spouse: He expects a lot from you.

Leo female with Piscean male
Friend: He's a bit too intellectual for you. Lover: You have to take the leading role. Spouse: He gives you plenty of love but doesn't make decisions.

VIRGOAN MALE
Virgoan male with Arien female
Friend: It mightn't be a lasting friendship. Lover: It might get very hot. Spouse: You're a compatible couple.

Virgoan male with Taurean female
Friend: You have the same ideas and outlook. Lover: The relationship is good at first but develops into a routine. Spouse: You have a solid marriage and happy children.

Virgoan male with Gemini female
Friend: You have plenty to talk about. Lover: The romance is very nice until one of you gets cold feet. Spouse: Although it's a great marriage, you get on each other's nerves.

Virgoan male with Cancerian female
Friend: You enjoy each other's company. Lover: She teaches you all you need to know. Spouse: She's really good for you – make the most of it.

Virgoan male with Leo female
Friend: She over-impresses you at first. Lover: She's too strenuous for you. Spouse: She's ruled by her heart whereas you're ruled by your head.

Virgoan male with Virgoan female
Friend: You have the same interests. Lover: Both of you are afraid of seeming to be too brazen. Spouse: Although it can be a good partnership, it isn't real marriage material.

Virgoan male with Libran female
Friend: You're too different from each other. Lover: If you maintain the novelty, she's okay. Spouse: She makes you a nice little nest.

Virgoan male with Scorpion female
Friend: Although you have a few arguments, the friendship is usually pretty good. Lover: You have to do a lot of hard work, but it gets better with time. Spouse: She wants you to be successful, so she pushes you hard.

Virgoan male with Sagittarian female
Friend: The friendship is very refreshing. Lover: It's a scintillating affair. Spouse: Don't let life become routine.

Virgoan male with Capricornian female
Friend: She's straightforward. Lover: If either of you are bold enough, she's nice. Spouse: It's a true, almost businesslike marriage.

Virgoan male with Aquarian female
Friend: You have fun exploring the friendship. Lover: You can satisfy each other quite well. Spouse: You make a good match and like to discuss things before you make a decision.

Virgoan male with Piscean female
Friend: She's a bit vague for you. Lover: She's very feminine – and you like that. Spouse: She's a good wife, and if you appreciate her your life is good.

VIRGOAN FEMALE
Virgoan female with Arien male
Friend: You're half-hearted about the friendship. Lover: Sometimes he's just too crude. Spouse: You have security.

Virgoan female with Taurean male
Friend: He's looking for a wife more than for a friend. Lover: He wants his comforts as well as the sexual side. Spouse: He requires his wife to be obedient.

Virgoan female with Gemini male
Friend: He takes you places but can be annoying. Lover: He can be very superficial. Spouse: He can be a bit immature at times – and unfaithful.

Virgoan female with Cancerian male
Friend: The friendship takes time to grow. Lover: He has lots of affection but no 'oomph'. Spouse: He provides a nice little nest – children in a nice little house.

Virgoan female with Leo male
Friend: Don't expect to have very much communication.

Lover: Don't judge a book by its cover – he disappoints you. Spouse: He spends too much money on the nice things in life.

Virgoan female with Virgoan male
Friend: It's a good, friendly association. Lover: If you want someone who's half-hearted, you've got him. Spouse: You nag each other to no effect.

Virgoan female with Libran male
Friend: He's a good companion for outings. Lover: He can make you really enjoy sex and romance. Spouse: He doesn't want any hassles.

Virgoan female with Scorpion male
Friend: The friendship is quite intense. Lover: If you don't have hang-ups, the affair is good. Spouse: Although he's hard to please, if you please him he's good.

Virgoan female with Sagittarian male
Friend: He's lots of fun to be with. Lover: He's an experimenter and quite good fun. Spouse: He's the boss, so expect plenty of arguments.

Virgoan female with Capricornian male
Friend: You can have good times with him. Lover: In his prime he's fantastic, but your worries increase later on. Spouse: Although he's true and solid, he tries to run your life.

Virgoan female with Aquarian male
Friend: He broadens your outlook. Lover: You know what each other wants. Spouse: He's a very good husband, and both of you remain reasonably free.

Virgoan female with Piscean male
Friend: Although he's a bit tentative at first, he's very nice afterwards. Lover: He's nice, but is he really with you in bed? Spouse: Although flare-ups happen often, they're quickly forgotten.

LIBRAN MALE

Libran male with Arien female
Friend: She can broaden your mind. Lover: She wants to both produce and direct the show. Spouse: She controls the marriage.

Libran male with Taurean female
Friend: She's a loyal friend. Lover: She's good for you. Spouse: She's a good homemaker, and she makes everything run smoothly.

Libran male with Gemini female
Friend: She's good company but she requires a bit of variety. Lover: She dictates the terms. Spouse: It's a very deep relationship.

Libran male with Cancerian female
Friend: The friendship has to be cultivated but grows well. Lover: She doesn't like one-night stands. Spouse: She's a good homemaker, but you have to take her out occasionally.

Libran male with Leo female
Friend: You have good, clean fun. Lover: There's plenty of romantic lovemaking. Spouse: You like the nightlife – but what about the children?

Libran male with Virgoan female
Friend: She can be a bit too cold and practical for you. Lover: There's no warmth in the affair. Spouse: She's a good homemaker, and she expects you to stay home with her and the children.

Libran male with Libran female
Friend: You're a good, complementary combination. Lover: There's no intensity in the affair. Spouse: You have a nice house, but there's no sparkle.

Libran male with Scorpion female
Friend: Stay clear of her. Lover: She's full of passion, even if you aren't – watch her sting. Spouse: She's too bossy, so give it a miss.

Libran male with Sagittarian female
Friend: She's warm, generous and true. Lover: She wants fireworks. Spouse: There's no stopping at home in this marriage – expect lots of adventure.

Libran male with Capricornian female
Friend: Take it easy – Rome wasn't built in a day. Lover: She might be too much trouble for the reward at the end. Spouse: She's better organised than you are.

Libran male with Aquarian female
Friend: She's good company for you – don't neglect her. Lover: The affair is nothing exceptional. Spouse: She's hard to keep entertained, and she requires variety.

Libran male with Piscean female
Friend: It's a quiet friendship. Lover: She's feminine, so treat her accordingly. Spouse: The marriage is based on love – there's no practicality.

LIBRAN FEMALE

Libran female with Arien male
Friend: He likes the outdoors and is rather blunt. Lover: It's 'Wham bam – thank you, ma'm.' Spouse: He'd like to put you in a golden cage.

Libran female with Taurean male
Friend: You're very well matched. Lover: Both of you are into rather earthy sex. Spouse: He's solid and a good provider.

Libran female with Gemini male

Friend: He's great, as long as you aren't jealous. Lover: It's all or nothing. Spouse: There's never a dull moment – it's nice, though.

Libran female with Cancerian male

Friend: He's hard to work out. Lover: He wants gentle sex – pamper him a bit. Spouse: He's faithful, and he likes home comforts.

Libran female with Leo male

Friend: He's a bit of a show-off, but you don't mind. Lover: You're both exhibitionists. Spouse: If you keep showering him with love, he stays true.

Libran female with Virgoan male

Friend: He might be a bit dull for you. Lover: The romance has no frills and nothing fancy about it. Spouse: If you treat him right, the marriage goes a long way.

Libran female with Libran male

Friend: You're good and kind to each another. Lover: In lovemaking, he's sweet, careful and gentle. Spouse: He's a sweet and gentle husband.

Libran female with Scorpion male

Friend: He keeps you guessing. Lover: He has a bit of the sadist in him – watch it. Spouse: He demands a lot, but it's great if there's real love.

Libran female with Sagittarian male

Friend: You have plenty of fun together. Lover: He likes to sneak in and out – the romance is quite marvellous. Spouse: As long as you can keep him interested in you, he's great.

Libran female with Capricornian male

Friend: He likes to be seen with you. Lover: He seems to be good, but is his heart in it? Spouse: You're well matched.

Libran female with Aquarian male

Friend: He's good to talk to. Lover: The romance is an exciting sex excursion. Spouse: If you keep him happy, he's good for you.

Libran female with Piscean male

Friend: It's a reasonably easygoing friendship. Lover: Neither one of you takes the initiative, because both of you are waiting for the other person to move. Spouse: Both of you are indecisive – who'll solve the problems in your life?

SCORPION MALE

Scorpion male with Arien female

Friend: You have too many arguments. Lover: You want more than she wants. Spouse: Expect plenty of fights, but don't sulk – speak up.

Scorpion male with Taurean female

Friend: As long as you try to lay down the law, it's a solid friendship. Lover: It's a good, solid relationship, and it improves all the time. Spouse: It's a solid, no-nonsense marriage – till death do you part.

Scorpion male with Gemini female

Friend: She's a bit flighty for you, but quite nice. Lover: You're very ill-matched in bed. Spouse: Although your knowledge of each other's sexuality is shallow, the marriage works if you're willing to grow together.

Scorpion male with Cancerian female

Friend: If both of you are mature, the friendship is all right. Lover: Be yourself and indulge. Spouse: The marriage is blissful, as long as you're frank with each other.

Scorpion male with Leo female

Friend: Both of you are a bit intolerant, and there are plenty of clashes. Lover: Although there's a lot of love in the romance, there are also fiery clashes. Spouse: If both of you learn to give and take, the marriage is okay.

Scorpion male with Virgoan female

Friend: There's no trouble if you treat her as an equal. Lover: She might be a bit too straight for you. Spouse: The marriage only just works.

Scorpion male with Libran female

Friend: The friendship is a bit too easy for you to mould. Lover: She's good in bed, but you have to treat her gently. Spouse: Although the marriage is difficult at first, if you love each other it's worth persevering.

Scorpion male with Scorpion female

Friend: Although you have the same outlook, you can expect quite a few arguments. Lover: This is a real duel – both of you love sex. Spouse: It's quite a serious partnership – don't let moods spoil it.

Scorpion male with Sagittarian female

Friend: She's more practical than you are. Lover: You want a deep relationship but she doesn't. Spouse: Even though you can expect to have fights galore, making up is nice.

Scorpion male with Capricornian female

Friend: You have great empathy for each other. Lover: The affair can turn into marriage. Spouse: It's a no-frills but sound marriage.

Scorpion male with Aquarian female

Friend: The friendship is rather superficial. Lover: The affair is only skin deep. Spouse: If you let her go her own way, it works out all right.

Scorpion male with Piscean female

Friend: Water mixes well with water. Lover: There'll be

no worries in the romance, but you have to be gentle with her. Spouse: Don't let temper flare-ups destroy your love.

SCORPION FEMALE

Scorpion female with Arien male
Friend: He's good fun but rather rough. Lover: He's the 'Hop on and see you later' type. Spouse: He takes care of you, but don't expect more than that in the marriage.

Scorpion female with Taurean male
Friend: He's good company for you. Lover: He's quite satisfying. Spouse: The marriage can work well.

Scorpion female with Gemini male
Friend: As a friend, he's a barrel of fun. Lover: He takes friendship into the cot. Spouse: You have to take charge completely in the marriage.

Scorpion female with Cancerian male
Friend: It's a pleasant friendship. Lover: He provides a full sex life for you. Spouse: He's a very good choice as a husband.

Scorpion female with Leo male
Friend: Although he's an exhibitionist, he isn't too boring. Lover: He always thinks he's tops and tries to show you he is. Spouse: As a husband, he isn't too serious for you.

Scorpion female with Virgoan male
Friend: You have similar interests and hobbies. Lover: He's a bit of a cold fish when it comes to romance. Spouse: He's simply a practical homemaker.

Scorpion female with Libran male
Friend: The friendship is quite charming. Lover: He wants to 'do it' with decorum. Spouse: You have to lead him all the way in the marriage.

Scorpion female with Scorpion male
Friend: It's a good, solid and lasting friendship. Lover: He's thrills and spills all the way. Spouse: The marriage usually doesn't work out.

Scorpion female with Sagittarian male
Friend: There are too many arguments for you to enjoy the friendship. Lover: He has plenty to give, but you haven't. Spouse: Although he isn't very thoughtful, he loves well.

Scorpion female with Capricornian male
Friend: You have to fit in with his plans. Lover: As long as you tell him your preferences, he's a satisfying partner. Spouse: The marriage is more like a business relationship.

Scorpion female with Aquarian male
Friend: This friendship is a no-no – you have too many opposing views. Lover: The affair is based purely on sex – you have nothing else in common. Spouse: Your ideas don't fit in with his.

Scorpion female with Piscean male
Friend: He can be quite entertaining as a friend. Lover: He seems to be full of loving. Spouse: He's just what the doctor ordered.

SAGITTARIAN MALE

Sagittarian male with Arien female
Friend: The friendship will be great but shortlived. Lover: The affair is a bit like a wrestling match. Spouse: You tend to outgrow her in marriage.

Sagittarian male with Taurean female
Friend: You don't have much in common. Lover: There's a boom then the romance fizzles. Spouse: She's the homemaker and nice to come home to.

Sagittarian male with Gemini female
Friend: Although it's reasonably good, there's a bit of rivalry between you. Lover: The romance is great but shortlived. Spouse: She's too airy-fairy for you, and you're also the restless type.

Sagittarian male with Cancerian female
Friend: She broadens your mind. Lover: She takes what she can get. Spouse: You might have to teach her to enjoy herself outside the home, otherwise she stays put.

Sagittarian male with Leo female
Friend: The friendship is great fun, but don't let it get out of hand. Lover: Although there are lots of sparks, they quickly burn out. Spouse: All's well if you keep the interest alive.

Sagittarian male with Virgoan female
Friend: She's too conservative for you. Lover: She knows how to 'do it', but there's no feeling. Spouse: She's a steady influence.

Sagittarian male with Libran female
Friend: You like each other. Lover: If you're a gentleman, she rewards you handsomely in bed. Spouse: She can be your tonic.

Sagittarian male with Scorpion female
Friend: She's after more than just holding hands. Lover: You have a hot one here. Spouse: You need plenty of stamina to keep up with her.

Sagittarian male with Sagittarian female
Friend: Two fires make a big bonfire – great stuff. Lover: You can burn each other out. Spouse: It's a perfect marriage, because you have the same outlook.

Sagittarian male with Capricornian female

Friend: She offers intellectual conversation, but that's all. Lover: If you find the right tempo, you can let her rip. Spouse: You lead at first, and she takes over later.

Sagittarian male with Aquarian female

Friend: You have good conversations and similar views. Lover: Both of you like little affairs – nothing serious. Spouse: It's a good match, and it includes plenty of outdoor living and social activities.

Sagittarian male with Piscean female

Friend: She just goes along with you. Lover: She can become a clinging vine. Spouse: Although she's a bit fancy free, the marriage is stable.

SAGITTARIAN FEMALE

Sagittarian female with Arien male

Friend: He's too much an outdoor-sport type for you. Lover: The affair becomes more of a wrestling match. Spouse: He's a dream husband.

Sagittarian female with Taurean male

Friend: He takes you out and treats you well. Lover: You enjoy his earthy nature. Spouse: You aren't the homemaker he's looking for.

Sagittarian female with Gemini male

Friend: He offers lively companionship. Lover: He's a very attractive bed mate. Spouse: Although there are plenty of disagreements, it's a nice working relationship.

Sagittarian female with Cancerian male

Friend: If you get him out of his shell, he's fun to be with. Lover: You have to acquire a taste for him. Spouse: He makes a good wife for you.

Sagittarian female with Leo male

Friend: He likes showing you off. Lover: There are plenty of good sex romps. Spouse: It's a very social marriage.

Sagittarian female with Virgoan male

Friend: He's quiet and shy whereas you aren't. Lover: He doesn't really set you on fire. Spouse: He might wear you down and turn you into a nervous wreck.

Sagittarian female with Libran male

Friend: He treats you like a lady. Lover: You enjoy his lovemaking. Spouse: He's very attentive and thoughtful – but you make the decisions.

Sagittarian female with Sagittarian male

Friend: It's a great friendship. Lover: You're nicely attuned to each other. Spouse: It's more like a brother-and-sister relationship.

Sagittarian female with Capricornian male

Friend: The friendship is too onesided – you do all the giving. Lover: You aren't very compatible. Spouse: He takes very good care of you – in fact, he keeps you locked up in a golden cage.

Sagittarian female with Aquarian male

Friend: It's a long and enduring friendship. Lover: He can take you to the top of the world. Spouse: You're well complemented.

Sagittarian female with Piscean male

Friend: Although he lets you make all the important decisions, he makes an issue of trivial matters. Lover: He wants you to be the aggressor. Spouse: You have to take charge, and he's too hard to live with.

CAPRICORNIAN MALE

Capricornian male with Arien female

Friend: You go places together. Lover: She can really get you going. Spouse: Don't heavy her – let love take its course.

Capricornian male with Taurean female

Friend: You have the same outlook. Lover: The romance is enjoyable and wholesome. Spouse: You're possibly the ideal match – a solid and happy couple.

Capricornian male with Gemini female

Friend: Although you're different, the friendship is quite enjoyable. Lover: She's all woman – but you fail to see it that way. Spouse: As a wife, she's a bit immature.

Capricornian male with Cancerian female

Friend: You argue constantly. Lover: It's a beautiful union. Spouse: You're perfect for each other, and both of you believe marriage gives you your purpose in life.

Capricornian male with Leo female

Friend: You indulge in mental fights. Lover: She probably thinks sex is only for making babies. Spouse: Although it's a nice, solid marriage, it lacks variety.

Capricornian male with Libran female

Friend: You take her too delicately. Lover: In her eyes, it's just an affair. Spouse: She makes you relax, and you make her efficient.

Capricornian male with Scorpion female

Friend: You're good friends but dreadful enemies. Lover: She makes you lose your inhibitions. Spouse: You aren't a good match, because there are too many obstacles.

Capricornian male with Sagittarian female

Friend: You have to keep your nose out of her business.

Lover: There are too many differences for you to enjoy your sex life. Spouse: She isn't a one-man woman whereas you're faithful.

Capricornian male with Capricornian female
Friend: After the shyness at the start, the friendship works well. Lover: You're the one who has conservative ideas about sex. Spouse: You have the same ideas about marriage, and yours is solid.

Capricornian male with Aquarian female
Friend: She makes fun of you constantly. Lover: You like her in bed – pity it's only for a short time. Spouse: You have a prim and proper marriage.

Capricornian male with Piscean female
Friend: She's loyal and a good companion. Lover: She wants you to dominate her. Spouse: She wants you to be a guide, not a tyrant.

CAPRICORNIAN FEMALE

Capricornian female with Arien male
Friend: It's a whirlwind friendship. Lover: He's like a bull at a gate. Spouse: He cares for you but wants time for himself as well.

Capricornian female with Taurean male
Friend: You can depend on him. Lover: It's just business as usual. Spouse: He works according to the rules and is very strict.

Capricornian female with Gemini male
Friend: He's a good side-attraction. Lover: His interest is getting you into bed. Spouse: He's too fickle.

Capricornian female with Cancerian male
Friend: You have to hold his hand sometimes. Lover: You have to play the leading lady. Spouse: It's a good partnership – you don't stifle each other.

Capricornian female with Leo male
Friend: He likes you, and you can teach him a thing or two. Lover: He thinks he's a lady killer. Spouse: He wants you to be his little show pony.

Capricornian female with Virgoan male
Friend: You're soulmates. Lover: Both of you find it hard to be emotional. Spouse: He's dull, and there's no excitement whatsoever.

Capricornian female with Libran male
Friend: If you're frank with him, the friendship is good. Lover: He doesn't want to engage in any strenuous activities. Spouse: Both of you make sure your offspring want for nothing.

Capricornian female with Scorpion male
Friend: Both of you feel superior. Lover: He gives you more than you can handle. Spouse: It isn't an easy partnership.

Capricornian female with Sagittarian male
Friend: He seems to live in a world of his own. Lover: He isn't a one-night-stand man. Spouse: He's better off single.

Capricornian female with Capricornian male
Friend: You have a lovely time together. Lover: There's no variety in the affair. Spouse: Everything is in its place and runs smoothly.

Capricornian female with Aquarian male
Friend: He's set in his ways. Lover: He wants new experiences constantly. Spouse: He wants you to fall in with all his whims.

Capricornian female with Piscean male
Friend: He's a dreamer – wake him up. Lover: He's too sleepy, and possibly too lazy for you. Spouse: He hates making decisions, and you might finish up wiping his nose for him.

AQUARIAN MALE

Aquarian male with Arien female
Friend: It's a nice, easygoing friendship. Lover: She wants a macho man – she isn't your cup of tea. Spouse: She isn't the homemaker type.

Aquarian male with Taurean female
Friend: She's too earthy for you. Lover: She does more than smother you. Spouse: Your lifestyle differs too much from hers.

Aquarian male with Gemini female
Friend: She's a happy-go-lucky friend. Lover: She's constantly up to new tricks – the romance is jolly good fun. Spouse: You're a great match.

Aquarian male with Cancerian female
Friend: She might treat you like a little boy. Lover: You might be a bit too distant for her liking. Spouse: You're counterweights.

Aquarian male with Leo female
Friend: She makes you feel great. Lover: You have great sex. Spouse: It's a good match, and both of you are keenly interested in sex.

Aquarian male with Virgoan female
Friend: The friendship is based on mutual intellect only. Lover: You can really fulfil each other's needs. Spouse: You can truly live for each other.

Aquarian male with Libran female

Friend: She's a good companion for you. Lover: She wants you to be a bit more forceful. Spouse: Although she isn't the world's best homemaker, she's great at social occasions.

Aquarian male with Scorpion female

Friend: She constantly hopes for more than friendship. Lover: She's serious about sex whereas you aren't. Spouse: At home, she wants you all to herself.

Aquarian male with Sagittarian female

Friend: It's a great and rewarding friendship. Lover: You can make beautiful music together. Spouse: If you keep the marriage interesting, it lasts.

Aquarian male with Capricornian female

Friend: She wants to stick her nose into your business. Lover: There are some nice hot moments. Spouse: She needs the marriage to run smoothly – one mishap and you're in big trouble.

Aquarian male with Aquarian female

Friend: The relationship remains very platonic. Lover: Both of you never seriously consider sex. Spouse: Although it's a good partnership, if sex isn't part of it it's dead.

Aquarian male with Piscean female

Friend: She's a kind and understanding friend. Lover: She might get too involved for your liking. Spouse: She's a bit of a scatterbrain but very kindhearted.

AQUARIAN FEMALE

Aquarian female with Arien male

Friend: Although he's the outdoor type, he's good company for you. Lover: He's too 'hot diggedy-dog' for you. Spouse: You're like a pair of wandering gypsies.

Aquarian female with Taurean male

Friend: He likes to run your affairs. Lover: He's down to earth. Spouse: He's a good breadwinner and homemaker.

Aquarian female with Gemini male

Friend: He's full of good humour. Lover: He's hot stuff. Spouse: He's the wanderer – he likes to roam around.

Aquarian female with Cancerian male

Friend: He's very moody. Lover: He's more interested in finding a wife than in being a lover. Spouse: He isn't a bad homemaker, but he's moody.

Aquarian female with Leo male

Friend: He's a very loyal friend. Lover: He's generous with niceties such as flowers and chocolates. Spouse: Although he's a bit of a prima donna, you can be quite happy together.

Aquarian female with Virgoan male

Friend: Stay away from him. Lover: There isn't much feeling in the affair. Spouse: The marriage might be a bit too clinical for you.

Aquarian female with Libran male

Friend: He's okay but a bit lazy. Lover: He's good in bed, and he tries to please you. Spouse: If you want an indecisive mate, he'll do.

Aquarian female with Scorpion male

Friend: He's too moody and domineering for you. Lover: Stay clear of him. Spouse: He isn't for you, and the marriage takes too much hard work.

Aquarian female with Sagittarian male

Friend: He has a great sense of humour and is nice to be with. Lover: He's terrific – both of you like the unusual. Spouse: He makes love to you almost like a breeze.

Aquarian female with Capricornian male

Friend: Expect clashes of the intellect. Lover: He's forceful but conservative. Spouse: He's solid and dependable.

Aquarian female with Aquarian male

Friend: You're soulmates. Lover: There's a lot of fiddling around but no substance. Spouse: You're weird characters together.

Aquarian female with Piscean male

Friend: You're quite nice together, but both of you are fickle. Lover: He has quite an imagination and can be fun in bed. Spouse: He loves deeply but is erratic.

PISCEAN MALE

Piscean male with Arien female

Friend: You have to get used to her ways. Lover: She dominates you – be her slave, if that's your scene. Spouse: You might have to swap roles with her.

Piscean male with Taurean female

Friend: She runs your life for you. Lover: Don't be wishy-washy with her. Spouse: She takes control and provides for you.

Piscean male with Gemini female

Friend: It's a nice friendship, but she loses patience with you. Lover: Expect to have a fling only – nothing serious. Spouse: You mightn't like it when she keeps pushing you, but she makes sure your children are looked after.

Piscean male with Cancerian female

Friend: The relationship might be just a bit more than platonic. Lover: As bed companions you're tremendous. Spouse: She's well balanced emotionally.

Piscean male with Leo female

Friend: For her, you might lack fibre. Lover: She wants a bit of a show in your romance. Spouse: Although she's good socially, she wants life's comforts.

Piscean male with Virgoan female

Friend: You have to be frank with each other and discuss your differences. Lover: It doesn't work. Spouse: There are too many differences for the marriage to work.

Piscean male with Libran female

Friend: You're very well suited. Lover. As bed mates you're very good. Spouse: You're a nice, sweet and gentle couple.

Piscean male with Scorpion female

Friend: You have to let her have her own way occasionally. Lover: It's a romance that's either bust or boom. Spouse: Although the marriage is full of strife, it works well.

Piscean male with Sagittarian female

Friend: She's very elastic. Lover: You have plenty of fun in the cot – for a while, anyway. Spouse: The marriage mightn't work, because your emotions get in the way.

Piscean male with Capricornian female

Friend: She might be a bit shy at first. Lover: Both of you might be too shy to start something. Spouse: It isn't a very good match.

Piscean male with Aquarian female

Friend: It's a very eventful relationship. Lover: She doesn't have enough substance for you. Spouse: There's no common ground for you to form a solid basis.

Piscean male with Piscean female

Friend: The friendship is too extreme for you. Lover: You have to take charge. Spouse: It's a marriage of two fuss-pots.

PISCEAN FEMALE

Piscean female with Arien male

Friend: He bosses you around. Lover: He gobbles you up. Spouse: He wants to make a doormat out of you.

Piscean female with Taurean male

Friend: Although he's dependable, you have to stop your dreaming. Lover: He's full of sex but not too much loving. Spouse: He wants everything to be in its proper place and time.

Piscean female with Gemini male

Friend: He can become a good companion. Lover: He talks you into getting into the cot with him – take him lightly. Spouse: You never quite know where you are with him.

Piscean female with Cancerian male

Friend: He's a firm and loyal friend. Lover: You're like two lovebirds. Spouse: You have a great home life with him and the children.

Piscean female with Leo male

Friend: Although he's a show-off, the friendship is good. Lover: If you tell him how great he is, he outdoes himself. Spouse: He might be too much in love with himself for the marriage to work.

Piscean female with Virgoan male

Friend: You're at opposite ends of the table. Lover: You have to click straight away, otherwise forget it. Spouse: If you don't click, don't try to make it work.

Piscean female with Libran male

Friend: It's a relationship based on artistic interests. Lover: It's a rather wet affair. Spouse: As a husband, he's a bit of a dag.

Piscean female with Scorpion male

Friend: He bewitches you. Lover: He wants to have you in his power. Spouse: As a husband, he's probably too one-sided.

Piscean female with Sagittarian male

Friend: He bolsters your self-confidence. Lover: He's in one hell of a hurry to hop into bed with you. Spouse: In marriage, he can be rather insecure.

Piscean female with Capricornian male

Friend: He benefits from the friendship more than you do. Lover: He seems to be distant. Spouse: He takes control and smothers you in the process.

Piscean female with Aquarian male

Friend: You have to keep up with him. Lover: He's sneaky – before you're aware of it, you're in bed with him. Spouse: He turns you into a nervous wreck because of his surprises.

Piscean female with Piscean male

Friend: You aren't a realistic couple, and you love dreaming. Lover: Both of you see more than there is. Spouse: He makes life more difficult than it really is.

Your best lover according to your star sign

Astrology can help you find that elusive lover you've dreamed of all your life. The fact is, though, that what's good for you in romance mightn't be good for your partner, so by reading the following guide, you might get closer to your night of nights. The guide is written from the point of view of the reader, you if you're an Arien, read the Aries section.

ARIES

As an Arien, you're highly sexed, so you probably get into trouble more than once. If you believe variety is the spice of life, the best love partner for you is a Sagittarian. You have many things in common in your attitudes towards sex; for example, you try to avoid permanence and lifelong attachment and live for the moment. The person you have to avoid is the Piscean: he or she wants to keep you forever and expects to have a longlasting relationship – something that isn't on your mind very often.

TAURUS

As a Taurean, you're romantic but down to earth and a slow mover. You should avoid the fire-sign people: Ariens, Leos and Sagittarians. You crave a deeply satisfying love life and want to have a partner for life. A Virgoan is a reliable love partner for you, and his or her commonsense approach to love appeals to you. Don't try to attach yourself to an Arien: you're simply incompatible.

GEMINI

As a Gemini, you have a complex personality because you're born under the sign of the twins: on the one hand you want excitement and romance, on the other stability and permanence. It isn't uncommon for Geminis to successfully conduct two love affairs at once, usually with two completely different partners. An Aquarian is a good love partner for you, because he or she is mysterious and therefore usually maintains your interest. You're usually bored stiff by a Taurean: his or her slow lovemaking doesn't appeal to you.

CANCER

As a Cancerian, you're worried not about your sex life but about your partner's fidelity. Because you crave romance, a Taurean is a good love partner for you: he or she is romantic and always reliable and also satisfies you. You're a bit too sensitive for any sex games, so you should avoid Geminis, whose whole existence is a game. Because you're warm and thoughtful, you're a nice, stable lover, and you have the knack of making people happy.

LEO

As a Leo, you have many chances to find love in your life because of your magnetic personality. However, you want only the person destined for you. An attractive Libran is the perfect love partner for you, because he or she is passionate but undemanding. Stay away from Virgoans, though: they're too ready to criticise you, which you naturally resent. Everything you do has to be the best, so you expect to be praised for your lovemaking.

VIRGO

As a Virgoan, you're easily aroused and you worry a lot about your love life. Because you're very selective, not many people come up to your standards. You're somewhat insecure by nature, so a secure Cancerian is the best love partner for you. Leos' fiery temper makes a love union with them impossible, so avoid them. The Cancerian's affectionate nature makes him or her the best bet for you.

LIBRA

As a Libran, you're as hard to please as Virgoans are: you're often intellectual and very moody, so it's often difficult to know what you want. A Leo can usually read your moods and satisfy you both mentally and physically. Much less emotional are Capricornians, with whom you have little in common, so stay away from them. The Leo's sexual fire burns brightly with you around.

SCORPIO

As a Scorpion, your life is full of sexual fantasies.

You have a powerful personality that's reflected in your sex life. The only love partner who really pleases you is another Scorpion, but it's a stormy affair. Stay away from Librans: they ruin you mentally, and because you have a very direct nature, you don't understand their many needs.

SAGITTARIUS

As a Sagittarian, you like to play hide-and-seek – and that game applies to your sex life too. If your prospective partner doesn't understand that you love to play games, the relationship won't work. A good match for you is therefore an Arien: he or she also likes to play and enjoys life the same way you do. The person born under the water sign of Cancer very soon cools your fire, and you don't have much in common with him or her anyway.

CAPRICORN

As a Capricornian, you're hard to please. You're therefore best suited to a Piscean, who's also a discriminating person. Both of you are sensitive and charming, so you should be able to satisfy each other – a mutual admiration society is what your romance could be called. The person who does nothing for you as a lover is the Aquarian: you're completely incompatible.

AQUARIUS

As an Aquarian, you tend to flaunt your sexuality, so some people would say you're shocking. You like to have explosive love affairs, and few people can resist you. Geminis are made for your kind of love. However, run fast if a Scorpion has set his or her sights on you: the relationship would be a disaster, because your freewheeling nature would be curtailed completely.

PISCES

As a Piscean, you're a sentimentalist, and you dream of having perfect love, both mental and physical. For you, a Capricornian is probably the closest thing to a perfect lover you can get. Both of you are sensual and imaginative in lovemaking, and the romantic atmosphere you create so well as a Piscean suits both of you extremely well. Don't bother taking an interest in a Sagittarian: as a lover, he or she would completely frustrate you.

Your man's love nature according to his star sign

Is he a loyal Leo, a scorcher of a Scorpion, a Piscean who can't stand pettiness or a Libran who loves to love? Find out what you can expect from the twelve men of the zodiac.

ARIES

In romance, the Arien man likes to get a head start. His enthusiasm for approval from the opposite sex starts early in life. He needs love in order to build his confidence in his own pioneering spirit, and he doesn't hesitate to take practical steps towards finding what he's looking for.

The Arien man is generally successful in his romantic pursuits. Although he might seem to be hard to get, he definitely isn't; in fact, he might become impatient if his love affair isn't moving along as smoothly as he thinks it should. Furthermore, he's probably a bit of a flirt when it comes to relating to females other than you in the same room. Nevertheless, fickleness won't necessarily be a part of his roving-eye nature. The fact is that because of his flair, it's rather difficult for him to continue granting his approval or disapproval to all women, even after he's married.

TAURUS

The Taurean man might act as though he's an ocean of love and be completely surrounded by expensive things. He has a very natural attitude towards love affairs. Although he's very passionate underneath, he's outwardly very direct in his approach to the whole matter. He's usually quiet, but when he believes he's being challenged, he can become possessive and very jealous.

The Taurean man also tends to become intellectually as well as emotionally involved in his romantic entanglements.

Although he will or might have many love affairs, once he falls in love it's for good. It's inherent in his nature to be loyal and faithful; in fact, he'll easily become rather stubborn if he encounters a disagreement about the question of fidelity. He takes his time when evaluating the inner qualities of the person who's the object of his pursuit, and he refuses to be rushed into making a decision. In love, what he's really looking for is a love that manifests itself through a really warm affection.

GEMINI

The Gemini man might be somewhat less sentimental than the Taurean. It's his nature to like variety in life, and this characteristic carries over into his love affairs. Basically, he doesn't like to feel either tied down or possessed. He'll probably go through many love affairs in order to have ample opportunity for the self-expression he finds very exciting.

KERRY KULKENS' GUIDE TO LOVE, SEX AND YOUR STARS

The Gemini man often fails to find love quickly, because of his tendency towards finding people's faults before finding their good points. He's gentle and sympathetic, despite his leanings towards flirting. He can also tease without actually showing a vital interest. Actually, his affections are ruled by his mind more than by his emotions. He's also willing to listen to points of view that differ from his own. With reference to his changeable nature, he eventually more or less catches up with himself and begins to lean towards loyalty and sincerity.

CANCER

The Cancerian man sometimes believes that love is only a conflict between reflexes and reflections: he often views it as being a whim of the moment. Nevertheless, he's indeed a dull person if he doesn't have romance in his life. He's almost always loyal and affectionate, and he can most certainly be self-sacrificing when the need arises. Although he might also give the impression he's restless, changeable and fickle, underneath he's looking for a good love life.

The Cancerian man might have to withdraw himself once in a while in order to regain his confidence so he can avoid adopting a nagging or domineering attitude. These attitudes are caused by his feeling insecure. He might find it difficult to find someone who measures up to his ideals. His standards are sometimes too high, and he's usually hurt when his love fails to live up to them. He might tend to develop a possessive nature that could lead to jealousy when he fails to see eye to eye with his love partner. He always intends to please you, so don't misunderstand him.

LEO

The Leo man is a fool in love. Although he loves deeply and sometimes not very wisely, he always loves well. Despite the fact he's conventional in most things he does, he's very likely to be totally carried away by love. At heart he's highly romantic, and he takes love affairs very seriously. He expects you to do the same, and he isn't a flirt. He doesn't like public displays of affection, because he believes they're beneath his dignity and that he'll lose the respect of the people who witness the demonstration.

The Leo man is more often than not the centre of attention, so control your tendency to be jealous. Because he's proud, he finds it rather difficult to understand how anyone could either deceive or fail him. He's ardent and passionate, and he'll give himself completely to whoever he's fixed his sights on. He's truly loyal to the person who returns his affections.

VIRGO

The Virgoan man sometimes believes that love is only the result of marriage, so he might be somewhat inhibited and disinclined towards romance and glamorous love affairs. He can so very easily be dominated by the person who wins his love. It's very important he make the right choice. He might suffer disappointment frequently in his love affairs and have difficulty finding someone who lives up to his expectations. He might, in fact, shop around when it comes to finding the right partner.

The Virgoan man won't readily admit he needs romance, because he likes to think his intellect comes first.

When it comes to affection, he tends to be somewhat undemonstrative. Basically, he's the type of man who makes an excellent companion rather than a romantic partner. He becomes capable of real love only once he feels sure of himself.

LIBRA

The Libran man believes that love sought is good but that love sought after is better. Although he might seem to be very mentally detached, he's a most passionate person. He has a physical side that makes him very fond of company, and he's usually affectionate, loving and very considerate. He tends to have strange ideas about his relationships with the opposite sex and sometimes becomes deeply involved in a secret or impulsive love affair.

The Libran man is prone to becoming a bit unstable emotionally, because his passions tend to burn red hot and ice cold in a matter of minutes. He usually presents himself as being highly refined – up to a point, after which he falls into a heap. However, if he fails to be constant in his devotion, remind him he's loved and appreciated.

SCORPIO

The Scorpion man loves wine, women and song, and if you think he doesn't, you're wrong. He's really dynamic and intense in his love affairs, as he is in everything else he's involved in. For his life to run smoothly, he has to be in love so he can have sympathy and understanding. He thrives on receiving compliments and expressing passion and spares no effort in making his love partner happy and secure.

The Scorpion man might sometimes seem to be overly sensuous. The fact is he rarely finds time for light flirtations because of the intensity with which he expresses his devotion. He's a proud and generous-natured man and expects complete reciprocation in all matters of love. He might also be a bit too possessive. However, he's simply unhappy unless he's involved in a romantic entanglement. He likes open displays of affection and is very capable of destroying obstacles that appear in the path of him and his love partner.

SAGITTARIUS

The Sagittarian man might believe that a man should love a little and a woman a lot.

However, he isn't possessive, and he's loyal to the woman he loves. Basically, he doesn't value personal possessive love very highly but instead tends to treasure universal love. For him, any romance has to bring him mental as well as physical satisfaction. On the other hand, his attraction to the opposite sex sometimes produces an unfortunate experience for him. The reason he might have many affairs before he marries is that he finds it impossible to be insincere in any romantic commitment he makes.

The Sagittarian man has to make absolutely sure he has the right woman. He tends to view his romances as being an outlet for both adventure and escape from reality. Although his high ideals mean a lot to him, he treasures his freedom highly.

CAPRICORN

The Capricornian man tends to be intellectual rather than emotional in his approach to love affairs. He's usually careful to do exactly the right thing and very conscious of his partner's feelings. There's never any danger his partner will be misled about exactly where she stands, because her position is determined right from the start. The affairs he does become involved in are always sincere, and he means what he says.

The Capricornian man won't necessarily take the lead in romance, despite the fact he usually knows what he wants. He might even be inclined to put his career before his romance. It's simply inherent in him to take life seriously. However, once he does allow himself to become committed to love, he tends to become rather possessive and to be made jealous easily. Despite these characteristics, though, constancy becomes one of his strongest qualities once he really falls in love.

AQUARIUS

The Aquarian man has a slight tendency to express a preference for universal love over personal love, because he believes romance is as much a meeting of minds as of hearts. He usually seeks out a woman who shares his mental interests, and when he finds the right one, he's faithful forever. If he suffers a disappointment, he falls out of love just as fast as he fell into it.

The Aquarian man tends to fall into worry and anxiety if he senses his love partner is trying to override his mental inclinations. When this happens, he resumes his search for the woman who has both intellectual and emotional resources and a temperament that's the same as his, because he simply won't tolerate anything else. He also insists on having his own personal freedom and privacy. Underneath all this, he's strongly affectionate when he believes he isn't being either possessed or crowded in; in other words, he can be easily led.

PISCES

The Piscean man believes that the only way to win victory over love is to run from it.

He's sincere and affectionate and won't tolerate any kind of pettiness. His standards are very high, and he's looking for a woman who's very careful of her appearance and who uses her intelligence as she should. He has no time for wasting talents.

The Piscean man thrives on receiving compliments and even on being flattered. His emotions run deep, and his feelings are rather easily hurt. He might be all too easily led into a romantic entanglement against his will, especially if the woman's personality is stronger than his. When this happens, both he and his love partner suffer, because he's entirely too sensitive to other people's feelings to hurt his lover's feelings. He therefore submits himself even if his heart isn't in it.

What the people of each star sign expect from sex

All of us have an interest in sex, be it personally or academically or simply to test our memory. It's believed that witches practise all sorts of abominations in pursuing and worshipping physical gratification of the flesh. For the mystical community, venerating phallic symbols and engaging naked in orgies could be viewed as being good, clean fun – well, almost, depending on what turns you on.

The people of all cultures have been preoccupied with sexual prowess at some stage of the cultures' development.

THE SUMERIANS

The Sumerians moulded figurines of goddesses who showed off their swollen belly and pendulous breasts as being the fruit of their sexual behaviour.

THE ANCIENT EGYPTIANS

For the Ancient Egyptians, the phallic god Min symbolised the male's procreative pore. Min reminded people that sexual behaviour is an integral part of the balance of nature.

THE ANCIENT ROMANS

The Ancient Romans threw themselves into sexual gymnastics, after which they took quite some time to recuperate – at least until after they'd indulged in the usual drunken bacchanalia.

THE ANCIENT GREEKS

The activities of the Ancient Greeks' deities up in Mount Olympus resembled a good week at a bawdy house. For debauchery, the god Zeus set an example that his loyal worshippers could never equal – although the Roman emperor Caligula would've given it his best shot.

EUROPEANS IN THE MIDDLE AGES

When the Middle Ages hit the Western world with a big thud, the church authorities made sure that people stopped enjoying themselves. Witches were burnt at the stake, and much female lore and wisdom was thereby lost to masculine values and authority.

THE VICTORIANS

By the time of Queen Victoria, sex was to be rigorously avoided at all times, except if sanctified by marriage. However, even for married women it was something to be endured. Naturally, a lady didn't move when her husband foisted the marital obligation on her – only a loose woman would gain any pleasure from the activity.

And they give witches a bad name! Well, we're fortunate that times have changed. Today and through astrology, we can find out what to expect from sex with all the people of the twelve zodiac signs.

ARIES

Ariens like to have a good time and don't have time for either prudery or pussyfooting around: what you see is what you get. As fire people, they're passionate and sexual and expect to get as good as they give. They're the sustained performers of the zodiac. Their planet is Mars and their symbol is the ram, so their animal nature is easily aroused and has to be quickly satisfied. In sexual matters, they like to take over, and they know what they're doing, so let them do it: you'll find the experience to be both challenging and exciting. If possible, rest up beforehand, because you'll need every bit of strength you can muster.

TAURUS

Taureans are very sexual. They have an earthy approach and aren't known for their subtlety. You'll know exactly what they have in mind. Their symbol the bull represents the healthy animal spirit that characterises their attitude towards sex. Because they're ruled by Venus, they want their loving to be sweet and simple: no frills and no fuss. They don't need bedroom gymnastics to get their thrills, just a willing partner and a comfortable bed.

GEMINI

Geminis are usually in two minds about how to approach sex, depending on the mood of the moment. They like fun and games and carry this liking into their sex life. The dull, pedantic approach isn't for them. Although they like sex, they also like to fool around, so they don't go in for a quick approach. Because they're ruled by Mercury, they'll have you up in the air one minute and down on the bed the next. Sex will be like a merry-go-round: you won't know whether you're coming or going – but the ride will certainly be worthwhile.

CANCER

Cancerians are ruled by the Moon and have a strong attitude towards sex: they enjoy it to the fullest, especially if it's used to comfort their partner. Cancerian crabs have a lot of sexual energy to share

with any partner who's passionate and intense. Their heavy release of emotional feeling follows through to a sexual involvement, so if you want a lighthearted approach, try elsewhere – Cancerians expect a total response.

LEO

Leos like all the drama and pussyfooting around that precedes the sexual union. Because they're ruled by the Sun, they're hotblooded and passionate, and real lions in the bedroom. Indulging in erotic games together and reading sexual-technique manuals will have you appreciating Leos' capacity for physical enjoyment. If you want a straightforward approach, the lion isn't for you.

VIRGO

Virgoans can have a very conventional attitude towards sex: the 'in bed, with the light off' approach. Although they're extremely sexual, they require a high standard from their partner. This attitude can be an inhibiting factor for full enjoyment of the physical union. If you can pass the physical test, Mercury-ruled Virgo the virgin is for you.

LIBRA

Librans like a lot of physical contact in a sexual relationship, including touching, caressing and kissing. They'll try novel methods to achieve a satisfactory sexual union. Their symbol is the scales and their planet is Venus, so they're turned on by physically attractive partners and sweet offerings of flattering words. For them, the setting in which to express sexual desires is important: having a water bed, satin sheets and little touches of elegance enhances the erotic capacity of these Venus-ruled people. If you're after quality, a Libran is for you.

SCORPIO

Scorpions are sexual and aggressive. You'll need to have a lot of stamina to keep up with their marathon bedroom lovemaking. They're ruled by Pluto and their symbol is the scorpion, so in sexual encounters they like to dominate.

They're very passionate and erotic, consummate lovers and masters of their art. They'll possess you utterly, so if you're looking for a passive partner, look elsewhere.

SAGITTARIUS

Sagittarians like plenty of action, and sex with them is likely to be an endurance marathon. They're ruled by Jupiter and their symbol is the archer, so they like to try different and stimulating techniques. You can look through the sex manual together and choose an array of techniques for the evening. The archer will want a very active partner who provides a lot of erotic stimulation. If adventure is what you're seeking, look no further.

CAPRICORN

Capricornians might fool you: they don't give the impression they're good in bed, but they are. They're ruled by Saturn and their symbol is the goat, so they can be as earthy and physical as any of the other people of the zodiac are. The frisky goat will expect to have a sensual partner who's receptive to his or her sexual needs. An athletic performance won't be required: just a good, plain romp between the sheets.

AQUARIUS

Aquarians need something different in order to stimulate their sexuality: ordinary, everyday sex is out of the question for them. These Uranian water bearers like their sex life to be full of surprises. They're capable of adding much variety to their approaches and techniques, and they also like their partner to be versatile. If you crave constant excitement and don't wear your sexual preferences on your sleeve, an Aqaurian is for you.

PISCES

Pisceans are very emotional and passionate and expect their mate to have the same response. These Neptune-ruled fish are happy to be a passive partner and to defer to a more aggressively sexual person. For them, lovemaking is a gentle event. They like a lot of physical contact, including caressing and kissing, and they're very demonstrative.

Turn on according to your partner's star sign

All of us attempt to have our sexual needs fulfilled, and how they're to be fulfilled has us tingling with anticipation.

If you want to go deep-skin diving in a waterbed, take a Scorpion along: he or she knows how to find hidden treasures.

Perhaps you need to escape into an erotic fantasy, in which case a Piscean is the perfect partner: he or she dresses up for effect – is it a whale or a minnow? You'll soon find out.

Looking for fireworks? Want some heat? You'll soon be burning up for your Arien lover – skyrockets in flight and big bangs will soon delight you.

If perfection turns you on, your Virgoan will show you the way – but scrub up first: he or she likes a clean body and sweet breath. When you're ready, prepare for a game of doctors and nurses – but make sure you bring your gloves.

Do you need to be dominated? A willing slave to a kind master? Leo is for you. He or she will have to be in control of you, body and soul.

For kinky sex, you can't go past Geminis: they're all over the place, and their feet never touch the ground. They have two ways of doing everything and like to have two things going on at the same time – but can you handle it?

If you prefer the romantic approach – wine, moonlight and a stroll on the beach – a Cancerian is for you. If you like making love on the sand then swimming in the nude, you'll be squeezed with delight by your crab.

Want to keep your feet on the ground? You must have a Capricornian. Hold on and wait for the earthquake to start.

If eroticism sends your pulses throbbing, try an Aquarian: the sultan of sex. Hire a camel, pitch a tent and watch the sun set in your erotic fantasy.

If you want to ride at a galloping pace on a strong stallion, a Sagittarian has the stamina. He or she can be a real beast.

If you fancy a fandango in the clover – or a bit of bull, especially the long-horn variety – a Taurean is for you. If you're looking for a stampede, wear red.

Want to swing? Like to go up and down? A Libran is for you, if you can keep your balance. He or she has the right angle: sharp and to the point.

The choice is yours now you know which zodiacal partner will make your sexual dreams come true. Have a lusty time!

ARIES

Ariens are the fastest people in the zodiac and gets things done in a hurry. They're very impatient, and they never work in low gear: even in sleep they're in full flight. Anyone who can't keep up with them might as well have a droopy bum. Aries is the sign of the inventor, and Ariens make new things out of old. They're possibly too easy with their money, and they expend too much energy in too many directions. They also get sick of their lover very quickly and always look for someone new.

Arien bosses give authority to their job and have excellent leadership qualities. However, Ariens are a bit too bossy when it comes to their love life. They're neither boring nor bored for very long. If you're interested in one, don't waste time: come on strong.

Turn up naked with a can of beer, and keep things short and sweet and straight to the point.

The best way to keep an Arien interested is to look sexy and perhaps either wear raunchy lingerie or acquire a tattoo in an exciting place on your body. Your ram will be too hot to handle, so hang on and wait for the fireworks.

TAURUS

Taureans like to break down the barriers. They're stubborn and always ready with an answer. Weak people find it hard to handle them. Taureans would rather hold their breath than admit to being wrong and would also rather poo their pants than say yes. Your kindly banker could be one of them, because money is one of their big interests. Sex is another one – especially kinky sex.

They might even have a dollar sign tattooed on one of their buttocks.

Don't get too fooled by your Taurean friend's easygoing nature: he or she uses it only to make you relax and then pounces. Taureans are usually honest and don't try to talk you into anything if you aren't interested. However, when you show that you are, watch out: here comes the bull. The best incentives for Taureans to perform well in bed are a good meal and some fresh water – and don't talk bull crap, otherwise they'll lose interest. In love, they're like a bull in a china shop: they quickly break down all the barriers and leave you shattered and on edge.

GEMINI

Geminis are very entertaining and good in all aspects of flirting. They're also very sexy, and everyone should have one for a pet. They're quick witted and fun, but you won't be able to put one over them if they don't want you to. Because they're good talkers, it can be hard to keep them quiet long enough to pose the vital question. Once you've done so, though, they're with you all the way.

Two problems most Geminis might have is that they have too many possibilities to choose from and that group sex is one of their hobbies. If you're planning to seduce a Gemini, wear a seductive scent and sexy clothes so you can be sure you'll be accepted. Don't let Geminis talk you into participating in weird arrangements if you aren't into weird arrangements. They like to play hide-and-seek games in bed. If you have the right balance, they have the right angle. They're kinky, and they always have two ways of doing things.

CANCER

Although Cancerians can have a complex personality, they're very honest and fear-minded people. They aren't very easy to please, they tend to be in a hurry, and they tend not to concentrate very much on what they're doing and who they're doing it with. If you get them burning, you're in for a treat. They're great at parties and fun to be with, providing they're in a good mood. Run if they're in a foul mood. They could be rough and ready. They don't take harassment from anyone and usually give as well as they get.

A sea voyage would be just the thing to get them interested: they'll rise to the occasion. Don't reveal your fears, otherwise your Cancerian will exploit them and make you suffer. Because Cancerians are crabs, they love to claw at you and squeeze you with delight – so if you don't want a crab, avoid them.

LEO

Leos have to show off, and their personality is obvious enough. They wear lots of frills and feathers and have a mane that's usually strongly coloured. They love drama, and you'd be wise to make a big thing out of your seduction number. Don't let them feel they're neglected, otherwise you'll have the world's greatest martyr on your hands. Although they aren't very selfish, you have to make sure they get what they believe is their due. They're very optimistic, and they'll wait for a good lover if they think he or she is worth it.

Don't let your Leo smoke or drink too much, because Leos can become excessive in their habits. They're born leaders, and you'll be happiest – and they'll excel – if you let them lead you to bed. They know how to give you a right royal affair. Dreams come true with them.

To keep the night flame burning, wear lots of orange and make sure you make the bed with orange-satin sheets.

If you like to play servant to a master, your Leo will take you over, body and soul. Try a command such as, 'Come here and dominate me, master!'

VIRGO

Virgoans are very critical but are usually more modest than brassy. They can make you do what they want very easily. They're very clean: there might be some kinky sex in store for you, because they might suddenly want to get up and have a sauna in the middle of it all. They're loyal, and they usually stay with the lover they've chosen at the time – and they expect you to do the same.

The best thing for you to do is stay clean and enjoy what you have. Don't insist on doing things your way – at least not very often. Virgoans can be a bit difficult if they don't do very well, so don't persist if the flame isn't burning. If you don't have enough class for your Virgoan, you might be out of the race. The most effective things to do are to scrub up clean, wear clean clothing, use a breath

freshener and leave no body parts undeodorised. Then start playing doctors and nurses: your Virgoan will soon fix what's ailing you.

LIBRA

Librans are swingers. Because they have a very unpredictable personality, you can expect almost anything. They have plenty of energy, so be prepared for a vigorous sex life and some special gymnastics. Although you could call them unreliable, they do deliver when the mood is right. You mightn't be their only lover either, but at least with them you get value for your money and something to think about in those lonely moments.

If your Libran lover is bored, he or she might stray and find something better, in which case it might be goodbye to you. Keep him or her interested by using some special effects and aids in order to improve your sexual performance. Use an aphrodisiac sometimes to add a bit of mystery. If you don't demand attention from your Libran, you'll get plenty of it from him or her. Librans like to play hide-and-seek games in bed. Give them the right balance and they'll give you the right angle.

SCORPIO

Scorpions have a strong personality and frighten the more timid among us – but it's all a sham: they're as insecure as the rest of us, and they want to be cuddled and loved like babies are. However, Count Dracula was a Scorpion, so if you beware the hidden menace in their personality you'll sail through your lovemaking with flying colours. You have to live and love by your Scorpion's rules – nothing less. Scorpions can be very long suffering and will never forget it if you do the wrong thing; therefore, make sure you mean what you say, otherwise you'll be on their black list for good.

Scorpions are red hot in bed, so your love life will be a wow and sex will come when you call. If you talk crap, you'll never see them again. Because they're a water sign, they like deep-skin diving in a water bed and lots of sex that has a fantasy aspect: everything from 'little French maid' to bondage and discipline – and leather underwear. Your Scorpion lover will want to possess you, body and soul, and will hate to think you've been with even one other person. He or she will have to know your every thought.

SAGITTARIUS

If you like horsing around, a Sagittarian stallion is for you. Sagittarians aren't known for their tact and might come on to you like a ton of bricks. However, you'll have to guide him or her towards the finer things in sex, and you'll have to use your imagination to make the encounter more fun. Although Sagittarians are always willing, the object of their desire mightn't remain the same, and they can stray just for the sake of it.

People who seriously want a Sagittarian have to use their charm and body in order to get their message across and then guide the archer to where they want him or her. Although Sagittarians have intuition and do use it, it mightn't always work in the right place at the right time. It's up to you to let them know, in your clever way, what you want them to do in order to arouse you. Give them the chance to relax, otherwise their parts might wear out. Sagittarians are a bit of a beast: half human, half horse.

CAPRICORN

Watch out for the earthquake: just when you're worn out, your Capricornian lover will remain very amorous and sexy. Locking the door would be a good idea, because Capricornians don't wish to be caught out by their wife or lover when they're with you. They love to be romantic, and many of them are musical, so creating a bit of mood is helpful when you're planning your seduction ritual.

If you want to get on with your Capricornian love, you'd better like his or her friends, otherwise you won't be around

for long. Don't irritate him or her with small talk while you're making love, because it'll soon result in a cooling off. Sex is a serious business for him or her, so cut out all small talk. Capricornians can be a bit hard to handle when they're in a bad mood, so if you handle them with kid gloves you'll get between the sheets with them in no time at all. Their favourite position is both feet on the ground: the closer to the floor the better.

AQUARIUS

Aquarians are the sultans of sex: truly exotic erotics.

Because they collect friends like some people collect stamps, there's always a new friend who takes their fancy, so you'll have to work hard to keep their attention. You can do almost anything you like as long as it interests them; even being a bit eccentric tickles their fancy.

It's no good trying to change their habits or ideas: if you try, you'll find yourself in the doghouse of their imagination, and there you'll stay – no more fun and games for you. If you're in love with an Aquarian man, don't criticise either his manhood or his use of it, otherwise you'll never hear from him again. Aquarians are one of only a few people who can successfully be your lover and friend at the same time – so hire a camel, pitch a tent and watch the sun set with your sultan of sex.

PISCES

Pisceans love to escape in an erotic fantasy and to dress up for effect, as the strong and silent type. You might think they're easygoing, but you're in for a surprise if you get to know them intimately. Even you might have to work hard before you get them into bed, but they usually turn on a good show. Let them choose the time and place, and take it from there.

Pisceans aren't known to spend their money uselessly, so they'll want value for their time and money. Make sure you deliver. Although their cool, calm exterior might fool you, the fire is burning within, and getting your share of it will be worth your while if you do the right thing by your Piscean lover. Use your imagination: set the scene and lead your Piscean into it. To entice a Piscean man, try wearing silver underwear and silver high-heel shoes. However, when you're with Pisceans, neither speak loudly nor attract attention: they don't want the world to know what's on their mind.

The divorce rate for each star sign

The people of some signs are definitely more prone to divorcing than others are. Taureans tend have the highest divorce rate, Virgoans and Librans the lowest.

ARIES

Ariens are warm and romantic and don't like to be alone, so they usually marry quite young, and often twice. Because they're strong and determined, if they do divorce it's usually because they've found their partner isn't up to their standard in either intellect or vigour.

Although the Arien man is very often a devoted husband, if his input isn't appreciated, he leaves. The Arien woman isn't happy being a homemaker only, and this preference doesn't sit too well with some men. Ariens usually have a slightly above-average divorce rate.

TAURUS

There are more divorcees in this sign than in any other. After divorcing, most Taureans marry again, often to a partner who's very similar to the first. They're often selfish, demanding and hard to please, because other people don't live up to their required standards.

The Taurean man likes the nicer things in life such as food and comfort, and if they're missing, he leaves.

The Taurean woman often marries a man who's weaker than she is — which isn't hard, because she believes all men are weak.

GEMINI

Geminis are often argumentative and get into quarrels, so it isn't surprising they have an above-average divorce rate. They're in love with change, so they make changes often. If they come from a happy home, they have as good a chance in marriage as anyone has. However, they have a bad temper and a fickle mind and are therefore often found in the divorce courts.

The Gemini man believes he's the boss, and if he finds someone who's willing to share this belief, he settles into marriage happily. The Gemini woman is often searching for a father figure and often marries a man who's either considerably older or more mature thinking than she is.

CANCER

Cancerians are busy and ambitious and therefore often marry later in life. Work and career are important for them, and other things come second. They can be hard to live with, because they want everything done their way and forget about the nicer things such as love and romance.

The Cancerian man loves his home and family and doesn't really approve of divorce – if it happens, it's usually his wife who wants it. The Cancerian woman likes to dominate her mate and often marries at least twice.

LEO

Leos don't divorce very often, but their second marriage tends to be happier than their first. They like the oldfashioned type of mate: the knight in shining armour or the nice girl next door. When their mate turns out to be just an ordinary person, they're often disappointed. This realisation can be such a shock to them that divorce results.

However, both the classical tall and handsome Leo man and the classical attractive and vivacious Leo woman almost always marry again. Their second marriage is usually better, because they're more knowledgeable and experienced.

VIRGO

Although Virgoans don't divorce very often, they sometimes become very disappointed in their mate. When they do divorce, they're so disenchanted they never marry again. They trust people only so far – anything more is too much.

The Virgoan man is a good family man and holds on to his wife strongly. Because he might sometimes be a bit dull, his marriage might have some problems. The Virgoan woman is a good wife and mother and often likes to make the two roles her career. Virgoans of both sexes do tend to complain a bit.

LIBRA

Librans don't divorce easily, and very few of them ever end up in the divorce courts.

They have a very low level of tolerance for being ridiculed, so anyone who loves one of them should never ridicule him or her in public.

Being ridiculed would be just about the only reason a Libran man would divorce his wife. The Libran woman is an ideal wife, and there aren't many reasons a man would divorce her. However, if a Libran of either sex does divorce for whatever reason, he or she tends to remarry soon.

SCORPIO

Because Scorpions often come from a happy home that had a dominant mother figure, they aren't likely to divorce very often. They usually choose a good partner and live happily ever after. They're very sexually active, so incompatibility might sometimes be the reason for divorce. They also tend to be moody, so their moodiness is a factor that can aggravate some relationships.

The Scorpion man is a hard worker and looks after his family and friends loyally. The Scorpion woman is usually the stronger partner and tends to marry a quiet man who likes to get his strength from her.

SAGITTARIUS

Sagittarians are very unreliable in love: they like to play with fire and to get their kicks from the emotions thereby created.

The Sagittarian man is the hunter and wants the entire attention of the person he's pursuing. He isn't very faithful to his wife, who he finds too dull, and he usually creates a situation whereby his wife leaves him. The Sagittarian woman is much the same and doesn't like the domesticity expected of her.

CAPRICORN

Although Capricornians are emotional, because of their fierce loyalty they don't divorce easily. They're often able to pick a good partner, and if divorce happens it's usually caused by the other partner. When the break-up occurs, it hurts their feelings, and it takes them a long time to recover.

The Capricornian man usually respects his partner and expects her to be a good mother and wife. The Capricornian woman is the ruler but is very subtle about it so the husband thinks he's the head. Capricornians of both sexes think the world of marriage and try hard to make it work.

AQUARIUS

Aquarians don't divorce very easily, because they're intellectual and both sexes think very carefully before they commit themselves. Although Aquarians are strong characters and hard to please, they usually manage to find a partner to suit them.

The Aquarian man likes a woman to be a woman so he can play the male of the species, but he's sometimes a bit unreliable and seeks another partner. The Aquarian woman dominates in the marriage, but when she has a milder man, she's happy. She sometimes likes to pursue a career instead of settle for a conventional marriage.

PISCES

Pisceans are reasonably restless, which might be the main reason their divorce rate is high. They like to play on people's feelings and want sympathy. Good looks often get their attention.

The Piscean man likes a strong woman who's independently wealthy. The Piscean woman likes a softer man she can mould to her liking. The partner's looks play an important part when Pisceans of both sexes are making their selection.

Acrophonology: the sexy
meaning in your name

A useful way of measuring people's passionate reaction to intimate attentions is to consider the first letter of their first name. Each letter represents a sound in the English language, and the sound can be joined to the energy force of each of the twelve signs of the zodiac.

Reveal your sexual nature and that of other people by reading the following table. Find the first letter of the name by which your lover calls you and of the name by which you call him or her. Read the description next to the letter even if the name is a term of endearment but a name he or she uses more often than your actual name.

LETTER   SEXUAL NATURE

A
Your physical needs come first. You're passionate and sexual, in a cool way. You don't like flirting and don't have the patience for a subtle approach. You tell it like it is, without pretence. Action is what you like, and you aren't particularly romantic: you like to get on with it.

B
You're very sexual and earthy. You love to be indulged and know how to pamper people. You like conditions to be favourable before you give yourself completely – even to the point of putting things off until circumstances meet with your utmost approval. You like new sexual experiences and will experiment when you're comfortable in a relationship.

C
You need to know you have a loved one – even if it's several loved ones. You love to be involved. Talking to your mate is very important, and you crave closeness and tenderness. Your lover has to be attractive and to have an indefinable sexual attraction. Although sex is important for you, you can go without for a while.

D
You're passionate and intense in your involvements. You prefer to have security before you can let yourself go. Your perseverance usually wins out when you want the object of your desire. You're a caring and loyal mate who helps people in need.

E
You like to flirt but more for the challenge than the deed. You're loyal when you have the right mate, and your mate has to be able to stimulate you mentally. You like bantering and bickering in order to liven up your relationships.

F
You're out for the best, and nothing less will do. You like dramatic relationships. Although you're idealistic, you enjoy the attention you receive through flirting. However, you should stop flirting when you've found the person you're devoted to.

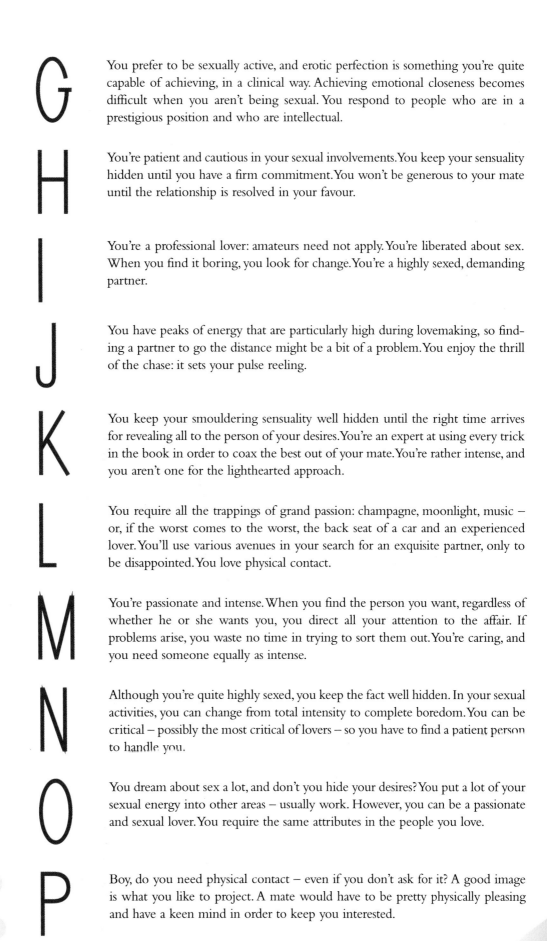

G

You prefer to be sexually active, and erotic perfection is something you're quite capable of achieving, in a clinical way. Achieving emotional closeness becomes difficult when you aren't being sexual. You respond to people who are in a prestigious position and who are intellectual.

H

You're patient and cautious in your sexual involvements. You keep your sensuality hidden until you have a firm commitment. You won't be generous to your mate until the relationship is resolved in your favour.

I

You're a professional lover: amateurs need not apply. You're liberated about sex. When you find it boring, you look for change. You're a highly sexed, demanding partner.

J

You have peaks of energy that are particularly high during lovemaking, so finding a partner to go the distance might be a bit of a problem. You enjoy the thrill of the chase: it sets your pulse reeling.

K

You keep your smouldering sensuality well hidden until the right time arrives for revealing all to the person of your desires. You're an expert at using every trick in the book in order to coax the best out of your mate. You're rather intense, and you aren't one for the lighthearted approach.

L

You require all the trappings of grand passion: champagne, moonlight, music — or, if the worst comes to the worst, the back seat of a car and an experienced lover. You'll use various avenues in your search for an exquisite partner, only to be disappointed. You love physical contact.

M

You're passionate and intense. When you find the person you want, regardless of whether he or she wants you, you direct all your attention to the affair. If problems arise, you waste no time in trying to sort them out. You're caring, and you need someone equally as intense.

N

Although you're quite highly sexed, you keep the fact well hidden. In your sexual activities, you can change from total intensity to complete boredom. You can be critical – possibly the most critical of lovers – so you have to find a patient person to handle you.

O

You dream about sex a lot, and don't you hide your desires? You put a lot of your sexual energy into other areas – usually work. However, you can be a passionate and sexual lover. You require the same attributes in the people you love.

P

Boy, do you need physical contact – even if you don't ask for it? A good image is what you like to project. A mate would have to be pretty physically pleasing and have a keen mind in order to keep you interested.

Q

Are you in training for the sexual Olympics? You're so robust, with energy to spare, that you require someone who can supply stimulus and activity. Mental stimulation barely matters. You can be a sad case in love, because you're very gullible.

R

Although sexual activity with your partner gives you security, you like to call the shots. You'll even teach him or her the finer points if his or her technique isn't terribly proficient. Ultimately, it'll be a meeting of minds that grabs your heart and soul and that clinches your partner for life.

S

S is for sizzler. Although you're highly sexed, you put business before pleasure. It's hard for you to get in the mood if you have financial problems on your mind – but if you haven't, wow! You're careful to keep your emotions in check, but when you let yourself go, you're virtually the ideal lover.

T

You love to be teased and stimulated erotically. You're sensitive and very private, and you like to assume the dominant role in bed. Although you can flirt in the right environment, a lover would find it hard to reach you on a mental level because you're often tuned into a fantasy world.

U

You have a strong sexual urge that requires quick release. You need to love and to spend a lot of time looking for the right person. You generate enthusiasm in your love affairs. Because you're able to put your loved one's needs above your own, you're a generous lover.

V

Way-out love affairs are your forte. You always attract unusual people who are almost always the wrong one. You eventually settle down with someone who's pretty 'ordinary' compared with most of the people you've been involved with. A love affair that has some suspense suits you best: it keeps you on your toes.

W

You exude sex appeal and use it to your best advantage. The objects of your desire will pursue you relentlessly until you accept them. However, your loved ones' impressions aren't always accurate, and you sometimes fall in love with someone for your ego's sake because the person builds up your confidence.

X

You're fickle, and that's why it's good there are so few of you: broken hearts would be littered everywhere. You take on several lovers at a time. Your mind and body never close down.

Y

You have to be the boss and are very pushy in initiating sexual contact. You have a strong desire to prove yourself. In love, Y is for yobbo. However, you make an exciting love and bed mate.

Z

You're easily aroused, especially after watching other lovers in action. You're full of passion, and you have to be the centre of your lover's attention.

Your birthday – sexually speaking

The day on which you're born can reveal – among other things – your likes and dislikes in love and lust. Are you born on the fourth and deeply sexual, or born on the twenty-first and lucky in lotteries? Read on for a titillating description of what you and your loved ones can expect from sex according to the day on which you were born.

THE FIRST

You have a warm and loving nature and strong sexual needs. You like to be loved and want to be in love all the time. If you're married to the right person, lovemaking is the best and keeps your marriage alive.

THE SECOND

You're a quiet person, even when with your loved ones. You need privacy and intimacy. If love or your emotions cause you trouble, seek professional advice.

THE THIRD

Although your love and sex life is usually vigorous, shyness sometimes creeps in. You love passion and like to talk about your life with your friends.

THE FOURTH

You're a deeply sexual person who could jump into bed with just about anyone. You really should look for quality, and you mightn't think too much in the height of passion; however, you learn later on.

THE FIFTH

Many people born on the fifth are different. Some are neither deeply sexual nor easily loved, some like to please, and some like the idea of loving but don't find the right person. Your jealousy is obvious even if your love isn't.

THE SIXTH

Although you're constantly in love, when trouble strikes, you go wild. You want to make your own rules but are wary of passionate lovers who openly show their feelings.

THE SEVENTH

You're unpredictable, you have many platonic friendships, and you like to think about fulfilment. You're creative and often artistic, and you have to have a more intelligent person as a lover.

THE EIGHTH

You want a dashing and courageous lover to sweep you off your feet. You have strong sexual feelings, and because you're inclined to like a lot of variation, you don't make a good partner.

THE NINTH

You're very sexy, you delight in making people look at you, and you enjoy being loved. You usually have a very deep and sensual voice that entices people.

THE TENTH

As a child you want love all around you, and as an adult you continue to need love from various people. When you're lucky and you've found the right circumstances, you do anything to keep love around you.

THE ELEVENTH

You're orderly, you're kind to animals, you obey the rules, and you usually do the right thing. For you, real love involves having high ideals and being devoted, and you usually think love is only for the young and beautiful.

THE TWELFTH

You're very demanding in love, and sex plays an important part in your life. Although you like to flirt and play games, when the real thing happens you're in it wholeheartedly. You like to have little romances such as holiday flings.

THE THIRTEENTH

Even when your relationship or marriage isn't happy, you try and make a go of it. You view love and sex in a practical way.

THE FOURTEENTH

Some of you worry too much and create much ado about nothing. If you do this in your love life, it never works. Even if you want marriage, it's usually somewhere in the future and it doesn't concern you.

THE FIFTEENTH

For you, life would be dull without love. However, you have a short attention span: 'Love 'em and leave 'em' is your motto. You don't like everyday life – you prefer going to parties and having fun.

THE SIXTEENTH

Your style of love is very hard to define. Many people are hurt because you seem to be interested in many other things. Sex doesn't play a major part in your life.

THE SEVENTEENTH

Your appearance tells people you're interested in sex. You're usually aggressive in both love and war, and you like to have a good time. You're the kiss-and-tell type.

THE EIGHTEENTH

You like privacy, you usually know what you want, and you don't change partners easily. Getting on with life is important for you.

THE NINETEENTH

You give yourself time to have fun and look around. Although you eventually do want to marry, in your marriage you have to have it all – love and sex – otherwise you might wander.

THE TWENTIETH

You find it hard to tell people what you think about and want in love and marriage. Although you take your time getting involved with someone, once you're aroused you're a true-blue lover.

THE TWENTY-FIRST

Although you're lucky in lotteries, you're unlucky in love. You're often charmed by a person's beautiful pair of eyes or handsome presence.

THE TWENTY-SECOND

You're ambitious, and you also want to have a terrific love life. You're the type of person who marries the boss's son or daughter and ends up being vice-president of the company.

THE TWENTY-THIRD

You can't tolerate either being with dull people or having a dull life. If you marry, your life has to be both fun and fast. You can fall out of love as easily as you fall into it.

THE TWENTY-FOURTH

You want to have a romantic love: candle-lit dinners and serenades under the window. You don't mind having sex as long as it's preceded by romance.

THE TWENTY-FIFTH

You're mysterious: although your sex drive is strong, your idea of sex is complicated. You're usually the type of person who remains single until late in life.

THE TWENTY-SIXTH

You love romance and fun and like to change partners often. Your sex is intense but shortlived, and you soon look for someone new.

THE TWENTY-SEVENTH

You like to exploit your popularity. Even though you believe in eternal love, your feelings aren't deep.

THE TWENTY-EIGHTH

You like to be the centre of attention, and many hearts are brought to your doorstep. However, you wait for the one and only before you give your true love.

THE TWENTY-NINTH

You can sometimes be cruel to your admirers: you play with them and then cast them aside. However, this habit doesn't last, and you eventually settle down to having some kind of domestic life.

THE THIRTIETH

You're an ideal partner who works hard to maintain happiness in your personal life and that of your partner.

THE THIRTY-FIRST

You should stop analysing everything and jump into life: love is what you make of it. If you want marriage, stop pretending, because if you don't find the right person immediately, you might simply settle for someone else and it could end up in the divorce courts.

CANDLES & CRYSTALS

The power of candles

Ceremonial burning of candles is practised in most of the world's religions. The people of many countries use candles as part of their cultural heritage. Burning candles in order to obtain psychic and spiritual power certainly isn't a new phenomenon: the people of ancient societies used the force of candles to ward off misfortune, and the benefits continue to apply today.

Even people who are sceptical about the benefits of burning candles have to admit they place candles on a birthday cake and make a wish. Although what these customs are isn't always impressed on our consciousness, the power of candles can in fact make our dreams come true.

A burning, bright flame makes a living energy rise that points and directs its force upward and outward. Candles excite our imagination: tapers are lit in holy churches, candelabras are set ablaze at sumptuous feasts, and fire torches are carried that bow to the wind. We look into the candles' flame and our consciousness is raised to ever higher levels. Our minds fuse with the flame's power and with its body that gives it life.

Candles' power in love and magic is exemplified by the discovery of Tutankhamen's tomb, including an alabaster vase that seemed to be opaque until it was lit from within using a candle. Lighting the candle threw into relief what couldn't be seen from the outside: an image of Tutankhamen and his queen joined in a fond embrace. When they were alive, the royal couple were illuminated by their love, symbolised by the candle. Without the candle, they faded into darkness. The 3000-year-old tomb demonstrates that love transcends death through candle magic.

Candle power can be used by everyone: no special gifts are required. You don't have to be either a witch or involved with the magical community in order to obtain maximum benefits from the art – you simply have to nurture a sincere wish to improve your life. The rest is easy.

Your candle's colour is of prime importance for your spell to be efficient. Your candles' shape and size don't matter – your success is determined by your using the right colour. You can use any type of candle, from a birthday candle to a candle you'd place on the table at dinner parties.

I use candle power in my own life. Every morning for seven consecutive days, I light a light-blue candle at sunrise. This practice protects you from evil influences, promotes harmony in your love relationship and is an antidote to quarrelling. I also burn one yellow and one brown candle for good luck and for restoring good fortune.

Following are some candle-burning rituals for you to follow. There's one important thing to remember, though: if you don't wish to leave your burning candle unattended, ***never, ever blow it out*** – snuff it instead, because blowing it out reverses the ritual. Also, it's best to let the candle burn right down in order to ensure your wish is granted.

To have financial luck

Light one brown, one yellow and one orange candle at the same time.

To keep financial problems from your door

Light three pale-orange candles, and remember that if you miss one day you'll invite a bad day.

To have luck in love and money

Light one red candle.

To start a favourable week

Light one orange and one blue candle, because the combination is powerful for good fortune.

To help avoid scandal and malicious gossip

Light one silver candle.

To establish a telepathic link and transmit your thoughts to a desired lover

Place one pink candle on each side of your bed, and burn the two candles when there's a full moon. Light the two candles at midnight, write your desired lover's name on two small sheets of white paper, and place one sheet of paper under each candle.

Burn the candles for three nights, and your beloved's affection will be yours.

To make the right decision about the future

During the night, burn one turquoise candle to ensure there'll be peace and optimism and that you don't make a foolish decision.

To win a legal battle

Burn one yellow and one blue candle an hour before you enter the courtroom, and the judge will decide in your favour.

To prevent harm or violence

Burn one yellow and one violet candle before you go to sleep.

To prevent robbery and assault

Burn one green candle at sunset every night.

To have maximum protection against crime

Burn one lime-coloured candle at sunset every night.

To help prevent financial loss and disaster

Burn one green and one red or gold candle. Burning these coloured candles also helps prevent disloyalty in a love relationship.

To restore harmony and stability if domestic turmoil erupts

Burn one green and one purple candle. This ritual will work quickly.

To break up a love affair

Burn one green and one black candle. This negative combination is quite powerful.

To make good fortune come to you

Burn one orange and one blue candle on a Monday.

To deprive an enemy of strength

Burn one orange and one black candle.

To make your rivals have financial disaster

Burn one orange and one green candle.

To attract financial gain, success, fame, honour and power

Burn one orange candle each morning when you wake up.

Crystals and their properties

HOW CRYSTALS ARE FORMED

Rock crystals are the children of the earth itself, having formed slowly and laboriously deep beneath the planet's surface in much the same way as a child forms within the womb. Crystals originate within the earth's core, in the restless, molten magma that's always seeking to reach the outer surface. However, only a very small proportion of the fiery mass of magma results in volcanic activity and lava flow: instead, most magma flows through the honeycomb-like subterranean fissures that form the planet's substrata.

Magma is a mass of molten rock and minerals and is accompanied with boiling waters, steam and gases. As these substances cool, they begin to form into crystals by building on the many minerals deposited within the fissures. This is how rock crystals and gemstones begin their development. They slowly form their light in the primeval darkness and take between twenty and thirty million years to achieve any real size.

MASCULINE CRYSTALS

The crystals that attract the most attention are the 'masculine', or 'positive', variety, because they have great clarity. Indeed, these crystals often emit the most intense energies and are therefore potent instruments in natural healing. Because of their level of clarity, they provide positive help for people who are somewhat confused and whose overall view of life is clouded by emotion. When these people can be persuaded to focus their attention on a masculine crystal, they're enabled to acquire a much clearer outlook on life and to thereby help their pent-up emotions to be released.

Equally, for people who through meditation wish to go beyond the mind, masculine crystals provide a powerful stimulus for the chakra system and thereby enable the desired goal to be attained. Exposure to masculine crystals results in activity, and these quartz formations are beneficial when either stimulus or action is required, especially when a person is suffering from physical exhaustion.

FEMININE CRYSTALS

For people who wish to activate their latent mediumistic qualities, a cluster of 'feminine' quartz crystals swiftly accelerates the person's spiritual momentum by activating the chakra centres related to intuition and clairvoyance.

Although the feminine varieties of quartz are often rather ugly because their appearance is either cloudy or opaque, they have unique properties. Whenever people are suffering from the effects of having an over-abundance of mental, emotional or physical activity that results in a painful headache or a migraine, feminine crystals help reduce the tensions.

CLEAR QUARTZ

The clear-quartz crystal stimulates brain functioning and makes the wearer's thinking capability clear and unclogged. It's designed to dispel negativity in the wearer's energy field and environment. It receives, activates, stores, transmits and amplifies energy.

Clear quartz is excellent for meditation. The milky or opaque variety is the receptive feminine force, and the clear variety is the stimulating male force. This type of quartz can help mend a broken heart and heal feelings of inadequacy.

ROSE QUARTZ

The rose-quartz crystal is commonly known as the 'love stone'. When it's worn as either a necklace or a brooch close to the heart, it attracts love and helps the wearer in developing his or her compassionate and forgiving side.

Rose quartz is a delicate-looking crystal that increases the wearer's fertility and can help people who are sexually and emotionally imbalanced. It helps clear stored anger, resentment, guilt, fear and jealousy and helps reduce stress and tension. It's therefore a great stone to have on your office desk. It can also enhance self-confidence and creativity. With reference to physical health, it's the type of quartz that's known to aid the kidney and circulatory systems.

SMOKY QUARTZ

The smoky-quartz crystal is a very powerful type of quartz, and you should be very careful when handling it. Exposure to it results in a great level of intensification within the subtle body of humankind. In turn, this action proves to be of great benefit for people who seriously wish to acquire full fourth-dimensional awareness or to attune to their higher self. Smoky quartz can also greatly aid the channelling process.

The energies projected by this irradiated variety of quartz are often overpowering and result in reactions that range from experiencing powerful pressure on the chakra points to experiencing heart palpitations. When palpitations occur, it's advisable to remove the smoky-quartz crystal from your immediate vicinity.

AMETHYST QUARTZ

Although amethyst-quartz crystals are much prized because of their great beauty, they have potent energies and are therefore indispensable for New Age healers and therapists. When amethyst-quartz clusters are placed in the treatment room, they emit a powerful, purifying energy that's stimulating for both the healer and the person who requires treatment.

Although the clusters' energy field might seem to be no less potent than the energy field projected by similar-size rock-quartz clusters, the benefits that accrue from using them in healing treatments are immeasurable. The energy that amethyst-quartz clusters generate has a beneficial effect on the nervous system and thereby provides healing therapists with a positive aid when they're endeavouring to treat related conditions.

When people are suffering from an irritating skin disorder, an amethyst cluster placed point-downward on the affected area soon brings relief. For people who have a painful eye condition, when the cluster is stimulated by a 'love' thought pattern and is held an inch or two from the eyes, a laser-like ray of healing energy is released that in turn eases the tension present within the eyes.

Amethyst quartz is also an invaluable aid for people who are endeavouring to counteract the effect of negative thought patterns, including fear and apprehension.

CLEANSING A CRYSTAL

When you've selected a rock crystal that's suitable for your requirements, you have to take some preparatory steps before you put the crystal to use. Regardless of why you've obtained the crystal, your main task is to physically cleanse it. When crystals are mined,

they're often encrusted with various forms of mineral matter that's removed by placing them in an oxalic-acid bath. From that point onwards, they're handled by people, each of whom in turn leaves his or her own mental or emotional imprint on them.

In order to eradicate these unwanted vibrations as well as any oxalic-acid residue, it's recommended the crystal be cleansed in the following way. Fill a glass container with one litre of warm water and add two tablespoons of sea salt as well as two tablespoons of apple-cider vinegar. When the sea salt has dissolved, place the crystal in the solution for about ten minutes then rinse it using cold water. The combined action of apple-cider vinegar and sea salt on quartz crystals is quite remarkable, because any unwanted residue is swiftly removed. If you have several crystals that require cleansing, you can increase the abovementioned measures.

ACTIVATING A CRYSTAL

Continually flowing from all forms of natural rock quartz is a stream of electromagnetic energy that's released into the atmosphere for the benefit of all lifeforms. This task is unconsciously undertaken by the crystals' elemental inhabitants, who are blissfully unaware of 'outer' experiences because they're caught up in their own crystalline world.

If you wish to capitalise on this source of power, you first have to dedicate both the crystal and its indwelling inhabitant to universal purpose, because in doing so you convey to the elemental intelligence a measure of awareness of the higher, or 'outer', planes of experience. In turn, the elemental intelligence wishes to become part of the 'outer' world, and, like a chick seeking to break free of its shell, releases ever increasing levels of electromagnetic energy in its bid to free itself from its crystalline form. The evolutionary process thereby continues.

To activate your crystal, hold it point-upward in your left hand, adjacent to the heart chakra, which is the seat of unconditional love. Project towards it a 'love' thought pattern for about five minutes.

This simple act establishes a rapport between you and the elemental intelligence, because the emotion of unconditional love has the highest and purest of vibrations, to which the crystalline structure's atoms and molecules pose no real barrier. In response, the indwelling elemental intelligence releases via the crystal's point a tingling flow of electromagnetic energy that's easily discernible within the area of the chakra.

In order to make sure a quartz crystal is fully activated and that the indwelling elemental energy completely co-operates, it's suggested you dedicate your crystal in the following way.

*I dedicate this crystal to
universal purpose.
From this moment on,
I undertake
To use its energies
To benefit all living things,
For I am one with the
creative source*

*And therefore one with
all lifeforms.
In that which I am,
I will now activate
The life energy within
this crystal,
So that its force may now be used
To serve universal purpose.*

CARDS

The significance of standard playing cards

Following are four tables in which I give the symbolic meaning of each of the thirteen cards in the four suits of an ordinary playing pack.

HEARTS

CARD	SYMBOLIC MEANING
Ace	You'll receive love, news about distant friends, and affection.
King	You're a good-hearted person who has strong affections.
Queen	You're a faithful, domesticated person who has a very loving nature.
Jack	You're a very stubborn person who has the reputation of Cupid.
Ten	Good fortune is coming your way, and you have the prospect of having a large family.
Nine	Riches and wishes are probably coming your way.
Eight	Love and marriage are soon to come for you.
Seven	A friend of yours might prove to be an enemy.
Six	You're easy prey for swindlers.
Five	You'll cause someone of weak character to be jealous.
Four	You're being too hard to please.
Three	You must be aware of anything you sign.
Two	Wedding bells are in the air.

DIAMONDS

CARD	SYMBOLIC MEANING
Ace	You'll receive either a ring or paper money.
King	You must be wary of your violent temper.
Queen	You're a very reasonable person.
Jack	You're easily offended.
Ten	You'll have plenty of money and children.
Nine	You'll receive a surprise connected with money.
Eight	You'll be married late in life.
Seven	Uncharitable tongues are around you.
Six	You'll be married early and quickly widowed.

Five	You're successful in business.
Four	You have trouble with friends.
Three	Unhappiness is caused by your husband or wife's temper.
Two	You have an unsatisfactory love affair.

SPADES

CARD	SYMBOLIC MEANING
Ace	Concern will arise in your love affairs.
King	You'll be successful in love.
Queen	You're fond of scandal.
Jack	You're a very kind person who wouldn't say a bad word about anyone.
Ten	Evil forces are in the air around you.
Nine	There's illness in your family.
Eight	You'll have some opposition from your friends.
Seven	You feel sorrow because you've lost a friend.
Six	Hard work will bring you wealth.
Five	Your bad temper will cause harm.
Four	Your family needs your attention.
Three	Travel and marriage are coming your way.
Two	There'll be a removal or possibly a death.

CLUBS

CARD	SYMBOLIC MEANING
Ace	You'll have wealth and a peaceful home.
King	You're faithful and true.
Queen	You have a great attraction to the opposite sex.
Jack	You're genuine and trustworthy.
Ten	You suddenly acquire riches.
Nine	You have jealous friends because your wishes have come true.
Eight	Love and money are coming your way.
Seven	Great happiness and fortune are arriving for you.
Six	You have success being in business with your children.
Five	You have an advantageous marriage.
Four	You have to be careful about falsehood and double dealing.
Three	You have more than one marriage that includes a lot of money.
Two	You have to avoid opposition.

A basic understanding of tarot cards

I've found that reading the tarot cards is both an accurate and an interesting way of divining the future and that my clients frequently request a reading.

The way in which the cards are placed to ascertain their correct meaning varies according to a person's individual needs and circumstances. The method I use in order to gain strong psychic power is to have the seeker shuffle the twenty-two major cards of the tarot deck.

I concentrate on the questions the client seeks knowledge about, and the client puts five cards down face-up. He or she then puts another card down on top of one of the other cards, because a clearer picture of a situation is sometimes required. He or she puts the cards down one after the other in their correct place until all twenty-two cards are down.

Tarot cards date as far back as Ancient Egyptian times, when Thoth, the Egyptian god of writing and wisdom, directed the scribes – the learned men of the time – to inscribe magical pictorial signs on clay tablets. The magical signs were the precursors to the tarot cards we use today.

The tarot cards are indicative of and represent in a symbolic way humankind's past, present and future. In the following table, set out the number and name of each card and outline each card's symbolic meaning.

THE STAR

THE MOON

THE SUN

NUMBER	CARD	SYMBOLIC MEANING
I	The Juggler	The will of God, and creation and quickening of life
II	The High Priestess	Duality and virginity
III	The Empress	Beauty and pregnancy
IV	The Emperor	Material things and worldly authority
V	The Pope	Sacred things and spiritual power
VI	The Lovers	Innocence, love and the union of opposites
VII	The Chariot	Exaltation and the spirit's passage towards contentment
VIII	Justice	Achievement of equilibrium
IX	The Hermit	Puberty and hidden light
X	The Wheel of Fortune	Karma and a building-up towards your destiny
XI	Strength	Strength that leads to ecstasy
XII	The Hanged Man	Release of the waters of life
XIII	Death	Resurrection
XIV	Temperance	Change and transformation
XV	The Devil	Dominance of pride, ambition and lust
XVI	The Tower Struck by Lightning	Bitterness, collapse, violence and destruction, imprisonment, or death
XVII	The Star	Intuition, hope and bliss
XVIII	The Moon	Loss of innocence, and the darkness of the womb
XIX	The Sun	The light of true intelligence
XX	The Day of Judgement	Aspiration to move from low to higher things
XXI	The World	Joy, and release from earthly existence
XXII	The Fool	Divine madness: the card that contains all qualities but has none

DREAMS

Your dreams and what they mean

Dreaming is usually defined as being the imagal, sensory, motor and thought processes that occur during sleep. What does this very technical-sounding definition really mean?

From the time we wake to the time we go to sleep again, our conscious mind absorbs and reacts to information delivered to our five senses: sight, smell, taste, touch and hearing. It's in the dream state that our subconscious retrieves the day's data and reviews it to be more in tune with how we really think and feel, deep down.

Our dreams are actually symbolic images, and although they sometimes seem to be very jumbled and almost as unreal as a Steven Spielberg movie, they always have a hidden meaning. I'm sure you've woken from a dream and tried to make sense of it. You might wonder whether you have a sixth sense that's trying to warn you about something, especially when you have a nightmare.

NIGHTMARES

Having a nightmare is a simple way of telling you you're fearful of something in your life that you haven't yet confronted. Although in your conscious state you might think nothing's wrong, your subconscious determines otherwise, because it's there that our true thoughts and feelings are stored.

DREAMS WE CAN'T REMEMBER

It could therefore be argued that the dreams we find it hard to remember are the result of our blocking an event or situation from our conscious because we either aren't prepared to deal with the issue or are too afraid to deal with it.

The longer we ignore our dreams, the more they recur, until our conscious recognises and deals with the message our subconscious is giving us when we're asleep. On the other hand, when you wake refreshed and clearheaded, the chances are that during your dream state you've examined an aspect of your life and clarified it, and therefore had a good night's sleep.

HAPPY DREAMING

Of the ways to prepare for happy dreaming, one effective way is to let go of all the day's stress and tensions before turning the light off. Listen to some soft music, meditate, or do what I like best: indulge in a hot bath laced with lavender oil. Remember that being happy during your waking hours will translate into having beautiful dreams. Being fearful and anxious will simply promote experiencing unpleasant images in your sleep.

COMMON DREAMS

It's said you should never tell your dreams while you're fasting and that you should always tell them first to a woman named Mary! In the following table, I set out some common dream subjects and their interpretation.

DREAM	INTERPRETATION
A hearse that bears white plumes	There'll be a wedding.
A wedding	Grief and death might follow.
A woman kissing you	You'll be deceived.
A man kissing you	You'll have friendship.
A horse	You'll be exceedingly lucky.
A priest	This is a bad dream.
The devil	This is a better dream.
Abortion	You'll suffer heartache.
A fighting army	There'll be a change in your life, especially to do with wealth.
An aeroplane	A wealthy marriage is in store for you.
A baby	This foretells prosperity.
Baldness	You're about to lose your heart but not your head.
A bed	This foretells illness.
Buying a bed	You'll have a change of address.
Birds	You'll have good luck.
Blood	An illness is on the way.
A boat	This is a happy omen.
A cat	This foretells false news and deceitfulness.
A clock	Many good investments will come your way.
A coffin	This foretells news of the marriage of either a near relative or a friend.
Dancing	A happy and fortunate event will take place.
Danger	This is a warning for you to look into both your business and your state of mind.
Death	This either is an omen of marriage or foretells news of a birth.
Eating	This is a sign both of good fortune and of quarrels and separations.
Entertainment	There'll be a slight illness in the family.
Falling	You'll suffer disappointment.
Falling into water	This foretells death or personal danger.
Falling from either a high place or a tree	Many troubles will follow.
Flowers growing	This foretells luck.
Flowers dying	This foretells illness.
Flying	This foretells a speedy journey, and good things in general.
A funeral	There'll be a wedding.
Ghosts	A close relative will be slightly ill.
Receiving a gift	You'll have a spell of bad luck in business.
Gold	Selfish ambitions have to be checked.
Hair either falling out or being cut	You'll gain financially.
Illness	A journey will take place that will be to your benefit.
Jewels	This is a favourable sign that brings plenty of good luck.
Love	This foretells prosperity, and happiness and success in love.

DREAM	INTERPRETATION
A key	A young child will play a part in your life.
A lot of kissing	You'll soon receive a present.
A ladder	This is a sign of warning: you'll incur debts from friends.
A letter	This indicates either good news and happiness in love or that a successful love is looming.
A girl in love	This is a bad omen.
Being loved by someone you dislike	This is a warning that you'll need a friend one day and have no one to turn to.
Marriage	Good fortune is coming.
Being present at your own wedding	This foretells divorce.
Finding money	This foretells a birth.
Losing money	This is a bad omen for love.
Nakedness	This usually means there's trouble ahead.
Being naked	This is a sign of poverty.
A woman naked	This is lucky.
A man naked in bed	This denotes deceit.
Numbers	There'll be worry in love affairs, and a bit of scandal.
The ocean	There'll be a trip overseas, and gossip.
Pain	Unexpected money will come your way: buy a Tatts ticket!
Being pregnant	This foretells sorrow and sadness.
A quarrel	Either unwelcome news or a visit from an unexpected friend awaits you.
A ring	This foretells a broken promise, as well as good news about a business prospect.
Singing	Unhappiness is in store for you.
Spiders	This foretells good fortune.
Killing a spider	There's enjoyment in the future for you.
A spinning spider	Money is coming to you.
Being bitten by a snake	Your adversaries will hurt you.
Killing a snake	You'll overcome your enemies.
Swimming	This foretells an unexpected death, as well as financial trouble.
Tears	These foretell great joy and unexpected happiness.
Losing an umbrella	An unlooked-for item will be found.
An undertaker	If you're married, it means the birth of a child; if you're single, it means success in love.
A voyage	You'll hear from a friend abroad and have luck in business.
Walking	You'll hear serious news from a close friend.
Washing	This foretells a change of either address or workplace.
Water	This is a sign of good fortune for your lover or spouse.
Yelling	This indicates treachery from a friend, and is also an omen of coming joy.

FEATHER
& FLOWER
POWER

The language of feathers

Wild birds' fallen feathers were once considered to be omens. In late summer during moulting time, the wise people strolled into the countryside to collect as many feathers as possible for their spells and rituals.

A grey feather meant peace of mind, a black feather death. The weather pattern ahead could be foretold through reading of a feather. If there was a multitude of feathers an early autumn was foretold, whereas if feathers were scarce an Indian summer was at hand.

Feathers are a feature of many occult uses. A wreath of chicken feathers placed on the victim's head is a warning of harm. The film *Four Feathers* referred to the custom of sending a white feather to a person who's betrayed a trust. A peacock feather bears ill-will and bad luck. A red-gull feather brings good luck, and a blue-gull feather promises success in love. If you present a traveller with a good-will feather, he or she will have a safe and pleasant trip.

In the following table, I set out the feather colours and what they represent.

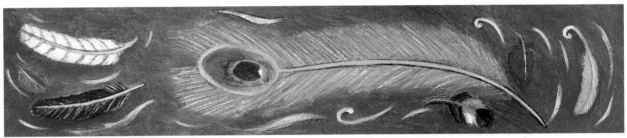

FEATHER COLOUR/S	WHAT THEY REPRESENT
Red	Good fortune smiles on you.
Orange	This is a promise of delights to come.
Yellow	This is a warning to be wary of false friends.
Green	Adventure awaits.
Blue	Love will enliven your days.
Grey	This represents peace of mind.
Brown	This represents good health.
Black	This represents either ill-tidings or death.
Black and white	Disaster will be averted.
Green and black	These represent fame and fortune.
Brown and white	These represent joy and mirth.
Grey and white	Your wishes will come true.
Blue, white and black	These represent a new love.
Purple	You'll go on an exciting trip soon.

Your lucky flower according to your birth month

In the following table, I set out the flower for each of the twelve birth months. It's said that if you have one of each flower that represents your family members' birth month, you'll have good luck and good fortune if your family members keep their flower in the house on the first Sunday of each month.

Birth month	Flower or plant	Birth month	Flower or plant
January	Carnation or snowdrop	July	Water lily
February	Primrose	August	Gladiolus
March	Daffodil	September	Aster
April	Daisy	October	Dahlia
May	Lily of the valley	November	Chrysanthemum
June	Rose	December	Holly

The fragrant language of flowers and plants

Flowers aren't only a decorative item; they have many powerful qualities. You can use them to add potency to any occasion. For example, if you're visiting someone in hospital, choose a bunch of irises that contains fennel, thyme and cedar, because it'll help the person get well. To enhance an office environment, a cheerful vase or bowl of buttercups does wonders.

In the following table, I list many flowers and plants and their associations.

Flower or plant	Association/s	Flower or plant	Association/s
Acacia	Secret love	Iris	Hope and messages
Almond	Hope, watchfulness and haste	Ivy	Friendship
		Jasmine	Amiability
Aloe	Superstitions	Lavender	Answers
Aspen	Fear and sensibility	Lilac	First love
Balm	Hatred	Lily	Purity and joy
Bay leaf	Change	Marigold	Sorrow
Birch	Grace	Mistletoe	Being overcome
Buttercup	Riches	Moss	Maternal love
Carnation	Admiration	Myrtle	Love
Chamomile	Energy	Nightshade	Secrets
Cedar	Strength	Oak	Hospitality
Clover	Fertility and luck	Pansy	Thoughtfulness
Daisy	Innocence	Periwinkle	Friendship
Dandelion	Oracles	Poppy	Sleep and comfort
Elder	Compassion	Primrose	Consistency
Evergreen	Worth	Rose	Beauty and love
Fennel	Strength	Rose – burgundy	Simple pleasures
Fir	Time	Rose – versicolour	Mirthfulness
Foxglove	Ambition	Rose – moss	Merit
Geranium	Recall	Sweet William	Treachery
Hawthorn	Hope	Thistle	Defiance
Heather	Solitude	Thyme	Courage
Holly	Foresight and good wishes	Violet	Steadfastness
		White poplar	Time
Honeysuckle	Fidelity	Yew	Faith and rebirth
Horse chestnut	Luxury	Zinnia	Friendship

FENG SHUI

No, it isn't beef and black-bean sauce!

Sometimes we find that regardless of how hard we work and what we do, it seems success, love and money are far away and almost unattainable. Is it bad luck, karma, our parent or even our horoscope that's to blame? Perhaps it is – but what if your living space and workplace were actually causing the trouble? If you could change your whole life by simply hanging a mirror in the right place or buying a potplant for that dark corner, I'm sure you'd do it today.

WHAT IS FENG SHUI?

The principles of feng shui – pronounced 'fung sway' – go beyond mystical interior design and are based on the principle that the way in which the fixtures and fittings are placed in our environment can dictate our wellbeing.

I won't get too technical here, because feng shui is an art that takes some time to fully understand and appreciate. Basically, it's split into to groups: *chi*, which radiates positive energy, and *sha*, which carries negative energy.

Chinese people avidly believe in feng shui and rarely make a move without consulting it. They believe the space we inhabit is alive with energy and that the energy influences what happens to us in life. Energy is around us all the time, and when the energy is positive, life is good. When the energy is negative, life is bad, and anything can happen because of our negativity.

RESTORING POSITIVE ENERGY

Using the art of feng shui helps restore positive energy, which in turn establishes and creates luck and harmony in our life. Energy is like our friend: it has both a personality and a behaviour pattern, as we have. It has to be nurtured, encouraged to grow, directed and guided through our space.

According to feng shui, energy prefers air that's circulating; light; reflections; and living matter, such as plants and animals. It doesn't like dark, cramped spaces in which it can't flow freely; dead or dying plants; and dirty and messy places. One of the best things you can do to restore the positive energy in your life is to clean up and organise the spaces in which you live and work.

Read on and discover both what to do and what not to do when you're arranging your home and office according to the principles of feng shui.

THE ENTRY

- Ensure that the front door isn't in a straight line with the back door; if it is, any negative energy will flow straight through and taint everything in its path. If you're faced with this problem, hang either a chime or a mobile from the hallway ceiling halfway between the two points. This will confuse the bad energy's path and redirect the energy out again.

- Hang a wind chime near your front and back entrance doors in order to redirect the bad energy.

- Ensure that your entrance doors open inwards and thereby enable the good energy to enter. If your doors don't open inwards, either re-hang them or use another door as the main entrance.

- If you have stairs approaching a door, place a talisman either at the head of them or on the half-landing.

- Place a mirror directly opposite your front door in order to reflect the bad energy and push it straight out again.

- Place a 'gloom guardian' such as a lion, tiger or dragon in the front or back entrance or in any part of the home in order to guard it.

- Ensure that a path that leads directly to your front door isn't straight: it should be either curved or zig-zag instead.

THE LOUNGE AND DINING ROOM

- Ensure that the chair used by the head of the family doesn't have its back to either a window or a door: if it has, the person is rendered vulnerable to intruders. You can, however, place the chair sideways to the window or door. If you can't do this, position a mirror so the door can be seen from the chair.

- Ensure that your lounge-room furniture follows the lines of the wall in order to enable the good energy to circulate.

- Ensure that your dining-room window faces a direction different from that of the dining table itself in order to stimulate the good energy's flow.

THE KITCHEN

- Ensure that your kitchen stove, which represents the element fire, doesn't adjoin either the element wood or the element water.

If the stove is placed next to wood, the danger of fire is enhanced, and if it's placed next to the sink, the Chinese character of disaster is produced.

THE BEDROOM

- Ensure that your bed doesn't receive direct sunlight, otherwise the excess of energising forces will disturb your sleeping.

- Don't put too many mirrors in the room, otherwise an over-abundance of stimulating energy will be produced and the bedroom will no longer be a place of rest.

THE BATHROOM

- Although most new houses have an en-suite bathroom, according to strict feng shui principles the bathroom shouldn't lead into the bedroom. This is because bedrooms require a smooth and gentle flow of energy, whereas in the bathroom it's important that the dark energy be replaced as quickly as possible.

- Ensure that all drainpipes aren't visible.

THE OFFICE

- If a room has no window and only one door, use it for storage only. This is because in this type of room the good energy can't circulate and is therefore stagnant.

- In order to radiate good money opportunities, place a jade pot near the office's entrance door.

GENERAL DIRECTIONS

- If your house is either a terrace or semi-detached so that one or more walls adjoin other premises, note which walls are joined, because they block any feng shui influences, both good and bad.

- In a dark corner of any room, in order to brighten up the room's energy, instal a mirror that will reflect the sun.

- For protection, place a large potted plant at the front of the premises' southernmost window.

- Instal potted plants in order to keep the good energy alive.

- Avoid having dead corners by filling them with cabinets, large plants or ornaments. This is because areas in which the current is unable to flow are dead.

FOOD FOR THOUGHT

Magical foods

When we think of food, we instantly think of what we like to eat and how to cook it – the last thing on our mind is, 'Gee, I wonder what magical things eating this food will bring.' There are many foods that we eat on a day-to-day basis which boast magical qualities thus promoting whatever it is we want in life.

In the table on page 99, I list the foods that have magical qualities. If you can't eat one of the foods, have either a picture or an ornament of it in the room in which you spend most of your time, or have its scent burning in an oil burner. In an office environment, having a bunch of bananas in a bowl at the reception desk promotes financial gain and effective public relations, because you're offering your visitors the fruits of your labour. In the home, it's ideal to have a big bowl of all the fruits on a bench or table and an attractive picture of pineapples on the kitchen wall.

THE POWER OF THE PIE

The humble pie that you might like to chomp on at your favourite sport event has a colourful history. In the seventeenth century, it was actually banned in England by Oliver Cromwell because it gave people pleasure. Cromwell ruined many a good party by raiding it and confiscating its pastry delights. In 1660, Charles II thankfully ascended the throne and made enjoyment of pies legal again throughout the land.

The reason the pie is round has its origin in Europe. Because cooks found that filling a square or oblong pan required too much fruit, they cut the pans' corners and made them shallow – and the round pie was born.

In magic, round pies induce spirituality, and square pies promote prosperity. Pies topped with intricate lattice-worked crusts are useful in protective diets. Choosing the fruits is important when you're making a pie: you have to choose them for their magical properties as well as for their taste.

Mince pies are particularly special, because throughout Europe and England they're baked and served on New Year's Eve, just after midnight. Traditionally, it's believed that a piece is eaten and a wish is made.

When you're reading the table, note that all the foods retain their magical qualities when in pie form.

FOOD	MAGICAL QUALITY OR QUALITIES
Apples	Love, healing and peace. To maintain these powers, eat an apple a day
Apricots	Peace and harmony. If apricots aren't in season, burn a few drops of their oil in a burner in order to get the same effect
Bananas	Financial gain and success
Blackberries	Money and sex
Blueberries	Safety; especially great for safe sex
Cherries	Love
Chocolate	Money and love
Coconuts	Spirituality
Custard	Spirituality
Lemons	Cleansing, and removing negative vibes
Limes	Domestic bliss, love and purification
Mince pies	Luck and money
Peaches	Love, health, happiness and wisdom
Pecans	Money and financial security
Pineapples	Love, healing, health, money, protection and happiness
Pumpkins	Money and healing
Raspberries	Happiness, love and protection
Rhubarb	Protection and love
Strawberries	Love and tenderness

Foods to ignite your lover

They say the way to a man's heart is through his stomach – well, feed your man the foods that suit his star sign and you're guaranteed to have a fantastic dessert! All foods have an aphrodisiac effect, and you have to pay attention to their presentation, colour and shape. Atmosphere also plays a big part in seducing the opposite sex through the eating of food.

When Venus is ruling, try oysters with crushed coriander; eat plenty of asparagus, beans, basil and capers; and drink champagne. When Mars is ruling, sit in a spa and eat strawberries with chocolate; and eat plenty of salad foods, including avocado.

Try and seduce the people of the twelve zodiac signs using food as follows.

ARIES

Ariens love fast, quick food, because they love speed and making little effort. Bacon, baked potatoes and all baked vegetables have a big effect on them. They like plenty of food and a good selection of desserts.

TAURUS

Taureans love plain and simple food – something that won't take long to prepare. Licorice is their weakness, as well as sarsparilla, cinnamon, ginger and chocolate. They also like plenty of good conversation to be made during the meal.

GEMINI

Geminis love foods that they can eat on the run and when walking down the street. Their favourite is chicken.

CANCER

Cancerians are into the atmosphere more than the food. Don't give them spicy food, though, and they love seafood and salad.

LEO

Leos love spicy food: the spicier the better. They need to eat food that makes them roar.

VIRGO

Virgoans are the hardest people of all to seduce, especially with food. Everything has to be perfect: the crockery, the cutlery, the food, the ambience, the wine, the music and the company. Make sure you haven't a hair out of place, a button missing or any distractions. Virgoans will eat anything as long as it's fresh and well presented.

LIBRA

Librans won't stay long enough to make a decision when it comes to food, so don't give them too much variety. When it comes to seduction, they'll try new things, but don't give them too much. They'll eat plenty of pasta and cheese.

SCORPIO

Scorpions love variety in their foods, and if they don't like something, they'll tell you: they don't have much decorum when it comes to offending you. They love seafood and salad, and a good start to a meal with them is shrimp salad.

SAGITTARIUS

Sagittarians like food that takes little effort to eat, because they have to do several things while they're eating. Impress them with your value-for-money tactic. The key to winning them over is to include plenty of variety on the menu.

CAPRICORN

Capricornians like to have a lot of effort put into their meals. They like home cooking, they don't like crowds, and they definitely aren't the smorgasbord type.

AQUARIUS

Aquarians aren't into variety: as long as you do the work, they're happy with whatever you choose to cook. They're fussy, and they won't eat unusual foods – so stick to bangers and mash.

PISCES

Well, this one is obvious: fish. Give them plenty of fish, chips and salad. They're usually vegetarian, or they eat very little meat.

NUMEROLOGY

Whatʼs your number, and what does it mean?

Numerology is the science of numbers, and the numbers are used to describe peopleʼs personality. Numerology complements astrology in determining a suitable partner for you. If youʼre armed with both astrology and numerology, your success should be assured.

Numerology in its basic form is the number of the personʼs birthday. To determine your numerology number, use the following example of a person born on 25 May 1968 and apply it to your birthdate.

25/05/1968:

2 + 5 + 5 + 1 + 9 + 6 + 8

= 36

3 + 6

= 9

This personʼs numerology number is therefore 9.

If your number is either 11 or 22, you donʼt have to add the two numbers (1 + 1 or 2 + 2) in order to produce one digit. This is because theyʼre what are called master numbers, and master numbers have the same characteristics as number 2 and number 4. If you have a master number, the world will certainly know youʼre in it!

Every birthdate conveys specific characteristics to a person. For example, a Sagittarian born on the fourth is an unreliable person in love relationships. Because number-four people are highly sexed, we can see that Sagittarian fours are a risk in the love stakes. The birthdate number accentuates the star sign, so the four combined with the Sagittarian personality is a difficult relationship unless the person is aware of the problems and can fight fire with fire.

Your birthdate influences both your character and your life. Have you noticed that some people are luckier that others or that some people have a stronger character? This isnʼt accidental; itʼs predetermined. Knowing what date people are born on can give us an insight into what we can expect from them. Some overseas companies take birthdates into account when theyʼre hiring people for an executive position. As is accurately stated in the old proverb, to be forewarned is to be forearmed. Iʼve therefore included birthdates in order to help you assess peopleʼs potential.

If the person has two numbers in his or her birthdate, simply add the numbers in order to arrive at the divining number.

ONES

The Sun is associated with the number one, so ones are sun people. Ones are positive, creative, determined and ambitious. They're also stubborn. They like to be unhampered. They make themselves respected and usually rise to positions of authority. They're compatible with twos, fours and sevens; their lucky days are Sunday and Monday; their lucky colours are gold, yellow and brown; and their lucky stones are topaz and amber.

TWOS

The Moon is associated with the number two, so twos are moon people. They're imaginative, artistic and romantic. They lack strong force and aren't physically robust. They often don't assume a leadership position but content themselves with taking second place. They're often clairvoyant, and they often have healing hands. They're compatible with ones and sevens; their lucky days are Sunday, Monday and Friday; their lucky colours are white, cream and green; and their lucky stones are pearl, moonstone and jade.

THREES

Jupiter is associated with the number three, so threes love authority, order and discipline. They're trustworthy, conscientious and proud but inclined to be dictatorial. They're often found in the public spotlight. They interact best with sixes and nines; their lucky days are Thursday, Friday and Tuesday; their lucky colours are mauve, purple, crimson and rose; and their lucky stone is amethyst.

FOURS

Uranus is associated with the number four, so fours are rebellious and often oppose generally accepted customs. They're sensitive, lonely and rarely successful in material matters. They don't acquire friends easily. They often forge a strong bond with ones, because Uranus is affected by the Sun; their lucky days are Saturday, Sunday and Monday; their lucky colours are grey, electric blue and half-shades; and their lucky stone is sapphire.

FIVES

Mercury is associated with the number five, so fives are prompt in thinking and making decisions. They're highly strung and quick to recover from misfortune. They crave excitement, and gambling holds a strong attraction for them. Business brings them good money. They attract a lot of friends of all the numbers; their lucky days are Wednesday, Thursday and Friday; their lucky colours are blue and green; and their lucky stone is diamond.

SIXES

Venus is associated with the number six, so sixes are artistic and generous, love the beautiful and are determined to the point of being obstinate. They're considerate of people who become devoted to them. They have a good friendship with threes and nines; their lucky days are Tuesday and Friday; their lucky colours are all shades of blue and pink; and their lucky stone is turquoise.

SEVENS

Neptune is associated with the number seven, so sevens are restless and independent and are original thinkers. They love travelling and are good at writing and painting. Fortune doesn't smile on them in financial matters. The number seven is in many ways associated with mysticism, so sevens are much more psychic than other people. Clairvoyance and intuition are two of their gifts. They have a good friendship with twos, because Neptune is affected by the Moon; their lucky days are Sunday and Monday; their lucky colours are green, white and yellow; and their lucky stones are cat's eye, pearl and moonstone.

EIGHTS

Saturn is associated with the number eight, so eights are intense and have great strength of individuality. They're often misunderstood, and they often lead a solitary life. They're buffeted by fate, and although they sometimes rise to a high position, they more often experience loss, sorrow and humiliation. Because they often seem to be cold and undemonstrative, they don't attract friends easily. They should avoid fours, because the combination brings either misfortune or tragedy; their lucky days are Saturday, Sunday and Monday; their lucky colours are grey, dark blue and black; and their lucky stones are dark sapphire and black pearl.

NINES

Mars is associated with the number nine, so nines are born fighters. They're impulsive, courageous and quick tempered. They make good leaders but resent criticism. Their home life is rarely peaceful, and they're peculiarly prone to accidents caused by fire and explosions. They get on best with threes and sixes; their lucky days are Tuesday, Thursday and Friday; their lucky colours are red, crimson and pink; and their lucky stones are ruby, garnet and bloodstone.

OMENS, SUPERSTITIONS & CHARMS

Charms for luck, love and wealth

This book would be incomplete without a discussion of the occult power of charms. I wear a Solomon's seal around my neck to ward off bad influences, and in this way my psychic powers aren't interfered with. I also wear a charm bracelet to attract luck, love and wealth.

A good-luck charm is essential to wear, and I've found that the most beneficial charms to wear, such as the pyramid and the scarab, come from Ancient Egyptian sources.

THE PYRAMID

The pyramid is a powerful charm to wear either on a bracelet or around your neck. It best embodies the search for immortality, which is a characteristic of all societies, both ancient and modern. Pyramid power exerts a strong energy force.

I believe this force was derived from the cosmos and harnessed by the Ancient Egyptians. I sleep blissfully under the pyramid edifice I have covering my bed. The vibrations that emanate from the pyramid are calm and relaxing. The pyramid is also a good sign for attracting favourable responses from people and is also helpful for dealing with people.

THE SCARAB

A scarab, or sacred beetle, is one of the better-known signs used in Ancient Egyptian amulets, and the Ancient Egyptians viewed it as being a symbol of rejuvenation. Wearing it results in a better, younger and wiser version of what we already are. It's a very powerful charm for a new you!

THE LOTUS

A lotus is another good-luck charm, because it imparts immortal power and eternal happiness to the wearer.

THE FOUR-LEAF CLOVER

This is a traditional good-luck charm that brings happiness and good fortune, as I discuss under 'Common superstitions and their origin'.

THE HORSESHOE

As also discussed under 'Common superstitions and their origin', the horseshoe brings a steady streak of luck. The prongs have to be pointing upwards so the luck doesn't run out, and the horseshoe has to be hung over a door.

THE RABBIT'S FOOT

This is another good-luck charm that many people either wear to great effect or have dangling from their car's rear-view mirror.

THE HEXAGRAM

A hexagram has to be worn in order to ward off evil and negative forces. I wear one, and so do members of my family. It derives from the time of Solomon and is also known as a Solomon's seal. Solomon used the seal to protect himself from demons and enemies and to control their malice. It's a particularly strong deflector of curses. It has to be made of a natural substance such as silver or copper and has to be handmade at a specific time in conjunction with the planets.

The seal has to be specially consecrated in order for the wearer to maximise its effectiveness. It's best hung on a leather, silver or copper chain. It also removes fear of the unknown. Copper is used because it absorbs positive forces.

AN IRON-ORE OR BLUISH-GREY STONE

These types of stone also have the magnetic properties of deflection and attraction. They increase your health, vigour and sexual attractiveness. If you carry them, they strengthen your magical powers.

Unusual superstitions and charms

The cat that serves nine masters has earned the right to transport its tenth owner straight to hell. Yes, many strange superstitions stem from the humble cat. Another popular belief about cats is that they have nine lives. This belief is a relic of the ancient legend that witches can turn themselves into cats a total of nine times before they exhaust their powers. In some instances black cats are thought to be lucky, but black-cat charms aren't a common means of luring good fortune.

Following are some other unusual superstitions and omens.

LIGHTING A PIPE

Pipe smokers who light their pipe from either a lamp or a candle will have an unfaithful wife or lover.

GETTING OUT OF BED

If you get out of bed on the left side, you should put your right shoe and sock on first in order to counteract the bad luck.

AN APRON THAT FALLS OFF

If a woman's apron suddenly falls off, it's an omen she'll have a baby within the year.

FINDING A BUTTON

If you find a button, you'll find a new friend.

MOVING INTO A NEW HOUSE

If you move into a new house, you can ensure you have good luck by walking into each room bearing a loaf of bread and a plate of salt.

UPSETTING A CUP OF MEDICINE

In Japan, it's a superstition that if a cup of medicine for a sick person is accidentally upset, the person will have a speedy recovery.

CURING ASTHMA

You can cure asthma by eating either raw cat's meat or the foam from a mule's mouth. If you find either cure to be just a bit too unpleasant, you'll find that having a diet of boiled carrots for a fortnight is just as effective.

CURING BALDNESS

To cure baldness, rub a liberal amount of goose dung into the bald patches! If you're a man, you might prefer to use the preventive measure recorded in another superstition: never cut your hair when the moon is rising, because if you do it will thin and fall out.

CURING CANCER

A quite useless superstition is that toads have the power to suck cancer from the system. Several people have swallowed either small toads or frogs in the hope the creatures will eat the disease away.

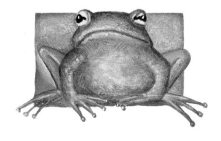

Common superstitions and their origin

Where do the supersitions we all recognise originate? Following is some information about eight items for which supersitions have developed and become prevalent throughout the Western world.

THE RABBIT

Rabbits are undeniably fecund, so they're an obvious choice for a fertility symbol. It follows that many people believe that either a rabbit or parts of a rabbit can confer fertility, improve sexual potency and even aid financial prosperity and bring good luck in general.

As any good Freudian would know, the rabbit's foot is symbolically associated with sex, so in folk belief, that part of the animal eventually came to be popularised as being the repository of good fortune. Many folk beliefs about the whole rabbit persist today. For example, in parts of Britain, if a rabbit crosses your path in front of you it confers good luck, if it crosses behind you it confers bad luck, and if it runs past a house it foretells a fire. A rabbit's left hind foot increases luck. With varying degrees of mockery, some people have added that a rabbit should be killed either at the full moon or in the dark of the moon, in a cemetery and by a red-haired, cross-eyed man or woman.

THE HORSESHOE

The horseshoe is made of iron, which is considered to be an infallible witch repellent. Its shape is roughly that of the new moon, or horned crescent. This highly powerful symbol has also been viewed as being a female sexual symbol. The best horseshoes have four nails on one side and three on the other. Horseshoes are made by blacksmiths, who for centuries were believed to have special powers because they worked with fire and iron.

Horses also have a place in magic, having in many cultures been a sacred beast. A horseshoe is especially lucky if it has been found on the road, and in Britain if it has been cast from a grey mare.

A small silver horseshoe on a charm bracelet is just as lucky as a full-size horseshoe, which is usually nailed up over a doorway in order to ward off evil. The horseshoe has to point upwards so it forms a U shape, whereby the luck neither spills out nor runs out.

THE FOUR-LEAF CLOVER

Four-leaf clovers draw most of their power from the mystical connotations of the number four, which in numerology constantly appears as the symbol of balance, unity and completeness.

The number three has also had lucky connotations, especially in the Christian era, because of its association with the Holy Trinity. A usually three-leaf plant, which in itself is lucky and therefore useful in keeping out supernatural evil, would therefore have its power immensely increased through addition of a fourth leaf.

THE NUMBER THIRTEEN

Today, most people fear the number thirteen because thirteen people dined at the Last Supper. However, the superstition is in fact much older and it's only in more recent times that the number has had unpleasant connotations. In the days of the witch hunts, witches' covens were supposed to have thirteen members. It's widely held that if you have a dinner party at which there are thirteen guests, one of the guests will die within the year.

SALT

Salt is a powerful magical substance, so the spilling of salt is a dangerous omen. Salt has played a part in ceremonies and rituals from the most primitive times. It was often included in sacrifices designed to appease a god or spirits. If you spill salt, you must throw the spilt salt over your left shoulder, in the eyes of the evil that follows you.

THE LADDER

Superstitious people fear walking under ladders not because they're worried something will happen but because the ladder has long been a symbol of spiritual ascent to heaven. You must detour around a ladder in order to avoid disturbing any spirits.

THE BLACK CAT

A female black cat personifies Hecate, the queen of witches. The powers Hecate had are said to have been passed on to female black cats, which is why if you cross a black cat's path you should turn back and start again as a sign of respect.

If a female black cat walks in front of you, you must walk backwards until you've passed the spot it crossed. It's difficult to determine cats' sex simply by looking at them, so don't take any chances.

UMBRELLAS

Sensible people believe that the taboo against opening an umbrella indoors is simply based on commonsense: if you keep the umbrella closed, you prevent breakages.

Animal omens

Following are eight well-known animal omens.

HEARING AN OWL HOOTING

If you hear an owl hooting in the forest before midnight, it warns of trouble to come. If you hear the hooting after midnight, it's a sign that death is near.

SEEING CROWS

If you see crows, remember:

One for sorrow;
Two for mirth;
Three for a wedding;
Four for a birth.

BEING VISITED BY A BLACK DOG

If a black dog comes to your home unbidden and takes up residence, welcome it, because you can be sure that good fortune will follow.

ARRIVAL OF A BLACK CAT

Although a black cat signifies bad tidings in a new quarter and is an omen of disaster in another, all witches know that

If a black cat arrives,
Good fortune thrives.

BEING VISITED BY A TRI-COLOURED CAT

A visit from a tri-coloured cat will bring good luck. If you can entreat the cat to stay, magic paths will open up before you.

SEEING A FROG IN THE EARLY SPRING

When you see a frog in the early spring, you should creep up behind it and use your finger to gently stroke its back. If you do, you'll know true love before the year's end.

SEEING A SPIDER

If you see a spider, in the morning you know shame; at midday pleasure and profit; in afternoon a gift it brings; in the evening joy and mirth.

ENCOUNTERING A FLOCK OF SHEEP

Either encountering or following a flock of sheep is a bad omen.

Weather patterns

It's long been recognised that witches have a sympathetic knowledge and understanding of the forces of nature. They have their own natural prognostications for recognising changes in the weather, as follows.

FAIR WEATHER

- Red sky at evening
- A crescent moon with its horns up
- An owl hooting after midnight
- Mist in the valley
- Red lightning
- Gnats sporting
- Smoke rising straight
- Wool-like clouds
- An evening rainbow

WINDY WEATHER

- A fiery sunset
- A sickle moon with sharp horns
- A surging sea
- Thunder in the morning
- Leaves rustling in the forest
- Spider webs in the air
- Thistledown floating on water
- Herons flying above the clouds
- Ducks flapping their wings

STORMY WEATHER

- Shooting stars
- A wolf howling
- A pale sun at sunrise
- Finches and sparrows chirping at sunrise
- Birds fleeing from the sea
- Bees not venturing from the hive
- Mice skipping around
- Dogs rolling on the ground

A HARD WINTER

- Trees holding their leaves
- Tough apple skins
- Early departure of birds flying south
- Wild geese flying low
- Long, shaggy hair on horses and cattle
- Weeds growing high
- A bountiful crop of acorns
- A large store of honey
- A narrow band of woolly-bear caterpillars

RAINY WEATHER

- Yellow streaks in a sunset sky
- Frogs croaking
- A dark mist over the moon
- Twinkling stars
- A red sky in the morning
- Crows agitating their wings
- Leaves showing their back
- Cows reclining
- Frisky sheep

PALMISTRY

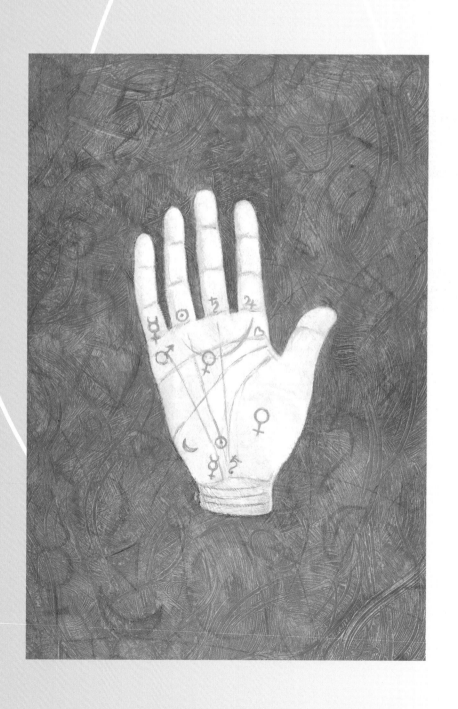

Understanding palmistry

The shape of our hand and the lines on our palm have always intrigued us. The lines are a window to our soul, and although some people view palmistry as being just a bit of fun or nonsense, chiromancy, as it is also called, is the most reliable source of information about a person's character and life path.

Our hands tell our life story, from how many children we'll have to how long we're expected to live. When we know what to look for and how to interpret it, we can gain fascinating insights into ourselves and other people.

I intend this part of the book to be a basic guideline for readers who are interested in palmistry. It will set you on your way, because it's easy to understand and straightforward. However, if you wish to pursue palmistry as a career, I strongly advise you undertake more-advanced studies in order to fully understand this ancient art.

Did you know that your non-writing hand is a guide to your past and that your writing hand delineates your present and future? When you're looking at a person's hands and fingers, use the following interpretations to reveal and perhaps understand more about him or her.

THE HANDS

- Firm hands indicate that the person is dependable.
- Soft and flabby hands indicate that the person loves the soft and easy life.
- Lean and firm hands indicate that the person is economical.
- Hollow hands indicate that the person has no business acumen.

THE FINGERS

- Tapering fingers indicate that the person is a bit of a dreamer, but they quite often indicate that he or she is also artistic.
- Square fingers indicate that the person is organised and honest but isn't very original.
- Pointy fingers indicate that the person is quite artistic and creative but very sensitive and that he or she might also be interested in religious and occult matters.
- Wedge-shape fingers indicate that the person is creative and very active. Depending on how flexible the hands and fingers are, these types of finger can also indicate a person's character.
- Fingers that bend backwards indicate that the person is impatient, but they usually indicate that he or she is quite well balanced.
- Fingers that can't bend backwards indicate that the person is stubborn but honest.

THE MOUNTS

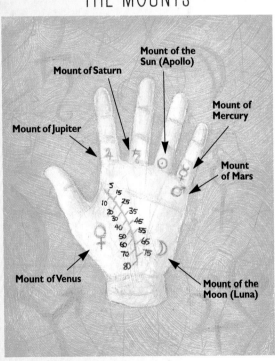

As illustrated, the palm of the hand has seven lumps, which are known as mounts. Each mount is named after a celestial body. Depending on the mount's extent, we're able to recognise various aspects of the person. To note the slight differences that occur takes a lot of practice and study. As well as the mounts, there are markings that resemble shapes such as stars, crosses and circles, all of which indicate something. We'll explore all the markings later.

THE MOUNT OF VENUS

Well pronounced

The person is very passionate and lively and has a great attraction for the opposite sex.

Not well pronounced

The person is coldhearted and usually pessimistic and miserable.

Very pronounced

The person is overly passionate, loves the good things in life without doing anything to earn them and is self-loving and self-centred.

THE MOUNT OF JUPITER

Well pronounced

The person is very much aware of his or her public status and cares very much about what other people think about him or her.

Not well pronounced

The person has very little confidence, if any.

Very pronounced

The person has a high opinion of himself or herself and can often be cruel.

THE MOUNT OF SATURN

Well pronounced

The person is a bit of a bookworm and is quiet and self-centred.

Not well pronounced

The person is cautious and reserved but can have a good sense of humour.

Very pronounced

The person is rather antisocial and can become a bit of a hermit.

THE MOUNT OF THE SUN (APOLLO)

Well pronounced

The person is slightly bad tempered but gets over things quickly and doesn't hold a grudge.

Not well pronounced

The person is quiet, peace loving and uninteresting.

Very pronounced

The person is vain and excessive and has an over-blown ego.

THE MOUNT OF MERCURY

Well pronounced

The person makes an excellent executive, will achieve success in a cut-throat type of business and doesn't have time for either frivolities or sentimentalities.

Not well pronounced

The person has no head for business at all.

Very pronounced

The person is a bit of a parasite, is always on the lookout for someone to exploit and is capable of becoming a hardened criminal.

THE MOUNT OF MARS

Well pronounced

The person is chivalrous and romantic but needs a lot of prodding, has quite a temper and can cause many troubles.

Not well pronounced

The person is rather cowardly or perhaps overly shy and lacks self-confidence.

Very pronounced

The person can be a real bully and boaster and tends to have a sadistic streak.

THE MOUNT OF THE MOON (LUNA)

Well pronounced

The person is very creative, is always looking for the unusual, loves to travel and has a good imagination.

Not well pronounced

The person is a bit of a wet blanket and has no imagination at all.

Very pronounced

The person is hypersensitive, is subject to fits of depression, often has strange dreams and tends to have psychic feelings.

THE MARKINGS

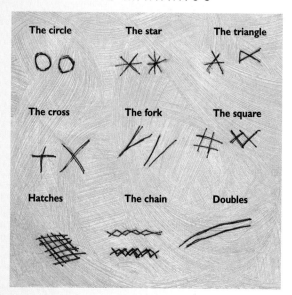

As illustrated, the hands have nine types of marking: the star, the cross, the square, the circle, the triangle, the fork, the chain, hatches and doubles. All the markings have different meanings, depending on where they're located. Let's look into their meanings.

THE STAR

Depending on where it's located on the hand, the star is a very important sign.

Located in the middle of the Mount of Saturn

Some fatal destiny is distinctly signified. This is a sign that the person's destiny has been decided and that he or she will have to play out the role assigned to him or her. The star is a significant sign, and the person will make a name for himself or herself.

Located to the side of the Mount of Saturn

The person will be in close contact with a person who'll make a name for himself or herself through some terrible fate.

Located in the Mount of the Sun (Apollo)

The person will probably gain a position of wealth and influence but not have real happiness. His or her position will probably come too late in life or be gained through loss of his or her health, peace of mind or friends.

Located anywhere on the sides of the Mount of the Sun

Again, the person will be brought into close contact with someone of great wealth and position.

Connected

The person will become famous through having real talent and working hard in an area of the arts.

Located on the Mount of Mercury

It's distinctly possible that the person has great ability as a scientist, businessperson or public speaker.

Located on the sides of the Mount of Mercury

The person will have a close association with someone who's a capable scientist, businessperson or public speaker.

Located on the Mount of Mars

The person will achieve great honours through being patient and courageous.

Located on the Mount of the Moon

The person will have great fame through expression of his or her imagination.

Located at the end of the head line

The person will be living too much in a dream world and by doing so could completely ruin his or her chances. Insanity might be the result of his or her fantasies. People who have suicidal tendencies also seem to have the star at this location.

Located on the Mount of Venus

The person will be successful in the area of passion and affection and will be very successful with the opposite sex.

THE CROSS

The cross isn't a very good sign to have on your hand, because it indicates you'll have to carry a cross, as Jesus did, throughout your life.

Located on the Mount of Saturn

The person will possibly have either a violent death caused by an accident or a disappointment in his or her life.

Located on the side of the fate line, towards the thumb

The person's career will be opposed by his or her relatives.

Located on the other side of the fate line

The person will have a distinct disappointment in a travel undertaking.

Located near or touching the head line

The person will possibly receive a serious head injury.

Located near the heart line

The person will possibly lose a loved one unexpectedly.

THE SQUARE

Located either on or just below the Mount of Saturn

The person will be saved from great danger in an accident.

The head line running through it

The person will have a great strain on his or her brain.

The heart line running through it

The person will have great trouble through love.

Penetrated by the life line

The person will to some extent be protected from death.

Located on the Mount of Venus

The person will be saved from trouble through love.

Located close to and a bit above the thumb

The person will probably be imprisoned during his or her life.

THE CIRCLE

Although the circle isn't a happy sign, it influences only the line or mount it's located on. Also, it quite often indicates hereditary evils. For example, if it's located on the head line, inherited mental illness is suggested.

Located on the life line

The person will experience an illness at the stage of life indicated on the life line.

Located on the fate line

The person will suffer a heavy and materially significant loss.

Located on the sun line

The person will be the subject of a scandal.

Located on the health line

The person will have a serious illness.

Located on the Mount of Jupiter

The person's ambitions will be hampered.

Located on the Mount of Saturn

The person will have bad luck.

Located on the Mount of the Sun
The person's artistic talent will be weakened.
Located on the Mount of Mercury
The person will be fickle.
Located on the Mount of Mars
The person will probably be cowardly.
Located on the Mount of the Moon
The person will lack imagination.
Located on the Mount of Venus
The person will be weak willed.

THE TRIANGLE

Located on the Mount of Jupiter
The person will handle people and matters successfully.
Located on the Mount of Saturn
The person will have a feeling for the occult and life's mysteries.
Located on the Mount of the Sun
The person will be practical and successful without becoming bigheaded.
Located on the Mount of Mercury
The person will be fickle and ruthless.
Located on the Mount of Mars
The person will remain cool in crises.
Located on the Mount of the Moon
The person will have great ideas and be imaginative.
Located on the Mount of Venus
The person will be calculating and have great self-control.

THE FORK

Ascending
The person will have abundant success.
Descending
The person will experience either lack of success or total failure.

THE CHAIN

Present
The person will have to overcome obstacles in his or her life, will suffer from anxiety and will struggle.

HATCHES

Hatches are usually noticeable on the mounts and indicate the following characteristics.
Located on the Mount of Jupiter
The person will be selfish and will wish to dominate.
Located on the Mount of Saturn
The person will be depressive and pessimistic and have bad luck.
Located on the Mount of the Sun
The person will be vain and stupid and will have a desire to be famous.

Located on the Mount of Mercury
The person will be fickle and ruthless.
Located on the Mount of the Moon
The person will be restless and suffer from malcontentment.
Located on the Mount of Venus
The person will be flirtatious.

DOUBLES

Present
These lines strengthen the quality of the line on which they occur and also indicate that the person will be highly strung and worry too much.
Excessive on the line on which they occur
The person might experience failure.

THE MAJOR LINES

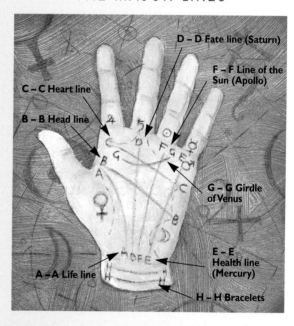

The palm has six very important lines from which can be read the person's character and personality as well as what life path he or she will have. The six lines are divided into two groups each: the major three lines and the minor three lines. The major three lines are the life line, the head line and the heart line. The minor three lines are the fate line, the health line and the sun line, and I discuss them later.

Although some people mightn't have all these lines, lacking them is very rare and is no cause for concern. The little cross-hatchings and other marks on the lines are also rather important.

Two other significant lines are the Girdle of Venus, which runs across the top of the palm, from the little finger to the index finger, and the chain-like lines around the wrists, at the bottom of the palm, known as the bracelets.

It has to be remembered that lines sometimes change and that the spot from where a line starts and finishes is very significant.

THE LIFE LINE

Curving around the thumb
The person will have a lot of physical activity in his or her life.

Solid all the way
The person will have a solid, steady and quite comfortable life.

Varying in depth and thickness
The person will have a varied life that has plenty of ups and downs.

Close to the index finger
The higher the line is towards the index finger, the more ambitious the person will be and the more able to stick to the task at hand.

Joining up with the head line
The person will be rather timid and cautious.

A gap between it and the head line
The person will be rather reckless and will act on impulse.

Tending to run towards the Mount of the Moon
The person will be a bit restless and would rather be somewhere else.

Broken and wavy
The person will have some type of mental or physical weakness.

Made up of chains
The person will have a rather poor disposition.

Another line running close by and parallel
The person will have a good, healthy disposition. This line is a sort of back-up.

Finishing in the fork
The person will have to depend on people's kindness in his or her old age.

THE HEAD LINE

A slight gap between it and the life line
The person will be a bit restless and rather active.

A rather wide gap between it and the life line
The person will be very restless and impatient and should work on these points in order to improve his or her social behaviour.

Joining up with the start of the life line and heart line
The person will experience real suffering.

Well defined and straight
The person will have clear and sound judgement.

Going all the way to the edge of the palm
The person will be a bit ruthless and will put business matters first and personal matters second.

The heart line also quite long
The person will be quite diplomatic and will succeed in his or her undertakings because he or she has this quality.

Short in length
The person will give up quite easily and will rarely finish anything he or she has started.

Weak in width
The person will be rather inactive and won't even start any projects.

Wavy in shape
The person will find it hard to face up to life's daily demands.

A chain shape
The person will be mentally ill either now or in the future.

Sweeping down and finishing in forks
The person will be a genius.

Lots of breaks in it
The person will probably suffer from deep depression.

THE HEART LINE

Strong in width
The person will be capable of true and faithful love.

Starting high
The person will be the jealous type.

Starting low
The person will have serene and rational love.

Starting very low
The person will have a cold nature.

Joining the head line
The person will let his or her head rule his or her heart.

Starting right under the Mount of Saturn
The person will usually encounter only one true and devastating love.

A wavy shape
The person will lack self-confidence, especially in love.

A chain shape
The person will be flirtatious and will find it hard to be faithful.

A duplicated heart line
The person will have a long and not very happy affair.

A duplicated heart line quite close to the heart line
Someone close to the person will probably die.

Not present
The person will have no love to spare for anyone except himself or herself.

THE MINOR LINES

THE FATE LINE (SATURN)

Present
The person will have good news.

Too long
The good news will turn sour.

Not present
The person will have the choice of making his or her own luck. Quite a few people have no fate line.

Starting at the life line
The person will have his or her dreams realised in time.

Starting at the Mount of the Moon
The person will be greatly influenced by other people.

A definite break in it
The person will have a definite change in luck.

THE HEALTH LINE (MERCURY)

Strong and well defined
The person will have a long and healthy life.

Short and rather weak
The person will have problems with his or her teeth.

Not present
This is good news: the person will have no health problems to worry about.

Ending near the ring finger (the fourth finger)
The person will probably have a good business.

Starting at the wrist
The person will travel a lot.

Badly broken
The person will have plenty of health problems.

A wavy shape
The person will have tummy problems and poor judgement.

A chain shape
The person will lose his or her hair.

A star on it
The person won't have more than one child.

THE SUN LINE (APOLLO)

This line indicates a person's intellectual and artistic nature.

Not present
The person will either have no interest in the arts or have no artistic talent at all.

Ending at the life line
The person will probably have a career in the arts.

A branch of it reaching the head line
The person will probably have a career in literature.

Rather weak and insignificant
The person will always be rather mediocre – or less – in what he or she does.

Finishing at the Mount of the Moon
The person will be motivated by his or her creative ability.

Ending at the heart line
The person will tend to be successful late in life.

A branch of it joining the Mount of Mercury
The person will probably be too materialistic to be a great artist.

THE OTHER LINES

THE GIRDLE OF VENUS

Present
The person will be surrounded by loving and caring people in his or her old age.

Clear and broken
The person will be brilliant and charismatic and quite popular with almost everybody.

Crossing the heart line
The person will possibly spoil a love affair because he or she has too many other interests.

Broken only
The person will have many disappointments in love.

Finishing near the Mount of Jupiter
The person will possibly be very witty.

THE BRACELETS

Each bracelet suggests a lifespan of about thirty years, so if there's a hint of three lines, the person can expect to live to about ninety years of age.

Clear and definite
The person will have a happy and varied life.

Weak in width
The person will be idealistic and a dreamer.

A chain shape
The person will be a hard worker.

To determine how many children you'll have, make a fist with either hand and by looking at the little finger, count the number of creases that appear on the side of your hand. Your hands should have the same number of creases, but if they don't, you'll have a decision to make. For example, if your left hand has two creases and your right hand three, you'll definitely have two children and the choice of having a third child.

PERSONAL GROWTH & DEVELOPMENT

Stop smoking according to your star sign

These days, smoking isn't about Marlboro men and sophisticated sexual predators: it's about immature behaviour and dumb decisions. The people of the twelve zodiac signs will have different ways of rising to the challenge of overcoming an addiction such as smoking, so read on and discover how you can quit for good.

ARIES

When the mood hits you, you might toss away your smokes, break all your ashtrays and give all your lighters away. Going cold turkey will probably be your best way to give up.

Although you'll quite openly assert that you've quit and that you're enjoying being a non-smoker, will you stay with it? The things we do on impulse quite often undo themselves in exactly the same way. There's no doubt you can quit, but keep in mind the fact that quite often your nemesis is lack of persistence. Therefore, before you allow your impulse to cause you to stop, make sure you fully recognise the sacrifices and losses involved.

Before you quit, outline both the benefits of not smoking and the dangers involved in continuing to smoke. Then use your head to stop and to make you remain a non-smoker. Why not challenge your mate, friend or business partner to a contest to see who can really quit? To meet a challenge or win a dare was probably why you started smoking in the first place.

Now you've shown you can smoke, show you can stop.

TAURUS

It mightn't be easy for you to stop smoking. Although you say that cigarettes have a good taste, how about the bad taste in the morning? Have you ever thought you might make a better lover if you didn't smoke?

You're stubborn and quite tenacious, so you resent any type of change. It isn't easy getting you to change your habits. Although stopping smoking might take quite an effort on your part, you're practical and you should therefore be able to see that the rewards are worth the effort.

Remember that once you're off the cigarettes, you have quite a good chance of staying off them. Look around you and consider taking up some other less harmful habit; however, don't make it either eating or drinking, because you also tend to go overboard with both. To reward yourself by having more sex could fill the bill quite nicely, and to chew gum might pacify you until you've quit smoking.

Buy yourself something new: something that's yours personally. However, you might want your gift to yourself to be something rather grand and expensive such as a new car, so you might be better off buying yourself something less expensive on a regular basis. Why not use wishing to take good care of yourself as your motivation for beginning soon?

GEMINI

You want to be busy, and your hands have to have something to do all the time. Sadly, as a Gemini, you're the person of the zodiac who should avoid smoking the most. You're inclined to run on your nerves most of the time, and you certainly don't need anything to stimulate your nerves even more.

You possibly started smoking to give your hands something to do and continued with the habit because you got a kick from it. You can become hooked and develop into a veritable nicotine field if you aren't careful. You can easily be the type of person who lights a cigarette from the butt of the previous one or who even smokes two cigarettes at the same time.

When you decide to quit, realise you'll have to have a substitute activity for keeping your hands busy. In brief, keep yourself amused if you truly wish to stop smoking.

CANCER

The reason you smoke might be either that your parents smoke or that smoking makes you feel content, secure and at home. As a matter a fact, you might do a lot of smoking at home, especially in the kitchen. You enjoy having a smoke after having a good meal.

It's through both reading and deep implantation in your emotions that you'll get a full understanding of the dangers of smoking. The threat of having a shorter life or of living with the fear that a fire could easily destroy your home will help you kick the habit.

Being deeply emotional will help you when you manage to convince yourself through practical reasoning that endangering your health and security by smoking is contrary to your plans.

If you believe you're unable to give up, have an after-dinner cigar or smoke a pipe instead. You'll find that your favourite foods taste better when you don't smoke, and you'll appreciate your meals much more. Because you appreciate quality, you might even reduce the quantity of food you consume now you're in search of good flavour.

LEO

You might believe that smoking makes you look better, and this is probably the reason you started smoking. However, smoking doesn't make you look any different – just worse. You very much want to be liked and accepted, so you'll perhaps stop smoking when you realise it's fast becoming unacceptable and that it's no longer the 'in' thing it used to be. More and more places are banning smoking altogether, it's receiving a lot of well-deserved bad publicity, and it's becoming a very expensive habit.

Consider also that your fingers and teeth are becoming an eyesore that's affecting your good looks. One of your wishes is to be viewed as being a strong-willed and self-willed person, just like a lion. To give in to a habit such as smoking is certainly no mark of strength. Because you usually enjoy being a pacesetter, you might find it easier to quit if you have a group of people trying at the same time. When you set yourself up as an example to other people, your pride is unlikely to allow you to shirk your duty.

Be generous to yourself and stop smoking as soon as possible. Show everyone how strong a Leo can be.

VIRGO

For Virgoans, smoking should never get to the point at which it's a problem, because they have an inbuilt awareness of the need to care for their health. Perhaps you offer the excuse that smoking gives you a bit of escapism from your rather pronounced and constant awareness of reality and of people's lack of perfection.

Virgoans should be warned that excessive smoking can play havoc with their nerves and very negatively influence their health. If you want to quit, start using two of your natural talents: awareness of detail and sense of practicality.

Start noticing the details of your habit: your stained fingers and teeth; your dry throat; your bad breath; the smell of your clothes, house and hair; and the filthy ashtrays.

After you've spotted these few details, bring your practical nature into the picture: start asking yourself relevant questions, such as whether or not smoking is sensible for a truly intelligent and practical person such as you. If you're honest with yourself, you should be able to drop the habit immediately. By giving up, you rid yourself of both worry and guilt. Once you've quit, you should have no difficulty adjusting to the change.

LIBRA

'Do I smoke or not?' is what you keep asking yourself, isn't it? I suggest you get a piece of paper and divide it into two columns. In the left-hand column, list smoking's advantages, and the right-hand column its disadvantages. This should help you decide to quit. You can then proceed to give up this filthy habit confident in the belief you've made the right choice.

Because you're always concerned about looking your best, it seems you can give up quite easily. Also consider the mess that smoking causes in your home and/or office. You can use your talents and time in a better way than cleaning up smoker's waste: consider expressing your natural artistic talents through painting, writing, making ceramics, doing needlepoint or some other creative pursuit that appeals to you. It's very important for your feeling of self-respect that you realise you've made an important decision.

Being indecisive is probably why you started smoking in the first place.

SCORPIO

If you make a decision to stop, you stop. Your strong desires can work marvels for you when you decide to stop. You might claim you smoke because you want to. Of course, if you're guilty of this, you're merely playing word games with yourself, and this is something you know even if you don't admit it.

If you have no desire to quit, there's nothing in the world that's powerful enough to cause you to cut down, much less stop. Because you're born under a water sign, your only hope of quitting is to use your emotions. If you can get turned on emotionally by the idea of not smoking, you'll be able to give up: you mightn't be as nice to kiss if you have smoker's breath.

You tend to do things all the way or not at all. If you do decide to quit, you will. No other person of the zodiac can smoke as many cigarettes and inhale as much and as deeply as you can.

SAGITTARIUS

Because you're always thinking about other things, it probably hasn't occurred to you that you're smoking too much or that you're endangering your health. If you have thought of it, you probably believe your good luck will keep you from suffering any ill-effects from smoking. You might be pushing your luck too hard if you believe you aren't vulnerable to the ill-effects. In order to stop smoking, you have to realise the danger involved in it. Pay attention to any reports you hear about it, because they'll aid you in quitting.

You're usually the type of person who does things in a big way, so you might be smoking much more than you realise. Start keeping a careful count of how many cigarettes you smoke per day: you might get quite a shock. You might also take note of how much money you're spending on smokes per week and per year.

Reward yourself by saving the money you spend on cigarettes and taking a trip instead. Your basic optimism and sense of humour can serve you very well in adjusting to a more rewarding and smokeless life.

CAPRICORN

You probably started smoking because you believed it gave you a more professional and grown-up look. By nature, you're inclined towards climbing high up the ladder of success, and you might have been persistent enough to make a lot of advances towards your goals. However, you know better than anyone that it hasn't been easy.

Now's the time to use your practical reasoning to consider that if you continue smoking, you might well be asking for additional setbacks in your progress. There's little likelihood that a person who smokes will gain any additional respect because he or she does so. Smoking is no longer the mark of either a professional or someone to look up to.

Remember that your position in life as a parent, a business leader or a civic or religious head is judged according to your habits. People tend to emulate you, so give them the correct image and they'll look up to you.

Turn your logical mind to other matters that can lead to pride, self-respect or greater accomplishment.

AQUARIUS

You might have started smoking in order to show you had either freedom of choice or independence. Although you at first might have believed that smoking did you some sort of good service in proving you had either of these things, in other people's eyes it only proved you had neither.

If you stop smoking, you can use your intelligence and originality to their best advantage. Although your friends and family might think your approach seems strange, the end result will be the same. You might prefer to quit among a group of your friends or relatives.

You might like to lay down some rules for the smokers you know, such as banning smoking at parties and social functions and in the presence of other members of your 'quit' group. This tactic mightn't help the other smokers, but it might help you. You could also ban yourself from smoking at parties and social functions.

Most Aquarians find that what works best for them is to go cold turkey. They usually make their decision to stop smoking at the most unexpected time or place. Remember that to give up smoking is to give you more energy, time, money and patience for moving about in your large circle of friends.

PISCES

You like to imagine that situations are as you'd like them to be rather than as they really are. However, you now find the statement that smoking is a health hazard emblazoned on every packet of cigarettes you buy.

In your attitude towards smoking, you might be inclined to be a bit wishy-washy: you alternate between being totally opposed to it and being totally in favour of it. If you wish to stop smoking, catch yourself out when you're in two minds about it and consider the facts about its bad aspects.

People who label Pisceans as being weak are wrong: you're anything but weak when faced with the facts and the truth. Remember that you have to be honest with yourself when you do announce you've quit: sneaking a smoke on the sly can be just as dangerous as smoking in clear view of other people. If you experience feelings of loss, seek to replace them by expressing your artistic talents and abilities more and by cultivating a greater awareness of your body's natural rhythms.

Hair and make-up tips according to your star sign

In this section, I tell you how to look after your skin, hair and face according to your star sign: how to make the most of your hair or hair type, and how to make the most of your face and eyes through working with your facial structure and knowing the best make-up to use.

ARIES

Hair	As an Arien, you love your hairstyles to be fascinating and alluring in order to accentuate your definite features and warm beauty. Guard against dry hair by using a shampoo that contains Vitamin F.
Face	Use a beige base.
Eyes	Use a pearl eye shadow, a black mascara and a grey eyebrow pencil.
Cheeks	Try a rose blush.
Lips	Try a light-plum lipstick.

TAURUS

Hair	As a Taurean, you love your hair to be glowing and well conditioned, so brush and condition it continuously. You also love your haistyles to be orderly and burnished in colour, so try a colourant such as chestnut or mahogany.
Face	Try a golden-sand base.
Eyes	Try a light-brown eye shadow and a black mascara that makes your lashes look super long.
Cheeks	Try a very soft-red blush, preferably the brush-on type.
Lips	Try a bright-rose lipstick.

GEMINI

Hair	As a Gemini, you love hairstyles you can wear at least two ways, especially ones that can convert from sleek and neat to flirty curls and back again. Try either a highlight or tips that are silvery or white mink in style.
Face	Try a beige-sand base.
Eyes	Try a turquoise or pale-blue eye shadow.
Cheeks	Try a blush that's a very light shade of pink.
Lips	Try a rose or orange lipstick.

CANCER

Hair	Try a lemon shampoo and lemon conditioner.
Eyes	Try a lavender or pale-purple eye shadow.
Face	Try a blonde-sand base that isn't too dark and a brown mascara that will enhance the length of your lashes.
Cheeks	Try a rose blush.
Lips	Try a plum or dark-rose lipstick.

LEO

Hair	As a Leo, you love hairstyles that make you look and feel elegant, and you love to be noticed and admired. Try a shampoo that hides any grey hairs and puts highlights in your hair.
Face	Try a base colour that isn't very dark, such as golden sand.
Eyes	Try a pale-green eye shadow and an olive-tone mascara.
Cheeks	Try a rose blush.
Lips	Try a rose lipstick.

VIRGO

Hair   As a Virgoan, you love to look well groomed and intelligent, so you adore hairstyles that make you look just that. Try an immaculate salon cut, and colour co-ordination.

Face   Try a pastel-beige base.

Eyes   Try a cream eye shadow that has olive highlights, and a brown mascara applied not too thickly.

Cheeks   Try a bone blush.

Lips   Try a rose or orange lipstick.

LIBRA

Hair   As a Libran, you like to wear pretty waves and curls for a party, to look glamorous and to be adored by everyone. Try a shampoo that gives your hair a luxury treatment and prepares it for styling.

Face   Try a dark-beige base.

Eyes   Try a blue eye shadow that has a green highlight and a brown or blue mascara.

Cheeks   Try a bone or beige blush.

Lips   Try a rose or plum lipstick.

SCORPIO

Hair   As a Scorpion, you love hairstyles that are clever, sophisticated and very flattering and that emphasise your mood. You don't have to do much except regularly treat yourself for dandruff.

Face   Try a light-colour base such as blonde sand.

Eyes   Try a prune eye shadow and a black mascara.

Cheeks   Try a frosty-peach blush.

Lips   Try a rose lipstick and lip liner.

SAGITTARIUS

Hair   As a Sagittarian, you love hairstyles that are easy to manage and non-frizz and that show off your hair's natural body and bounce. For you, the ideal style is a soft perm that will put bounce rather than frizz in your hair.

Face   Try a light-beige base.

Eyes   Try a silver-slate eye shadow and a black mascara.

Cheeks   Try a peach or apricot blush.

Lips   Try a pale-pink lipstick.

CAPRICORN

Hair   As a Capricornian, you love hairstyles that show your natural beauty, and you constantly control your hair's condition. Try conditioning your hair continuously and a gentle-care styling lotion.

Face   Try a soft-beige base.

Eyes   Try a slate-grey eye shadow, a black mascara and a brown eyebrow pencil.

Cheeks   Try a deep-pink blush.

Lips   Try a rose lipstick that isn't too bright in colour.

AQUARIUS

Hair   As an Aquarian, you're never satisfied with the same hairstyle, and you're never seen wearing the same style all year round. Try warm fashion hair colours.

Face   Try an elegant beige base.

Eyes   Try a soft-pearl eye shadow and a brown mascara.

Cheeks   Try an apricot blush.

Lips   Try a rose lipstick.

PISCES

Hair   As a Piscean, you love hairstyles that include wild curls or romantic waves, and you usually highlight your hair by tinting it with unusual colours. Try a lightener that gives you a natural, unleashed look.

Face   Try a blonde-tint base.

Eyes   Try a shimmering-pearl prune eye shadow and a brown eyebrow pencil.

Cheeks   Try a prune blush.

Lips   Try a rose lipstick.

Develop your psychic powers in twelve easy steps

Have you ever had a hunch that turned out be accurate? Have you ever thought about someone, the phone suddenly rings and it's him or her? You might jokingly say, 'Gee, I must be psychic.'

Well, in fact you are psychic; all of us are. There are simply different levels of psychic ability, depending on whether or not you make a conscious effort to tune into it. Each one of us has that sixth sense that makes us psychic, as well as a spiritual relationship with ourselves that causes us to be aware of our 'hunches' and 'gut feelings'.

Some people, for whatever reasons, delve into the psychic then choose to drop out. When I was a child, some things occurred that scared me and almost caused me to 'drop out'. Naturally, I didn't, because I had an incredible desire to learn and grow and to use my psychic ability to help not only myself but other people.

PSYCHIC CHILDREN

Our psychic ability is most strong when we're children. When our mind hasn't been tarnished by outside influences, and prejudices haven't yet set in, we're able to absorb a lot more effectively without passing judgement. However, it's during this innocent stage of life that parents dictate whether or not their child will be free to nurture his or her gift.

If, as a child, you experienced deja vu flashes or premonitions and later told your parents, chances are your parents dismissed them, and in time you'd have done the same. Your parents probably thought you had an imaginary friend. In some extreme cases, the parents think the voices in their child's head are demonic and dangerous, and they therefore seek out their church for help in cleansing the child's 'possessed' body.

However, if, as I did, you had understanding parents who were open to spiritualism and self-awareness, these occurrences were discussed so you could accept them as being part of your life and you could expand on the special gift you had.

EXPLORING YOUR PSYCHIC ABILITY

The psychic dimension is extremely powerful, and if you believe you're psychic and you wish to explore your ability, you can purchase books that will help you do so. Full psychic ability takes quite some time to develop, especially before you can practise it on a professional basis.

If you hear voices telling you things – and when I say 'voices' I mean not little people talking in your head but feelings from within – don't ignore them. Train yourself to listen to your inner voice, and when it tells you something that turns out to be accurate, thank it and tell it to stay with you.

My grandmother told me that the voice we hear inside us is usually that of a family member who has passed on and is with us as our guide. I strongly believe this is the case.

MEDITATION

Meditation is a wonderful tool for helping you to tune into your psychic ability. Although some people like to complicate this simple art by offering long, ambiguous explanations, it simply means being calm and relaxed. It's in the meditative state that we're in tune with our mind and body and we're able to ask our voice questions we're in search of answers to.

TWELVE EASY STEPS

Following is an easy way of developing your psychic ability. Don't expect miracles overnight, because it takes patience and perseverance. It comes easier for people who've already tuned into their power.

STEP 1
Make sure you're alone and that you won't be distracted. Take the phone off the hook and put a 'Do not disturb' sign on your door.

STEP 2
Don't rush anything: it might take several attempts before you see or feel anything. You can't develop your psychic ability if you don't have patience.

STEP 3
Never use your psychic ability for personal gain: to do so is unethical.

STEP 4
In order to accept your ability, give in return.

STEP 5
Before you start, cleanse the room by lighting a white or mauve candle and two sticks of sandalwood incense. Have the candle and incense burning for at least one hour before you start.

STEP 6
Sit in front of a mirror and look at yourself. Remember step 2 and be patient. At some stage, you'll see your features change, as your spirit guide takes over your appearance.

STEP 7
Practise step 6 for only about fifteen minutes at a time, not for several hours. If you have to, take several months to achieve the step, because it's only after you've had success that you can move on to the following steps.

STEP 8
Ask your guide for answers to your questions. Start off by asking some easy questions.

STEP 9
Remember to thank your guide even if you get no answers.

STEP 10
Keep a record of what happened so you can refer to it later. Your guide will sometimes give you an answer to a question you haven't yet asked.

STEP 11
Snuff out the candle – never blow it out – and let the incense burn out by itself.

STEP 12
Sit down and relax or meditate for at least twenty-five minutes before you go about your normal routine. It's important you absorb what you've achieved.

RUNES

Understanding the ancient art of runes

Have you ever stopped to think why we use the letter X in place of a kiss? Or wondered why we follow an arrow to whichever way it points? Believe it or not, both these day-to-day symbols evolved thousands of years ago, in the days of the Vikings, from the ancient art of runes.

The word runes derived from the words 'whispered secret', and runes remained shrouded in mystery for hundreds of years. However, in their heyday, they were read in a bid to predict and sometimes influence the weather, the harvest, births, deaths and even war.

Today, more and more people are studying and practising this secret and revelatory art to try and find the answers to their past, present and future. Reading runes is an alternative to reading tarot cards.

Runes comprise of twenty-five alphabetic-scripted stones. Each stone has a meaning and through its interpretation points the person towards the hidden forces and motivations that shape his or her present and future.

The X we use to represent a kiss is actually the rune for Partnership and Giving.

The arrow we follow actually represents the Warrior rune, which describes taking action and undergoing a passage with total trust. When the Warrior rune is reversed, it represents danger – pretty much the same outcome as if you decided to go against a pointing arrow, especially when you're driving on a freeway!

Although few people recognise the mystical art of runes, its decorative motifs are found both on many accessories and in past and current architecture. Once you're familiar with the age-old art, you'll want to consult the runes every day, as I and my many clients do.

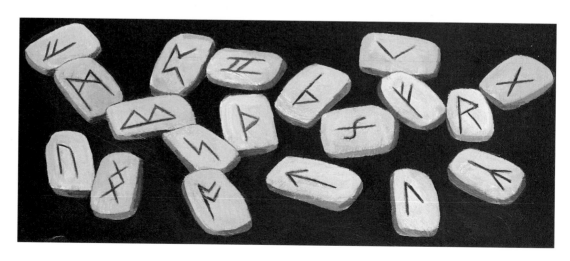

KERRY KULKENS' GUIDE TO LOVE, SEX AND YOUR STARS

What each rune signifies

READING THE RUNES

In a favourite spot of your home, lay out a special piece of fabric on either a table or a section of floor on which you wish to play the runes. You can light either a white candle, which promotes spirituality, or a sandalwood-incense stick, which promotes harmony. Take a few breaths, and make sure you compose yourself so you're totally at peace and stress free.

Try and focus on the issue about which you wish to seek guidance. If you don't have a specific issue, simply ask, 'What do I need to know in my life right now?'

Reach into your rune bag and juggle the stones about before you draw one out. Nine of the runes read the same regardless of how you take them out, and the other sixteen can be read either upright or reversed. When they're reversed, the focus is on blocking or slowing movement and the fact that care has to be taken.

There are three main types of reading, as follows.

ODIN'S RUNE

This is the most practical and simple reading to undertake. Simply draw out one rune from the bag on a daily basis in order to determine what your day holds. Odin's rune is also an effective reading if you're suddenly presented with a stressful situation and you require an immediate answer. You don't have to bother laying out your cloth and lighting the candle: simply find a quiet place for consulting the rune.

THE THREE-RUNE SPREAD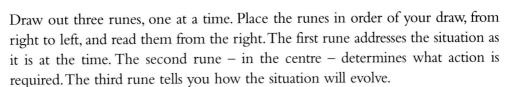

Draw out three runes, one at a time. Place the runes in order of your draw, from right to left, and read them from the right. The first rune addresses the situation as it is at the time. The second rune – in the centre – determines what action is required. The third rune tells you how the situation will evolve.

THE CELTIC CROSS

You have to draw out six runes in order to make a cross as shown in the illustration. The first rune sits on the right-hand side and tells of the past. The second rune represents you in the present, and the third represents your future. The fourth offers you the foundation of the issue at hand and the forces involved. The fifth tells you which obstacles might lie ahead, and the sixth shows you how to deal with them.

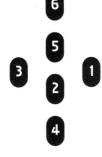

If after a Celtic Cross reading you're unclear about what the message means, draw a seventh rune, which will be your rune of resolution.

Remember to place your runes in numeric order when you draw them.

RUNE		WHAT IT SIGNIFIES
The Self	ᛗ	This rune signifies a time of major inner growth. It tells you that through having good self-esteem, you'll form many relationships.
Partnership	ᚷ	This rune signifies that a union or some form of partnership is at hand. A true and everlasting partnership will evolve only if you remain an individual during it.
Signals	ᚠ	This rune's keynote is receiving: messages, gifts and signals. The messages will come in unexpected forms. Remain aware and open to receiving, because even a timely warning is viewed as being a gift.
Separation	ᛝ	This rune signifies breaking away as well as gains and benefits. However, the gains will come from surrendering something, and this surrendering enables you to become more of the person you really are.
Strength	ᚢ	This rune signifies endings and beginnings. It tells you that you've outgrown your surroundings and that you're in search of something new.
Initiation	ᛈ	This rune is on the side of heaven and the unknowable. It has associations with the phoenix: the mystical bird that consumes itself in the fire then rises from its own ashes. A secret matter looms.
Constraint	ᛏ	This is a difficult rune. The need to deal with severe constraint is its lesson. Delve deep within yourself and recognise what troubles you with a smile, because only then will you recognise what's set you back and restrained you.
Fertility	ᛜ	This rune signifies new beginnings, new life and new paths. It's a powerful rune that strengthens you in your need to finalise something in order to clear away the old and free yourself from a rut, habit or relationship. It signifies preparations for a new life.
Defence	ᛇ	For this rune, patience is the counsel. In order to have a new life, you have to nurture it and not act hastily. Through inconvenience and discomfort, growth will occur.
Protection	ᛉ	This rune signifies that new opportunities and challenges are evident in your life, and it requires you to control your emotions so the opportunities and challenges can occur.
Possessions	ᚨ	This rune signifies fulfilment, ambitions, rewards and love. You're being asked to assess what makes you happy: is it wealth and possessions or self-determination and growth?
Joy	ᚹ	This is a fruit-bearing rune. It signifies that you have unblocked negative energy and that something lovely is emerging from the depths. Your soul is illuminating within.

RUNE		WHAT IT SIGNIFIES
Harvest		This rune signifies that good things are to come, provided you prepare the ground, plant the seeds and cultivate with care. Don't hasten your harvest; be patient.
Opening		You've found light at the end of your tunnel, and now you're free to receive and experience the joy of non-attached giving.
Warrior		This rune is the Spiritual Warrior, for whom the battle is within you. Patience and singlemindedness are required. You have to be willing to undergo your passage with compassion and total trust.
Growth		This rune signifies a blossoming and ripening in a broad field: in relationships, family matters, your inner self and even the world. Modesty, patience, generosity and fairness are called for.
Movement		This rune signifies movements and transitions. It could mean a physical shift, a new dwelling place, a new attitude or a new life. It could also signify movement by way of improving or bettering a situation.
Flow		This rune signifies flowing of emotions, careers and relationships. Let yourself live, be free and don't over-evaluate situations.
Disruption		Change, freedom, invention and liberation are all attributes of this rune; expect the unexpected when you draw it out. Events might be totally out of your control as you come out of a type of long sleep.
Communication		This rune signifies communications with the attunement of something that has two sides and two elements, and with the ultimate reunion that comes at the end of a journey. The journey is the soul's journey, and the communication is between what's above and what's below.
Gateway		This rune signifies there's work to be done both inside and outside yourself. Non-action is the counsel, so now isn't the time for making decisions. Make sure you've let go of the past before you step through the gate to the future.
Breakthrough		This rune signifies that a major shift or breakthrough in the process of self-change is evident and that it requires radical trust as you head emptyhanded into the void. The rune often introduces a major period of achievement and prosperity.
Standstill		This rune signifies the passive period that precedes a rebirth, so be patient. You might be powerless to do anything except submit, surrender or even sacrifice some long-cherished desires. Cleanse away the old in time for the new.
Wholeness		This rune signifies a time for regeneration. It's a time for regrouping and letting in light to a part of your life that's been in the dark or shut away.
The Unknowable		This is a blank rune that marks both the end and the beginning. It's the rune of total and utter trust. Obstacles can become gateways that lead to fresh starts. The work of self-change is progressing in your life.

Spells, Rituals & Potions

Understanding witchcraft and witches

WHAT IS A WITCH?

Some people have a misconception about the word witch: they think a witch is female and a warlock male. They're wrong: the word warlock is an Americanism and actually means 'traitor' or 'breaker of oaths'.

The word witch actually means 'the wise one who has knowledge'.

The knowledge is mainly of herbs and natural cures for ailments.

Witchcraft and witches have long been instrumental for people in searching for and capturing elusive love. In order to secure the object of their desire, people from all social strata often sought a witch to weave a spell and provide a potion and an amulet. They left nothing to chance, so that success was guaranteed.

Witches peered into a crystal ball in order to find the face of a person's loved one. They also read the person's palm in order to pinpoint the year he or she could expect to marry and to determine how many children he or she would have.

BLACK MAGIC AND WHITE MAGIC

Many people wrongly believe that witchcraft is black magic, which is practised for evil purposes and directed at innocent people. It isn't only evil; it's dangerous, because the evil often rebounds on the black magician, who seldom benefits from his or her powers.

The magic I write about in this book is white magic, which usually means magic used for the good of humankind. Although I provide some mischief-making spells, the spells don't endanger innocent people and some of them are quite fun to conduct.

WILL THE WITCHCRAFT WORK?

Witchcraft is as old as humankind. Some people have always believed in it; some have called it superstition. You can decide whether or not it works for you. No one can give you a guarantee your spells will work. However, you have to have an element of faith in both yourself and the spell you're conducting.

You don't have to be a witch to practise witchcraft. In this section of the book, I outline the basics of casting spells. If in performing a ritual there are parts that make you lose concentration, go over the ritual a few times until you're adept at it. You have to have complete concentration.

WHEN DO YOU CAST A SPELL?

You shouldn't cast any spell until at least three hours have elapsed since you've consumed any food or drink, except water. It's sometimes necessary to fast for twenty-four hours before you cast a special spell, because doing so gives the spell extra strength.

WHERE DO YOU CAST A SPELL?

If the spell is long, make sure you conduct it in a place you can work in without interruption. If you're casting the spell at home, make sure you pull the blinds down, lock the door and unplug the phone. If you cast the spell out in the wilderness, especially under your favourite tree, as I do, your spell will be given even more potency because trees are known to carry spirits and exude powerful energy.

WHAT THINGS DO YOU REQUIRE?

When you're casting a spell, try to achieve the right atmosphere. Preferably work by either candlelight or the glow of an open fire. If you can't use either of these, use subdued electric lighting. Create the right mood. A good aid is also burning of incense such as sandalwood.

WHAT APPROACH DO YOU REQUIRE?

Although your tools and surroundings are necessary, the most important aspect is yourself, because any spell's strength depends on the faith you have and the feeling you put into the spell. Your approach has to be right. Be clearheaded and align your inner self before you conduct the spell. Conduct it when you're neither angry nor emotional, because you have to exercise good judgement during it.

Love, sex and romance spells

Women who wish to light the flame of love have called on the powers of witchcraft for centuries. Luckily, love spells are fun and easy to cast, even for the beginner. Women in love have no trouble calling up the moods and images that trigger magic.

Following are some simple spells for catching the man or woman of your desires. When you cast them, remember that more than any other type of magic, love magic has to be kept secret from your prey. The trick is to catch the person at his or her right moment. Don't spoil anything by telling anyone about your plan.

To make an image is one of the oldest ways of casting a spell. The method is based on the principle of sympathetic magic, whereby the image or other item such as a photo, a nail clipping, a lock of hair or an item of clothing serves as a proxy for the real person or thing.

THE TRADITIONAL LOVE DOLL

If you wish someone to fall in love with you, use a doll to represent him or her. It's best to make the doll yourself, out of natural material such as wax, wood, clay or straw. It's better still to make a rag doll. Although you can buy a readymade rag doll, it won't be as powerful as one you make yourself.

First, obtain something from the body of the person you're pursuing: a lock of hair, a nail clipping, some skin and so on. To do this adds potency to the spell.

Make the doll on the first day of a new moon. While you're calling out your quarry's name, scratch or write his or her name on the doll. Your blood is the best substance to write with, but if you're squeamish, it's acceptable to use red ink mixed with a drop of your blood.

Using either a rose thorn or a pin, gently prick the doll where the heart is located, and say:

As this thorn pierces your heart,

So let it be pierced with love for me.

Alternatively, wrap the doll in three different-coloured ribbons, and as you wrap, say:

Thread bind;

Body entwine;

Heart find linked to mine.

You can also make a doll out of bread and eat a piece of it each night while saying:

As you become a part of me,

So let me become a part of you.

Always use the same doll and conduct the spell for fifteen minutes each night until there's a full moon. Start again on the first day of the next new moon.

If the person doesn't react, light a red candle and slightly singe the feet while saying:

For you I yearn;

For me you burn.

This should get a quick response.

When you aren't casting the spell, keep your doll wrapped in a clean cloth made of natural – not synthetic – fibre and hide it in a safe spot.

THE MODERN-DAY LOVE DOLL

Although synthetic fabrics usually aren't used, there's nothing to stop you from using a photo. In this case, you use a different method for casting the spell.

At the new moon, place a photo of you on top of the photo of the person you desire. Using red cotton, sew the two photos together while saying:

Face to face;
Heart to heart.

Keep the two photos sewn together, wrap them in either a black or a red natural-fibre cloth, and hide them. Take them out at each new moon and repeat the abovementioned words three times. Keep doing this until you've achieved your goal.

MY SPECIAL LOVE POWDER

If you know the person, invite him or her to dinner at your home and feed him or her the following powder.

Ingredients	Method
An ounce of dried leeks	*Mash the three ingredients into a powder and put*
An ounce of dried rose petals	*the powder in a tightly closed box. Keep the box on*
An ounce of dried coriander seeds	*you at all times, and as soon as you get the chance,*
	put a bit of the powder in the person's dinner food.
	Then sit back and wait for the results.

A LITTLE STEAL FOR THE BETTER

Another way of getting the person you desire is to steal something from him or her. However, you have to return it to him or her when you've conducted the spell in order for the spell to last. It's best to pick an item you can wear: a belt, a scarf, a tie, a sock and so on. Wear the item close to your skin, day and night, for a week. Sleep with it and touch it often. When you give it back, part of your spirit will have entered it and the person will soon be having deep thoughts of you.

If unbridled passion is what you want, try to touch the back of the person's neck without his or her knowing, and whisper softly:

Hands set him (her) on fire
With the wildest desire.

If you do this often enough, the person will soon be filled with an uncontrollable passion for you.

TO MAKE SOMEONE FALL IN LOVE WITH YOU

Spell number one

You can perform great magic using a strand of hair of someone you desire and conducting the spell on the night of a full moon. Using a red-silk thread, twist together the person's strand of hair with a strand of your hair. To strengthen the spell, smear a drop of your blood on the two strands of hair. Tie the ends of the strands together to form a ring. If the hair is too short to do this, put it in either a locket or a small red-silk bag. Keep the locket or bag next to your skin until the person is yours.

Spell number two

Before sunrise, pick either a blade of grass or a leaf from the person's garden and put it in your mouth. Turn to the east and say:

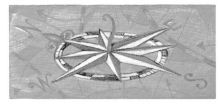

Let the moon rising
Be my true love's guide.
Then turn to the west and say:
And the moon setting
Find him (her) at my side.

Spell number three

Pick a rose petal, rub it with a spring onion and wrap it around a pinch of ground cinnamon. Using a sharp knife, cut out two small heart shapes from either red paper or red cardboard. Sew the two heart shapes together with the rose petal inside them and pin them to the left side of your underpants.

Spell number four

Sprinkle salt around yourself. On a small piece of plain paper, first write your name and birthdate and then write the name and birthdate of the person you desire. Make sure you write your name after the person's name. Draw a heart around the two names and birthdates. Burn a red candle, and light the piece of paper with it. Allow the piece of paper to burn until only the ashes remain.

Spell number five

You'll require the following ingredients for this 'herbal tea'.

Ingredients	Method
A glass of chilled red wine	*Mix all the ingredients in a saucepan. After the*
A teaspoon of rosemary leaves	*mixture has boiled, let it simmer and count to a*
A teaspoon of aniseed	*hundred. Remove the mixture from the stove and*
A teaspoon of cloves	*let it cool. Strain it through a sieve and return it to*
A teaspoon of honey	*the boil until sweet vapours rise. Pour the mixture*
A teaspoon of orange rind	*into a cup, give it to the person you've chosen and*
A pinch of ground cumin	*say it's a new herbal tea.*
Three green leaves from rose geranium	

TO MAKE SOMEONE REMAIN FAITHFUL

Simply obtain a lock of the person's hair and a sprinkling of the ashes of an item of his or her clothing you've burnt. Rub the hair using the ashes and some honey taken from a wasp's nest.

TO MAKE SOMEONE KEEP LOVING YOU

This one's a bit bizarre. Mix ambergris, powdered cypress wood and the marrow from the bones of a white dog's left foot. Perfume the mixture using musk, and wear it when you're around the person so he or she gets a good smell of it.

TO MAKE A WOMAN LOVE YOU

Find a black agate set in silver and wear it around your neck for seven days. At the end of the time, offer the agate to the woman you've chosen. The agate is one of the birthstones for Gemini.

TO MAKE A MAN LOVE YOU

Take the peels of two lemons and wear one of them all day in each pocket of an item of your clothing. At night, rub the four legs of your bed using the lemon peels. The man you've chosen will appear in your dreams and present you with two lemons.

TO BECOME PREGNANT

Try this spell if you're a woman who longs for a child. Obtain a bag of sunflower and pumpkin seeds. At the new moon, eat five of each type of seed. Continue eating the seeds until there's a full moon. If you haven't become pregnant before the next new moon, start the spell again.

TO GET YOUR LOVER BACK AFTER A TIFF

Using red ink, write your name and your lover's name on a piece of paper. Encircle the two names three times and bury the piece of paper. Your lover will soon turn up offering all kinds of apology.

TO REKINDLE YOUR LOVER'S INTEREST IN YOU

Write your lover's name on a piece of paper and put the piece of paper either under the phone or in an inconspicuous place near the phone. At the new moon, light a pink candle when you think your lover is most likely to ring you. Let the candle burn for half an hour while you're calling up your lover's image. Conduct this spell for seven days.

TO MAKE YOUR MARRIAGE PARTNER LOVE YOU FOR SEVEN YEARS

Hang a bunch of yarrow over the marital bed. If your partner doesn't react from that point onwards, put a pine cone under his (her) pillow or under his (her) side of the bed.

If you want something more dramatic, put a drop of your blood on a chicken's heart and bury the heart in a place your partner often uses.

TO FIND OUT WHETHER YOUR LOVER IS FAITHFUL

Put a piece of iron ore under your lover's pillow. If he or she is faithful, he or she will embrace you. If he or she isn't faithful, he or she will fall out of bed.

TO MAKE YOUR LOVER COME BACK

For seven times for seven nights at seven o'clock, say:

> *Hide in darkness,*
> *Out of sight*
> *Until the next moon's*
> *Seventh night.*
> *Then go and find*
> *The one I seek,*
> *As he must return*
> *Within a week.*

TO MAKE A WOMAN ADORE YOU

Sprinkle some olives with cayenne herb and dried mustard seed. Your darling will adore you in no time.

TO MAKE A MAN MORE PASSIONATE

You have to conduct this spell when the sun is passing through the sign of Leo (the lion). I don't recommend it unless you're desperate and dateless.

Grind half a dozen sage leaves until they're in powder form, then place the powder in a glass container. Bury the container in a heap of human faeces or ordinary compost and expose the material to the sun for thirty days.

When the thirty days have passed, you'll find there's a mass of writhing worms in the material. Immediately build a blazing fire between stacks of red bricks. When the flames soar high, place the worms on the blaze until they're burnt to a crisp. Pick up the worms and put them back in the glass container in the same place as before for another ten days.

When the ten days have passed, remove a small amount of the powder and place it under your tongue. From that moment onwards, you'll be irresistible to women.

TO SEDUCE SOMEONE

On a full-moon night, light a red candle while you're thinking about your prey. Repeat three times:

> *Light the flame;*
> *Bright the fire;*
> *Red is the colour*
> *Of desire.*

TO PUNISH AN UNFAITHFUL LOVER

At midnight, light a brown candle. Using a needle, prick the candle three times while saying:

> *Twice, thrice*
> *The candle is pricked by me;*
> *Thrice the heart*
> *Shall broken thee.*

Money, success and power spells

TO MAKE MONEY

Bury a silver coin and a drop of your blood in a clay pot then plant a shrub in the pot. Look after the shrub extremely well: if it grows, so too will your money, but if it withers, your money will dwindle.

TO SUCCEED AT BETTING AND IN LOTTERIES

Rub a green candle with sandalwood oil. Using a red pen and a piece of green paper, write down what you're betting on, and if you're buying a lottery ticket, write down the ticket number. Light the candle and burn the paper in the flame. Make sure you don't blow the candle out: let it burn down completely, then carry on your person the candle's stub and the paper's ash and place your bet. If you've bought a lottery ticket, carry it on your person until the lottery's drawn.

TO SUCCEED AT PLAYING CARDS

Conduct the 'betting and lotteries' spell before you start playing a game. Before the game, rub a bit of sandalwood oil on the cards. Alternatively, rub a silver ring with sandalwood oil and place the ring on your left hand. Make sure the ring and oil touch the cards.

TO MAKE SURE THAT MONEY ARRIVES

If your palm is itchy, it means money is on its way. To make sure the money arrives, either put your itchy hand in your pocket or scratch your hand on anything made of wood or clay.

TO GAIN WEALTH AND IMPORTANCE

On a sheet of white paper or parchment, write:

> *Lo, ma, na, pa,*
>
> *Quoa, ra, sata, na.*

Place a coin in the middle of the paper or parchment. Fold the four corners of the paper or parchment to the middle, fold again, and fold a third time until the paper or parchment has a firm grip over the coin.

On a Sunday when the sun is bright, seek out a dirt road that forms a crossroads. In the centre of the crossroads, bury the paper or parchment and coin. Using your left foot, stamp the ground firmly three times and make signs of the cross over the spot. Go, and don't look back.

On the following day at the same time, return to the spot and dig up the paper or parchment and coin. Don't fill in the small hole, but remove the paper or parchment and coin. Go, and don't look back.

You'll never experience ill-fortune if you carry the paper or parchment and coin with you at all times.

TO GAIN POWER OVER SOMEONE

Although this spell is a bit more ambitious, with practice you might succeed. Obtain a small wooden-framed mirror. Make a ring of ivy around the mirror and place the mirror face-up in a bucket of water. Leave the bucket and mirror outside overnight where the moon will shine on them.

On the next morning, take the mirror out of the bucket and put it in a secret place. When the person you wish to gain power over comes near, look into your mirror then look into the person's eyes. Continue doing this until you notice that the person is following your suggestions more and more. One day, you might have complete control over him or her.

TO HAVE GOOD FORTUNE

Before sunrise on the first Tuesday of a full moon, search
for a four-leaf clover. When you've found one, recite:

> *Christmas,*
> *Factus est obediens*
> *Usque ad mortem,*
> *Mortem autem crucis.*
> *Propter quod dues*
> *Exaltavit jeschue.*

Good fortune will follow if you carry the four-leaf clover with you at all times.

TO NEVER BE SHORT OF MONEY

It's important it be remembered that all fortune that results from these spells should be shared with poorer people.

If you fail to do this, ill-fortune will plague you.

This spell isn't an easy one, especially if you're the squeamish type. During the month of
March, take a dead mouse, dry its skin and make a purse out of the skin. Using a hawk's feather
for a quill and a bat's blood for ink, write:

> *Rosguilla dunstallum.*

Note how much money you put in your purse each time, and regardless of how much you
spend, you'll always find a similar amount in your purse.

TO BRING GOOD FORTUNE FOR THE YEAR

Greet the first new moon of the new year by wearing silver coins in your shoes. You're bound
to have good fortune for that year.

TO WIN A LAWSUIT

Remove a quill from a white goose and place some fern seeds in it. You'll have victory over
your adversary.

TO CHASE AWAY A WOMAN WHO'S TRYING TO STEAL YOUR MAN

Witches have a creed:

> *Don't get mad;*
> *Get even.*

In the smelliest place you can find, put a doll that represents the other woman. The woman
should very soon be feeling ill at ease in her home or workplace or wherever she's been trying
to trap your man. As a result, she'll move away.

TO SILENCE A GOSSIPY NEIGHBOUR

Sew up a doll's lips and chant the following spell:

> *If nothing but ill*
> *From your lips can fall,*
> *Let there be nothing*
> *From them at all.*

Luck and protection spells

TO PROTECT YOU FROM EVIL FORCES

The magic square is a simple little numbers square in which the numbers add up to fifteen every which way. It's a lucky combination:

438

951

276

Writing the combination on a piece of paper and carrying it around on your person will protect you from evil forces in general.

If you fear a specific person, write his or her name down on a piece of paper and write the numbers below the name. The person won't be able to do either you or your loved ones any harm as long as you carry the piece of paper on your person. If you're a woman, you'll find it particularly powerful if you carry the piece of paper in your bra, face-down in the left-hand cup.

TO PROVIDE PROTECTION DURING TRAVEL

If any member of your family or a friend of yours intends to travel, put a dozen hazelnuts and an item of the person's clothing under his or her pillow. The hazelnuts will bring him or her good luck during the trip, and the item of clothing will make sure he or she returns home safely.

TO PROTECT YOUR HOME FROM INTRUDERS

Get up before sunrise. Place a pinch of pepper both at your front door and on a rear-window sill. While you're placing the pepper, say:

Pepper rouge:
Knave or thief,
If you break this bond,
Find grief.
I mean it for
This sill and door
And all through
the house
For ever more.

TO MAKE A WISH COME TRUE

This spell features the wishing tree. Write your wish on either a piece of ribbon or a piece of red material. If you tie your wish to a tree's branch, the spirit that's dwelling in the tree will grant the wish.

TO AVERT TRESPASSERS

If a person or an animal trespasses on your property, find his or her footprints and hammer a nail through the imprint. The person or animal will develop an aversion to your land and leave you in peace.

TO PROTECT YOUR CHILD FOR THE DAY

Throw a handful of either sand or salt after the child as he or she is leaving home. The thrown sand or salt will form an invisible protection shield around the child until he or she returns at day's end.

TO PROTECT YOUR CHILD FROM BAD INFLUENCES

Collect some sea shells and wrap them in an item of the child's clothing. Pull out enough strands of your hair for braiding them with a silk thread. Braid the strands of hair and wrap them very tightly around the child's item of clothing that contains the shells. Hide the item in the room in which you spend most of your time. The child will never forget the things you've taught him or her as long as the item remains hidden.

TO REVERSE A THEFT

If someone has stolen something from you, face a mirror towards your front door. The evil spirits will chase the person until he or she has returned the stolen item.

TO PREVENT FIRE

When the moon is full, light a red candle. Using a glass of water, quickly douse the flame while you're saying:

Fire bright,
Fire cease;
Stay away
And leave this home
In peace.

Keep an unlit red candle handy, because you have to recast the spell at each full moon.

Mischief-making spells

TO ANNOY SOMEONE WHO'S BOTHERING YOU

Every day, pour some water over a weeping-willow branch. Each time, catch the water in a bucket, re-use it and save it. Do this for seven consecutive days. At the new moon, pour the water at the front gate of the person's home. He or she will very soon be suffering a few minor annoyances: lost items, minor injuries, car troubles and so on.

TO BRUISE AN ENEMY'S EGO

Saw a branch from a one-year-old tree while you're saying your enemy's name. At sunset, bring the branch home and put it on the floor. Beat the branch as hard as you can on the floor while you're calling your enemy's name. On the next morning, your enemy will be feeling stiff and sore.

TO GET BACK AT SOMEONE

This is an old spell for getting back at someone who's done you wrong. Using a new knife and while you're cutting a lemon into quarters, whisper:

> *As the fibres of this fruit fall*
> *asunder,*
> *So too the bands of your strength.*

Your wrongdoer will immediately feel a sharp pain and general weakness throughout his or her body.

TO MAKE MISCHIEF

In this spell, you use a needle that's been used to sew up a dead man's winding sheet. Place the needle under a dining table while you're whispering:

> *Cordial;*
> *Nerdac;*
> *Degon.*
> *Thereafter, a mysterious and*
> *unbearable horror will prevent*
> *anyone from eating at the table.*

TO MAKE MISCHIEF

Using a new knife, cut asunder a lemon while you're speaking words of hatred and malice against your enemy. Regardless of how far away your enemy is, he or she will feel a cutting anguish in his or her heart and a cold chill throughout his or her body.

TO AVENGE YOURSELF

On a Friday, obtain a strand of hair from the person who's harmed you. Each day for nine days, make a knot in the hair. On the ninth day, wrap the knotted hair in a sheet of white paper and beat it. The person will feel each blow through a series of sharp pains.

Health spells

TO PREVENT A COLD

By the light of a pale-blue candle, peel a small raw potato. While you're doing this, concentrate hard on keeping free from colds. Carry the peeled potato on your person all through winter.

TO RECOVER QUICKLY SPELL ONE

Place some tea leaves, lavender, ginger, salt, garlic and lemon rind on a piece of blue-velvet cloth. Using a red-satin ribbon, wrap the combination up in the cloth. Keep the parcel under the sick person's pillow. When the person wakes, he or she should smell the parcel until he or she is better.

TO RECOVER QUICKLY SPELL TWO

Rub a light-blue candle in bay-leaf, rose, sandalwood and tea-tree oil. Burn the candle every morning until the sick person feels better.

TO STOP SMOKING

Find a cigarette and say:

I have the knowledge that you kill;
Help me stop before I'm ill.

Rub some clove oil on the cigarette's filter, then light the cigarette and begin smoking it. You'll soon stop smoking.

Love potions

Each of the four elements – fire, earth, air and water – is sensitive to different smells, so each of the following four potions is custom-made to suit that element. It's important you use the essential oil, not the plant's fragrance. You can rub the potion on to an item of clothing worn by either your lover or your intended lover. You can also either burn it in an oil burner or lace a hot bath for two with it. Use it in any way that will appeal to your lover's senses.

A LOVE POTION FOR THE FIRE SIGNS
Aries, Leo and Sagittarius

To one ounce of olive oil, add:
Twelve drops of orange oil
Four drops of cinnamon oil
Two drops of clove oil
Two drops of amber oil
Six drops of musk oil

A LOVE POTION FOR THE EARTH SIGNS
Taurus, Virgo and Capricorn

To one ounce of olive oil, add:
Four drops of patchouli oil
Twelve drops of musk oil
Two drops of cedarwood oil
Six drops of jasmine oil

A LOVE POTION FOR THE AIR SIGNS
Gemini, Libra and Aquarius

To one ounce of olive oil, add:
Twelve drops of lavender oil
Eight drops of sandalwood oil
Eight drops of vanilla oil
Eight drops of honeysuckle oil

A LOVE POTION FOR THE WATER SIGNS
Cancer, Scorpio and Pisces

To one ounce of olive oil, add:
Four drops of jasmine oil
Six drops of sweet-pea oil
Four drops of vertivert oil
Four drops of lotus oil
Four drops of violet oil

SOME APHRODISIACS

If the zing's gone out of your love life, you might need an aphrodisiac more than you need a new partner. Read on and discover a few secret substances and spells that are known to work. I wish you well in your pursuit of love!

DILL SEEDS
These are a very good libido booster.

ROSE PETALS WITH WINE
This combination is also very good for helping things along.

A EUCALYPTUS STICK
If you grind a small eucalyptus stick into powder form and add whatever incense you're burning, your potency will be increased. A eucalyptus stick is also good for impotence if placed under the bed.

CRUSHED FENNEL SEEDS
These make a powerful aphrodisiac.

GINSENG ROOT
Asian people have always considered this to be helpful. They also believe that ginseng promotes longevity. Ginseng is best taken as a tea and is especially good for both middle-aged people and people whose sexual desire is flagging.

LAVENDER
This has always been considered to be a real turn-on for men. It's best to put some lavender oil in a nice, warm bath and let the two of you enjoy it together.

A BLADE OF GRASS
If you're a man, try putting a blade of grass in your mouth, turning to the east and then turning to the west. While you're doing this, say the following incantation:
> *Where the sun goes up shall my love be by me!*
> *When the sun goes down there, by here I'll be!*

A SHOE
Take a shoe from the person you love, fill it with rose petals and hang it over your bed in order to make sure the feeling is mutual.

A PLAIT
Make a plait out of some of your hair and the hair of the person you love in order to ensure you stay together.

A CLOVE OF GARLIC AND A HYACINTH BULB
Take a clove of garlic and a hyacinth bulb and plant them together in a pot you've never used before. While you're planting, keep repeating the name of the person you love. Every morning and night, say the following incantation over the pot:
> *As this bulb grows,*
> *And as this blossom blows,*
> *May the heart be turned on to me.*

STIMULATE YOUR SENSES

Aromatherapy and its uses

In this table I list some common and not-so-common ailments and what essential oil is best to help the condition. When purchasing oils, make sure they are good quality essential oils and not incense oils.

AILMENT	ESSENTIAL OIL	USES
Abscesses	Chamomile	Hot compress
	Lavender	Hot compress
	Myrrh	Hot compress
Acne	Bergamot	Local wash
Acute bronchitis	Bergamot	Room fragrance and steam inhalation
	Eucalyptus	Room fragrance and steam inhalation
	Frankincense	Room fragrance, inhalation and massage
	Lavender	Room fragrance and steam inhalation
	Marjoram	Hot compress, room fragrance, inhalation and massage
	Rosemary	Hot compress, room fragrance, inhalation, steam inhalation and massage
	Sandalwood	Room fragrance, inhalation, steam inhalation and massage
Arthritis	Chamomile	Bath, hot compress and massage
	Lavender	Bath, hot compress and massage
	Pine: small dose	Hot compress and massage
	Rosemary	Bath and massage
Asthma	Cypress	Room fragrance, inhalation and massage
	Jasmine: small dose	Room fragrance, inhalation and massage
	Lavender	Room fragrance, inhalation and massage
	Marjoram	Inhalation and massage
	Melissa: small dose	Inhalation
	Rosemary	Room fragrance and massage
Bleeding gums	Cypress	Gargle
	Lemon: small dose	Gargle
Boils	Chamomile	Hot compress
Build-up of toxins	Cypress	Bath, cream and massage
	Fennel: small dose	Bath, cream and massage
	Grapefruit: small dose	Cream and massage
	Juniper: small dose	Bath, cream and massage
	Rose	Bath, cream and massage
Catarrh	Frankincense	Bath, hot compress, room fragrance, inhalation and massage
Chest infections	Jasmine: small dose	Bath, hot compress, room fragrance, inhalation and massage
	Pine: small dose	Room fragrance, inhalation and steam inhalation
Chronic bronchitis	Benzoin	Bath, inhalation and massage
	Myrrh	Bath, inhalation and massage
	Frankincense	Bath, inhalation and massage
Colds	Cinnamon leaf: small dose	Bath, room fragrance and inhalation
	Eucalyptus	Bath and inhalation

Colds (continued)	Orange: small dose	Bath, inhalation and steam inhalation
	Peppermint: small dose	Bath, inhalation and massage
	Rosemary	Bath, inhalation and massage
Congestion and catarrh	Cedarwood	Bath, room fragrance, inhalation and massage
	Cypress	Room fragrance and inhalation
	Eucalyptus	Bath, room fragrance, inhalation, steam inhalation and massage
	Frankincense	Room fragrance and inhalation
	Myrrh	Bath, inhalation and massage
	Peppermint: small dose	Room fragrance, inhalation and steam inhalation
	Pine: small dose	Room fragrance, inhalation and steam inhalation
	Sandalwood	Room fragrance and steam inhalation
Coughs	Cypress	Hot compress, room fragrance, inhalation and massage
	Eucalyptus	Hot compress, room fragrance, inhalation, steam inhalation and massage
	Lavender	Hot compress, room fragrance and inhalation
	Sandalwood	Hot compress, room fragrance, inhalation, steam inhalation and massage
Diarrhoea	Chamomile	Bath, inhalation and massage
	Geranium	Bath, inhalation and massage
	Lavender	Bath, inhalation and massage
	Neroli	Bath, inhalation and massage
Earache	Chamomile	Hot compress and massage
	Lavender	Hot compress and massage
Excessive appetite	Bergamot	Bath, room fragrance, inhalation, massage and perfume
	Fennel: small dose	Room fragrance and inhalation
Fevers	Basil: small dose	Room fragrance, inhalation and massage
	Eucalyptus	Bath, cold compress, room fragrance, inhalation and massage
	Ginger: small dose	Bath and massage
	Juniper: small dose	Room fragrance, inhalation and massage
	Lavender	Bath, cold compress, room fragrance, inhalation and massage
	Lemon: small dose	Room fragrance, inhalation and massage
	Orange: small dose	Room fragrance, inhalation and massage
	Peppermint: small dose	Bath, cold compress, inhalation and massage
	Rosemary	Bath, room fragrance, inhalation and massage
	Tea tree	Bath, room fragrance, inhalation and massage
Flatulence	Bergamot	Bath, hot compress, inhalation and massage
	Chamomile	Bath, hot compress, inhalation and massage
	Fennel: small dose	Bath, hot compress, inhalation and massage
	Melissa: small dose	Bath, inhalation and massage
	Nutmeg: small dose	Massage
	Orange: small dose	Inhalation and massage
	Rosemary	Bath and massage

Foot ache	Peppermint: small dose	Foot bath
Haemorrhoids	Cypress	Bath, cream and local wash
	Geranium	Bath, cream and local wash
Hayfever	Chamomile	Inhalation and massage
	Eucalyptus	Inhalation and massage
	Lavender	Inhalation and massage
	Melissa: small dose	Inhalation and massage
Headache	Basil: small dose	Room fragrance, inhalation and massage
	Chamomile	Cold compress, room fragrance, inhalation and massage
	Lavender	Cold compress, room fragrance, inhalation and massage
	Lemongrass: small dose	Cold compress and massage
	Peppermint: small dose	Cold compress and massage
High blood pressure	Chamomile	Bath, room fragrance and massage
	Lavender	Bath, room fragrance and massage
	Marjoram	Bath, room fragrance and massage
	Neroli	Bath, room fragrance and massage
	Rose	Bath, room fragrance and massage
	Ylang-ylang	Bath and massage
Indigestion	Basil: small dose	Massage
	Bergamot	Bath, hot compress, inhalation and massage
	Black pepper: small dose	Massage
	Chamomile	Bath, hot compress, inhalation and massage
	Fennel: small dose	Bath, hot compress and inhalation
	Ginger: small dose	Hot compress and massage
	Marjoram	Bath, hot compress, inhalation and massage
	Peppermint: small dose	Bath, hot compress, inhalation and massage
	Petitgrain	Bath, inhalation and massage
	Rosemary	Inhalation and massage
Infected wounds	Bergamot	Bath, cold compress and local wash
	Geranium	Bath, cold compress and local wash
	Lemon: small dose	Cold compress and local wash
	Myrrh	Cold compress and local wash
	Niaouli	Local wash
Intestinal cramps	Marjoram	Bath, inhalation and massage
Kidney disorders	Cedarwood	Bath and massage
	Clary sage: small dose	Bath, inhalation and massage
	Geranium	Bath, room fragrance, inhalation and massage
Lack of appetite	Bergamot	Room fragrance, inhalation, massage and perfume
	Chamomile	Room fragrance, inhalation, massage and perfume
	Fennel: small dose	Room fragrance and inhalation
	Ginger: small dose	Room fragrance and inhalation
Low blood pressure	Black pepper: small dose	Massage
	Rosemary	Bath, inhalation and massage

	Peppermint: small dose	Inhalation and massage
Lower-back pain	Chamomile	Bath, hot compress and massage
	Rosemary	Bath, hot compress and massage
	Lavender	Bath, hot compress and massage
Low milk supply (lactation)	Fennel: small dose	Bath and massage
	Jasmine: small dose	Bath and massage
Low vitality	Cinnamon leaf: small dose	Bath, inhalation and massage
	Clary sage: small dose	Bath, room fragrance, inhalation and massage
	Fennel: small dose	Bath, inhalation and massage
	Geranium	Bath, room fragrance, inhalation and massage
	Juniper: small dose	Bath and massage
	Lemongrass: small dose	Bath, room fragrance, inhalation and massage
	Petigrain	Bath, room fragrance, inhalation and massage
	Rose	Bath, room fragrance, inhalation and massage
Migraine	Basil: small dose	Room fragrance and massage
	Lavender	Cold compress, room fragrance and massage
	Rosemary	Room fragrance and massage
	Peppermint: small dose	Cold compress and room fragrance
Morning sickness	Lavender	Inhalation
	Mandarine	Inhalation
Muscular pain	Black pepper: small dose	Massage
	Lemongrass: small dose	Massage
	Marjoram	Massage
Nasal infections	Tea tree	Inhalation and steam inhalation
	Eucalyptus	Room fragrance, inhalation and steam inhalation
Nose bleeds	Lemon: small dose	Cold compress
Painful periods	Chamomile	Bath, hot compress, inhalation and massage
	Clary sage: small dose	Bath, hot compress, inhalation and massage
	Jasmine: small dose	Hot compress and massage
	Lavender	Bath, hot compress, inhalation and massage
	Marjoram	Bath, hot compress, inhalation and massage
Palpitations	Neroli	Inhalation and massage
Postnatal depression	Clary sage: small dose	Hot compress, room fragrance and inhalation
Premenstrual tension	Bergamot FCF	Bath, hot compress, inhalation and massage
	Chamomile	Bath, hot compress and inhalation
	Geranium	Bath, hot compress, inhalation and massage
	Rose	Bath, hot compress, inhalation and massage
Rheumatic pain	Chamomile	Bath, hot compress and massage
	Eucalyptus	Bath, hot compress and massage
	Ginger: small dose	Hot compress and massage
	Lavender	Bath, hot compress and massage
	Marjoram	Hot compress and massage
	Rosemary	Bath, hot compress and massage

AROMATHERAPY AND ITS USES

AILMENT	ESSENTIAL OIL	USES
Scanty periods	Basil: small dose	Bath and massage
	Juniper: small dose	Bath and massage
	Myrrh	Bath and massage
	Peppermint: small dose	Bath and massage
	Rose	Bath and massage
Shortness of breath	Frankincense	Inhalation
Skin irritations	Chamomile	Bath and cream
	Lavender	Bath and cream
	Melissa: small dose	Bath and cream
Sore throat	Benzoin	Steam inhalation
	Tea tree	Massage, steam inhalation and gargle
	Lavender	Massage, steam inhalation and gargle
	Lemon: small dose	Gargle
Splinters	Chamomile	Cold compress
Swelling	Chamomile	Bath, cold compress and massage
	Cypress	Bath, cold compress and massage
	Geranium	Bath, cold compress, inhalation and massage
	Juniper: small dose	Bath, cold compress and massage
	Patchouli	Bath, cold compress and massage
Tension	Chamomile	Bath, room fragrance, inhalation and massage
	Lavender	Bath, room fragrance, inhalation and massage
	Marjoram	Bath, room fragrance, inhalation and massage
	Melissa: small dose	Bath, room fragrance, inhalation and massage
	Rosemary	Bath, room fragrance, inhalation and massage
Thrush (candida)	Lavender	Bath and local wash
	Myrrh	Bath and local wash
	Tea tree	Bath and local wash
Toothache	Chamomile	Hot compress
	Clove bud	Hot compress
Travel sickness	Ginger: small dose	Inhalation and massage
	Lavender	Inhalation
	Peppermint: small dose	Inhalation and massage
Urinary disorders	Eucalyptus	Bath, hot compress and massage
	Fennel: small dose	Bath, hot compress and inhalation
	Juniper: small dose	Bath, hot compress and massage
Vaginal pruritis	Bergamot	Bath
	Sandalwood	Bath
Varicose veins	Cypress	Bath and cold compress
	Lavender	Bath and cold compress
	Juniper: small dose	Bath and cold compress

Incense and its uses

In the first table I list the types of incense and their uses, and in the second table I list incense aids and their uses.

INCENSE	USE
Boronia	Useful for people suffering from nervous strain, either as an air freshener or burnt in their bedroom before they retire
Caraway	Used on the body by ancient priests before they performed sacred ceremonies
Cardamon	Useful for asthmatics if they burn it in their room before they retire
Cassia	Enriches the atmosphere and for use during the day
Cedarwood	For use before meditation and as a masculine perfume
Cloves	Useful for people who either have a speech impediment or stutter
Frankincense	Essential for success in performing church rituals and in meditation
Geranium	Used by many women in order to add a feminine influence to the house
Ginger	Makes a dinner party successful by giving the home a warming feel
Jasmine	Used for weddings and festivities and for a feminine influence
Lavender	Relieves feelings of fatigue, depression and irritation
Lemon	Useful for clearing the mind of unwanted thoughts
Lemongrass	Used for psychic work and meditation
Mace	Used in waiting rooms and invalids' rooms
Neroli	Helpful for the nervous system, for elevating consciousness and for gladdening the spirit
Orange	Rids kitchens, dining rooms and halls of odours
Origanum	Used for increasing appetite, and to be used before meals
Patchouli	Used for meditation and contacting spirits
Pine	Useful if burnt when people are listening to music, relaxing and attending a musical gathering
Rose	Creates a beautiful effect on people's emotions and a peaceful atmosphere
Rosemary	Helpful for poor eyesight, memory and concentration
Sage	Helpful for the nervous system and concentration
Sandalwood	Used for inspiring and elevating consciousness
Sassafras	Used for psychic protection
Tea tree	Used on children who don't co-operate

INCENSE	USE
Verbena	Used near plants and flowers on verandahs and patios
Vetiver	Helpful for driving away evil influences
Ylang-ylang	Used for meditation and as a suitable evening incense

USE	INCENSE AIDS
Concentration and willpower	Bay, cedarwood, ginger and sage
Meditation	Lavender, rose, sandalwood, patchouli, ylang-ylang and jasmine
Relaxation	Cardamon, cajeput, lavender, pine and lemongrass
Purification	Caraway, cinnamon, lemon, lime and sandalwood
Devotions	Neroli, rose, ylang-ylang, boronia and jasmine
Psychic work	Bergamot, lavender, lemongrass, letitrain, sandalwood and verbena
Healing	Bay, rose, juniper, vetiver, sandalwood, mandarine and lemon
Music and speech	Cloves, pine, geranium and spearmint
Memory and mental stimulation	Rosemary, pine, thyme and sage
Mealtimes and dinner parties	Ginger and orange
Weddings and festivities	Neroli, rose, boronia and jasmine
Children	Tea tree, ginger, rose and verbena
Feminine influence	Cedarwood, juniper, pine and ginger
Daytime use: for sun-type meditations	Cassia, pine, cloves and orange
Evening use: for moon-type meditations	Ylang-ylang, patchouli, lavender and jasmine

Herbs and their healing qualities

Following is a list of common and not so common aliments and which herbs and foods are best for either a remedy or prevention.

AILMENT	HERBS AND FOODS
Acne	Alfalfa, kelp, echinacea, dandelion root, burdock root, chaparral, valerian, gentian, yellow-dock root, capsicum (cayenne), lecithin and aloe-vera gel
Anaemia	Chlorophyll (liquid from fresh green vegetables), dry beans and peas, yellow-dock root, red-clover blossoms, comfrey, dandelion, red beets, burdock root, mullein leaves, kelp, dulse,* alfalfa, raspberry leaves, blackstrap molasses and bee pollen
	Eat grapes, prunes, raisins, dates, apricots and sesame seeds: foods that are high in iron, and drink almond milk – almonds blended with water then strained.
Arthritis	Yucca, alfalfa, brigham tea, comfrey (root and leaves), horsetail, chaparral leaves, black cohosh, celery seed, valerian root, burdock root, scullcap, wormwood, kelp, cayenne, sarsaparilla root and angelica
	Use distilled drinking water, and drink broth made from potato peelings for its high potassium content.
Asthma	Comfrey, fenugreek, lobelia, juniper berries, horsetail, licorice root, horehound, ginger, wild-cherry bark, pleurisy root, black cohosh, coltsfoot, royal jelly, mullein, chickweed, saw-palmetto berries, chamomile, slippery-elm bark, kelp and oranges
	Eliminate pasteurised dairy products.
Bad breath	Alfalfa, chlorophyll (either liquid or from vegetables), peppermint, rosemary, sage, myrrh and acidophilus
Bladder problems	Marshmallow, asparagus, corn silk, horsetail, white-oak bark, burdock root, golden seal, parsley, dandelion, fennel, uva ursi, slippery elm, chamomile, rose hips and juniper berries
	Eat watermelon and its seeds, drink plenty of liquids and eliminate coffee. Cranberry and apple juices are excellent.
Blood pressure	**High:** Cayenne, garlic, siberian ginseng, black-cohosh root, kelp, alfalfa, gotu kola, hawthorn berries, myrrh, angelica, evening-primrose oil, wheatgerm and lecithin. **Low:** Parsley, dandelion, angelica, shepherd's purse, golden-seal root, ginger, garlic and ginseng
	Eat watermelon and its seeds, and eliminate animal products and salt.
Blood purification	Red clover, burdock root, garlic, yellow-dock root, dandelion, licorice, echinacea, chaparral, barberry, sarsaparilla, yarrow, comfrey and golden seal
	Lemon beet, carrot juice, apples and grapes are also good.
Bones: for strengthening and rebuilding them	Alfalfa, arnica, comfrey leaves, horsetail, oat for straw, kelp, parsley, burdock root, chaparral, slippery-elm bark, irish moss, almonds, sesame seeds, chlorophyll, spirulina and freshly ground coconut
	Eat leafy greens for their high calcium content.
Bronchitis	Golden seal, coltsfoot, comfrey root, myrrh, chickweed, mullein, slippery moss, ginger, elecampane, red sage, yerba santa and pleurisy root
	Eliminate pasteurised dairy poducts.
Burns and scalds	Burdock, chickweed and comfrey
	Apply aloe-vera gel (either fresh or bottled) or a comfrey poultice, or Vitamin E oil, or linseed oil, or calendula (marigold) cream.

---

* Dulse is a combination of various dried seaweeds. It's very concentrated, and an ounce (28.3 grams) of it has the highest vitamin and mineral count of any food class. It's especially consumed by vegetarians because it's one of the few vegetable sources of Vitamin B$_{12}$. It provides all the sea's minerals and trace elements in proportions that are very similar to the ones found in human blood.

AILMENT	HERBS AND FOODS
Cancer	Red-clover blossoms, burdock root, yellow-dock root, golden seal, parsley (fresh), onions (fresh), blue violet, myrrh, echinacea, slippery elm, comfrey, poke root, dandelion root, rock rose, agrimony, pau d'arco, chickweed, sorrel, chlorophyll (preferably wheatgrass juice) and bee pollen
	Eliminate animal products.
Childbirth: to ease it	Black cohosh, blue cohosh, squaw vine, red-raspberry leaves, shepherd's purse, spikenard, passion flower, licorice root, comfrey root and kelp
Cholesterol: to lower it	Hawthorn berries, cayenne, garlic, golden seal, kelp, black-cohosh root, apples, lecithin and pectin (found in fruits and vegetables)
	Eliminate red meat, animal products, salt, fried foods and coffee.
Circulation: to improve it	Blessed thistle, cayenne, garlic, ginger, black cohosh, gentian, chickweed, blue vervain, comfrey, golden seal, rose hips, horseradish, Vitamin E and lecithin
Colic	Mistletoe, ginger, catnip, fennel, angelica, chamomile, wintergreen, anise, blue cohosh, peppermint and motherwort
Colon: cleansing and laxative	Red clover, barberry bark, psyillium husks, ginger root, chlorophyll, cascara sagrada, slippery elm, aloe-vera juice, butternut bark, rhubarb root, irish moss, garlic, buckthorn bark, golden seal, cayenne, lobelia, fresh fruits (especially apples, figs, grapes and prunes) and acidophilus
	East fresh, raw, high-fibre foods, and drink lemon juice and green-vegetable juices.
Dandruff	Burdock, kelp, sage, nettle, yarrow, bayberry, chamomile and yucca
	Rub jojoba oil into the scalp.
Depression	Gotu kola, kelp, spirulina, bee pollen, ginger, black cohosh and evening-primrose oil.
Diabetes	Ginseng, spirulina, garlic, huckleberry leaves, golden seal, parsley, gentian root, licorice root, dandelion root, blueberries, raspberry leaves, juniper berries, kelp, bladderwrack, yarrow, uva ursi, comfrey root, marshmallow root, buchu leaves and lecithin
	Eat avocadoes, and drink almond milk – almonds blended with water then strained.
Diarrhoea	Red-raspberry leaves, comfrey, slippery-elm bark, psyillium husks, kelp, ginger, cayenne, coltsfoot, chamomile, marshmallow, mullein, St John's wort, bayberry bark and cranesbill root
	Eat bananas.
Digestion	Papaya leaves, papaya, peppermint leaves, ginger root, catnip, comfrey, fennel seeds, sunflower seeds, cayenne and dandelion
Earache	Chickweed, black-cohosh root, golden-seal root, lobelia, scullcap, angelica, brigham tea, licorice root, yellow dock, mullein and hops
	Put a bit of warm olive oil or garlic in the sore ear.
Energy, vitality, strength and endurance	Licorice root, siberian ginseng, fo-ti, dandelion, peppermint leaves, ginger root, garlic, parsley, gentian root, red-clover blossoms, yellow dock, gotu kola, kelp, bee pollen, damiana, acacia, spirulina, pumpkin seeds and sesame seeds
Eyes	Evening-primrose oil, eyebright, golden seal, bayberry bark, red-raspberry leaves, angelica, alfalfa and spirulina (high in Vitamin A)
	Eat carrots, yams and leafy greens, and drink carrot juice. For a soothing eyewash, make a tea from eyebright, borage flowers, golden-seal root, red-raspberry leaves and rosemary. Strain the tea well and let it cool before you drink it.
Fasting	Licorice root, spirulina, bee pollen, fennel and hawthorn
	Drink fruit and vegetable juices and distilled water.
Female problems	Squaw vine, blessed thistle, false unicorn, uva ursi, ginger, marshmallow, raspberry leaves, cramp bark, golden-seal root, black cohosh, lobelia, queen of the meadow and dong quai
Fever	Sage, peppermint, valerian, vervain, dandelion, chamomile, fenugreek, lobelia, yarrow, angelica, wintergreen, nettle and parsley

AILMENT	HERBS AND FOODS
Fingernails: to strengthen them	Horsetail, irish moss, comfrey, kelp, dulse, oat straw, alfalfa and chlorophyll
	See the footnote on page 151 for a description of dulse.
Food poisoning	Charcoal tablets, lobelia tea, elecampane, wheat bran, apples, alfalfa, kelp and fennel
	Drink broth made from potato peelings. These suggestions are for mild cases only – in an emergency, contact your doctor.
Gallbladder problems	Horsetail, dandelion, parsley, peppermint, ginger root, red clover, milkweed, golden seal, fennel, barberry, cramp bark, garlic, horseradish and hydrangea
	Drink beet and apple juices, and drink three tablespoons of unrefined olive oil mixed with lemon juice in order to cleanse the gallbladder. Eliminate animal protein and fried foods.
Glands	Garlic, fo-ti, siberian ginseng, black cohosh, licorice root, mullein, lobelia, parsley, kelp, saw-palmetto berries, alfalfa, yellow dock, echinacea, slippery elm, dandelion, oat straw, figs, raisins and sunflower seeds
Hair	Horsetail, alfalfa, sage, rosemary, nettle and indian hemp
	Eat dulse and kelp: they're high in vitamins and minerals, and use only natural hair-care products. See the footnote on page 151 for a description of dulse.
Hayfever	Comfrey, yerba santa, parsley, Mormon tea, mullein, lobelia, chaparral, burdock root, marshmallow, bee pollen and raw honey
Headache	Basil, blessed thistle, ephedra, ginger, wild lettuce, valerian, peppermint, thyme, rosemary, white-willow bark and wood betony
Heart problems	Hawthorn berries, cayenne, garlic, ginseng, lecithin, motherwort, rosemary leaves, borage, blue cohosh, blessed thistle, angelica, valerian root, dandelion, barberry, evening-primrose oil, dulse, kelp, bananas and Vitamin E
	Eliminate fried foods, salt, red meat and dairy products, and use unpasteurised apple-cider vinegar in drinks or on salads: it's high in potassium, which strengthens the heart. See the footnote on page 151 for a description of dulse.
Haemorrhoids	Bee pollen, comfrey, collinsonia root, parsley, aloe vera, bistort root, buckthorn bark, myrrh, burdock, uva ursi, cayenne, garlic, and red and green cabbage
	Apply Vitamin E oil.
Immune system	Echinacea, siberian ginseng, golden seal, myrrh gum, yarrow, cayenne, rose hips, watercress, garlic, onions, spirulina, bee pollen and green vegetables
Infections	Echinacea, golden-seal root, pau d'arco, comfrey root, marshmallow, yarrow, cayenne, lobelia, bugleweed, plantain, black walnuts, myrrh gum, blue vervain, cinchona, garlic, kelp, watercress, onions, bee propolis (a natural antibiotic) and chlorophyll (from either green vegetables or supplements)
Insomnia	Valerian root, hops, scullcap, catnip, lady's slipper, passion flower, celery juice and raw honey
Kidney problems	Uva ursi, juniper berries, nettle, parsley, marshmallow root, apples, chamomile, alfalfa and ginger
	Eat watermelon and its seeds, and drink distilled water. Cranberry and apple juices are excellent.
Liver problems	Dandelion, apples, red beet, onions, horsetail, angelica, golden rod, lobelia, liverwort, parsley, celandine, oregon grape, comfrey, blessed thistle, wild-yam root, carrot juice, grapes and apricots
	Mix apple juice, cayenne, lemon juice and two to three ounces of olive oil in a drink, for cleansing the liver.
Longevity	Bee pollen, spirulina, ginseng, gotu kola, licorice root, fo-ti, cayenne and garlic
	Also refer to the herbs and foods for 'Energy, vitality, strength and endurance'.
Lungs	Slippery elm, bayberry bark, chickweed, coltsfoot, ginseng, marshmallow, blessed thistle, lungwort, lobelia, comfrey, angelica and yerba santa
Memory	Gotu kola, ginseng, rosemary, periwinkle, blessed thistle, chlorophyll, alfalfa, almonds, bee pollen, sesame seeds and lecithin

AILMENT	HERBS AND FOODS
Menopause	Kelp, sage, black cohosh, damiana, red raspberry, dong quai, chamomile, wild yam, kelp, black cohosh, blue cohosh, squaw vine, alfalfa, evening-primrose oil and peppermint tea
Nursing: to stimulate milk production	Fennel, blessed thistle, horsetail, borage, dandelion, alfalfa, red raspberry and spirulina Drink almond milk – almonds blended with water then strained – and plenty of pure water. To dry up milk, eat yarrow, parsley, sage, black-walnut bark and wild-alum root.
Osteoporosis	Kelp, horsetail (for its silicon content), alfalfa and oat straw Also refer to the herbs and foods for 'Bones'. Eat plenty of leafy greens, and either greatly reduce or eliminate your intake of animal protein and pasteurised dairy products.
Pain	Solomon's seal, chamomile, mint, catnip, mullein, wood betony, valerian, nettle, horsetail, cayenne, wild lettuce, white-willow bark, scullcap, kelp, blue vervain, angelica and wild yam
Poisoning	Poison oak, ivy, mugwort (grows near poison oak), Solomon's seal, myrrh, echinacea and black-walnut extract Apply either aloe-vera gel or Vitamin E cream.
Premenstrual tension	Dong quai, evening-primrose oil, kelp, black cohosh, licorice root, raspberry leaves and passion flower
Prostate problems	Parsley, juniper berries, gotu kola, horsetail, slippery-elm bark, saw palmetto, corn silk, pumpkin seeds, kelp, golden-seal root, uva ursi, gravel root, bee pollen and lecithin
Senility	Gotu kola, siberian ginseng, cayenne, alfalfa, kelp, pumpkin seeds, peppermint, scullcap, lecithin and nutritional yeast Eat high-fibre, fresh, raw foods, and either reduce or eliminate pasteurised dairy products and refined foods.
Sexual rejuvenation: male	Ginseng, saw palmetto, licorice root, fo-ti, ginger, sarsaparilla, bee pollen, lecithin, gotu kola, damiana, pumpkin seeds, sesame seeds, pistachio nuts and figs
Sexual rejuvenation: female	Saw palmetto, damiana, ginseng, onions, periwinkle, dong quai, fenugreek, sage, licorice root and eggplant
Stress and tension	Valerian root, celery, spearmint, vervain, chamomile, catnip, peppermint, passion flower, hops, rosemary, scullcap, mistletoe, wood betony, lobelia and bee pollen
Thyroid problems	Golden seal, bayberry bark, irish moss, cayenne, gentian, black cohosh, poke root, white-oak bark, molasses, parsley, kelp, watercress, black walnut, sarsaparilla, apricots, dates and raisins
Tumours and cysts	Dandelion, red clover, golden seal, bistort root, comfrey root, yellow dock, slippery elm, borage, kelp, evening-primrose oil, blue violet, chickweed and red root Eat lots of fresh, raw foods, especially grapes.
Ulcers	Cayenne, angelica, slippery elm, myrrh gum, irish moss, bayberry, licorice root, golden-seal root, comfrey, alfalfa, sage, blue violet and chickweed Drink carrot, cabbage and aloe-vera juice, and broth made from potato peelings: it's high in potassium, which helps neutralise acids.
Weight reduction	Spirulina, alfalfa, parsley, fennel seeds, chickweed, lecithin, bladderwrack, licorice root, safflower, irish moss, kelp, dulse, sassafras, burdock root, black walnut and papaya See the footnote on page 151 for a description of dulse.
Worms and parasites	Black-walnut hulls, garlic, violet, chaparral, pink root, wormwood, butternut bark, buckthorn bark, carrot, sage, wormseed, pumpkin seeds, sesame seeds, freshly ground coconut and apricots
Yeast infections	Juniper berries, squaw vine, golden-seal root, myrrh gum, witch-hazel leaves, comfrey root, buchu leaves and garlic Drink these herbs in tea form.

Magical uses of herbs, berries, roots and spices

In the following table, I list the herbs, berries, roots and spices that help you on your way to becoming well versed in the art of magic.

HERB	MAGICAL USE
Adam and Eve roots	According to voodoo legend, if you and your lover have contact with the roots, you'll be bound together forever.
Angelica	This is used for protecting your house from ghosts and hexes.
Basil	This guarantees fertility and makes a good love charm.
Bay leaves	These are used for warding off witches and vampires.
Belladonna	It's believed that if you chew the leaves of a belladonna plant, your pupils become enlarged.
Bergamot	This is used for making people succumb to your control.
Bethel	If you throw two bethel nuts into running water, you're given the power to grant a wish.
Blood root	This is used for protecting you and yours.
Buckeye root	If you wrap some money around a piece of buckeye root, your money will increase.
Bugle	If you dry and powder some bugle and sprinkle it on a grave, you'll dream of the deceased person and he or she will tell you the future.
Burdock	This is used as a bath perfume for purifying the soul.
Cactus	When you're making a doll for magical purposes, it's better to use cactus thorns than pins.
Calamus root	This is used for gaining control over a person.
Caraway seeds	These are used in Christmas cakes for keeping the eaters safe for the year ahead.
Celery seeds	If students chew celery seeds, the seeds will help them concentrate on their exams.
Chamomile	This is a popular herb for settling the nerves.
Clover	Four-leaf clovers bring both good luck and good fortune.
Cloves	These are used for stopping people from talking about you.
Comfrey	This should be carried by a person who's travelling, because it's said to keep the person safe.

HERB	MAGICAL USE
Coriander	This is used either as a love potion or in the bath in order to cure cramps and colds.
Corn	If you hang corn over your door, it'll bring excellent crops that year.
Elm bark	This is a cure-all tea.
Fern	If you dry it and rub it on your head, it'll cure a migraine.
Ginseng	This is used for prolonging your youth.
Hydrangea root	This is used as a courtroom charm in order to get a person released from gaol.
Irish-toad moss	This is carried or burnt in order to bring the carrier both good luck and money.
Lavender	This is used as a perfume in order to attract men.
Leeks	These are used as a good-luck charm and for keeping evil at a distance.
Licorice	'If you offer a person licorice slyly, you'll make him or her agree with you entirely.'
Magnolia root	This is used as a charm for keeping your lover faithful.
Mandrake root	This is used as a good-luck talisman.
Marigold	This is used for attracting people to you.
Mistletoe	This is a powerful all-purpose charm.
Myrtle	'If you throw myrtle at your lover's feet, you'll make him or her walk to your door and no other.'
Nettle	This is used for removing curses from you.
Parsley	This is used for making you more appealing to the opposite sex.
Pistachio nuts	These are often given to zombies in order to bring them out of their trance.
Rhubarb	This is supposed to be good to consume if you've lost a lot of blood.
Rosemary	If you lay some rosemary under your pillow, you'll have good dreams.
Snake root	This is a very popular sexual stimulant.
Thyme	It's believed that thyme gives a person clairvoyant powers.
Violets	These bring a change of luck and fortune.
Wahoo bark	This is used as a charm against exorcism.

Lucky colours

Colours have always had a wide significance in Western society, such as that black is for funerals and white is for weddings. They symbolise both the forces within us and the forces of nature. Our grandparents, for example, might have worn red-flannel clothing in order to ward off colds and chills, because they believed in the magical properties of the colour red. Another example is that hospitals have the colour blue in their operating theatres instead of the traditional white, because blue is healing.

Following is a list of colours and their magical properties.

Red
Red stimulates the human body. Too much of it can make a person irritable. Chinese brides traditionally wear it at their wedding.

Orange
Orange restores our willpower if we're at a low ebb. It activates good forces. Wear it and have it in your furnishings.

Yellow
Yellow stimulates the mind. It's good for increasing the appetite and increasing our vitality. Wear it if you're undertaking intellectual activities.

Green
For me, green is a colour of hope, although some people believe it's an unlucky colour. I think they're wrong: it's a calming and peaceful colour, and it's widely echoed in nature.

Blue
Blue is a healing colour that embodies the broad expanse of the limitless sky.

Indigo
Indigo is the colour of midnight and the depths of deep space. It's a deeply religious colour that conjures up the spiritual in humans and the universe.

Purple
Purple is the colour of psychic protection, and royalty has traditionally used it as the colour of garments worn in religious ceremonies.

The occult community has also coloured the heavenly bodies through the twelve star signs as follows. Use these colours as a guide for cultivating your star sign's power.

ARIES	Scarlet	LIBRA	Emerald green
TAURUS	Red-orange	SCORPIO	Green-blue
GEMINI	Orange	SAGITTARIUS	Blue
CANCER	Amber	CAPRICORN	Indigo
LEO	Yellow-green	AQUARIUS	Violet
VIRGO	Green-yellow	PISCES	Crimson

Following is a list of the colours that have been attributed to the ten visible planets. See which colour is associated with your planet, and feature it prominently in your home and workplace.

THE SUN	Orange	JUPITER	Violet
MERCURY	Yellow	SATURN	Indigo
VENUS	Green	URANUS	Silver-grey
THE MOON	Blue	NEPTUNE	Blue-green
MARS	Red	PLUTO	Black

The fragrance for each star sign

When it comes to stimulation, our sense of smell is the second-most powerful sense, after touch. Use the following list to get your senses reeling – or the senses of your friend or loved one.

One way to stimulate Geminis is to give them a huge bouquet of irises and carnations. They'll be impressed by the gesture, and the smell of the flowers will drive them wild. Taurean partners who love food find that a cake lavished with vanilla essence is irresistible. Have some fun with the information in the list when you're exploring what fragrances turn on the twelve people of the zodiac.

ARIES   Ginger or neroli

TAURUS   Jasmine or vanilla

GEMINI   Iris or carnation

CANCER   Jasmine or ginger

LEO   Musk or lavender

VIRGO   Vanilla or cedarwood

LIBRA   Rose or sweet pea

SCORPIO   Patchouli or musk

SAGITTARIUS Daphne or water lily

CAPRICORN   Sandalwood

AQUARIUS   Daffodil

PISCES   Violet

STONES,
SYMBOLS
& SHAPES

Magical stones

Occultists and magicians maintain that specific stones hold magical properties for the person who owns the stones. The famous hope diamond has brought extreme bad luck to all its owners: throughout its troubled history, death and financial ruin have been its legacy. On my charm bracelet, I wear an amethyst and a topaz encased in silver. You'll discover why when you read the following table.

STONE	MAGICAL PROPERTIES
Agate	The agate will act as a repellent against the bite of a scorpion or a poisonous snake. It should be worn by people who are born under the star sign of Gemini.
Amethyst	When the amethyst is either made into a person's drinking cup or bound to the person's navel, it'll definitely prevent him or her from becoming drunk. It gives the wearer the gift of being able to prophesy. If a wife wears it, it will ensure she keeps her husband's love. It should be worn by all people who are born in the month of February.
Aquamarine	The person who wears the aquamarine will be endowed with courage and strength. It's a cure for laziness, and it also quickens the intellect. It should be worn by all people who are born in the month of March.
Balasius	Balasius can heal arguments between friends.
Calundronius	Calundronius destroys enchantments and gives the wearer power over his or her enemies.
Carbuncle	Carbuncle purifies the air, represses luxury and preserves the wearer's health.
Chalcedony	Chalcedony removes evil spirits, and the person who wears it will make a fortune in the area of law.
Chelidonius	Chelidonius is a good talisman against melancholy and periodical disorders such as corns in winter and rashes in summer.
Crystal	Crystal will increase a nursing mother's milk supply. If a person dons it before he or she retires at night, it will grant him or her pleasant dreams.
Diamond	The diamond is believed to ward off witches, madness and terrors of the night. It will bring victory to the person who wears it, and it's a cure for both sleepwalking and insanity.

STONE	MAGICAL PROPERTIES
Draconite	Draconite makes the wearer invincible.
Emerald	For a woman, the emerald brings safety in childbearing. It's a symbol of kindness, and it also brings happiness in love and domestic affairs.
Garnet	The garnet brings health and promotes happiness for the wearer. It repels epidemics and is a very lucky talisman for people who are born in the month of January.
Lignite	If a person wears lignite around his or her neck, he or she will be protected from witchcraft.
Lippares	Lippares is worn by people who wish to have a successful hunting trip.
Malachite	Malachite is a 'preserver of the cradle', which means it protects infants from sickness.
Moonstone	The person who wears a moonstone will have both good will and lasting friendships, because it's the symbol of happiness. It should be worn by people who are born in the month of June.
Onyx	Only men should wear onyx, because it's the symbol of virility. An onyx ring shouldn't be worn on the smallest finger of either hand, because if it is, it'll bring only scorn on the wearer.
Opal	The opal will both lighten spirits and make the wearer have good cheer. It should be worn by people who are born in the month of October.
Pearl	The pearl will both comfort the wearer's heart and make him or her remain chaste. It should be worn by people who are born in the month of June.
Ruby	The ruby is a sign of freedom, charity, dignity and divine power. It brings very good luck to people who are born in the month of July.
Sapphire	The sapphire both protects the wearer from his or her fears and grants a man power and vigour. It should be worn by people who are born in the month of September.
Sardonyx	Sardonyx will bring the wearer good luck.
Topaz	Topaz will both preserve the wearer's chastity and elicit sympathy for him or her.
Turquoise	Turquoise prevents bad accidents for the wearer while he or she is on horseback. It'll also prevent him or her from encountering danger in general.

Stones and their healing qualities

PROBLEM	TREATMENT STONE
Allergy	Aquamarine
Anaemia	Haematite or red coral
Arthritis	Malachite or magnetite
Asthma	Amber, tiger eye, cat's eye or rutilated quartz
Backache	Rock crystal
Bedwetting	Jade
Bladder problems	Bloodstone, jasper or jade
Bleeding	Haematite, chrysoprase, sapphire, rock crystal or chalcedony
Blood pressure: high	Sodalite or lapis lazuli
Blood pressure: low	Carnelian
Blood poisoning	Carnelian
Bronchitis	Rutilated quartz, aquamarine or amber
Burns	Amethyst
Childbirth	Chrysoprase, bloodstone or jade
Colds	Aquamarine
Colic	Malachite
Cramps	Ruby, carnelian or rock crystal
Depression	Lapis lazuli, garnet, chalcedony, tourmalinated quartz, amber, tiger eye or rock crystal
Diabetes	Carnelian
Diarrhoea	Rock crystal
Dizziness	Rock crystal or tourmaline
Drunkenness	Amethyst
Epilepsy	Emerald, jasper, pyrite or lapis lazuli
'Evil eye'	Turquoise, amber, carnelian, cat's eye, tiger eye or hawk's eye
Fear	Amber
Feet: odour	Amethyst
Fever	Ruby or carnelian

PROBLEM	TREATMENT STONE
Gas pains	Rock crystal, cat's eye or bloodstone
Hair problems	Onyx, lapis lazuli, aventurine or agate
Hayfever	Aquamarine
Headaches	Amethyst (the most popular and successful stone of all)
Heart problems: rhythm	Garnet, agate, onyx, rock crystal, olivine, beryl, topaz or magnetite
Haemorrhoids	Bloodstone or topaz
Intelligence: to increase it	Emerald, tiger eye, chrysoprase or rose quartz
Infertility	Moonstone
Insomnia	Amethyst, topaz, sapphire or aquamarine
Kidney problems	Jade or rock crystal
Liver disease	Topaz, aquamarine, beryl, turquoise or gold
Menstrual problems	Malachite, moonstone, rock crystal or peridot
Migraine	Amethyst
Miscarriage: to prevent it	Moss agate or ruby
Motion sickness	Rock crystal
Nose bleeds	Bloodstone or haematite
Personality disorders	Peridot
Poisoning	Malachite, agate, diamond or chalcedony
Psoriasis	Aventurine
Rashes	Aventurine
Sinus problems	Aquamarine
Stomach problems	Beryl, bloodstone, jasper, moonstone or aquamarine
Swollen glands	Aquamarine
Taste improvement	Aquamarine, topaz or sapphire
Teething problems	Amber
Temper tantrums	Turquoise
Tension	Rock crystal, tourmaline, topaz or sapphire
Throat problems	Aquamarine, beryl, chrysoprase or pyrite
Tiredness	Rock crystal
Toothache	Malachite or aquamarine
Warts	Tourmalinated quartz

Which stone for which month?

Stones for attracting good influences are worn according to your star sign. These birthstones have their origin in the breastplates worn by ancient priests in the area now known as Israel. The breastplates featured four rows of jewels, three jewels to each row. The jewels represented the twelve months of the year and corresponded to the twelve signs of the zodiac. They are listed as follows.

JANUARY Garnet

FEBRUARY Amethyst

MARCH Bloodstone or aquamarine

APRIL Diamond

MAY Emerald

JUNE Pearl or moonstone

JULY Ruby

AUGUST Sardonyx or peridot

SEPTEMBER Sapphire

OCTOBER Opal or tourmaline

NOVEMBER Topaz

DECEMBER Turquoise or zircon

Magical symbols and shapes

In the following table, I list twelve items that have a magical power that's derived from their shape. You can buy a readymade item, but the item will have a more powerful effect if you make your own and impart some of your own power to it. Use any natural material, such as wood, clay, stone or wax.

ITEM	MAGICAL POWER
Acorn	A dried acorn is excellent for people who wish to maintain a youthful appearance.
Arrowhead	A stone arrowhead is a powerful force against evil spirits.
Bee	A bee's shape brings success in a business.
Beetle	A beetle brings money to its owner.
Cat	A black cat is the best-known good-luck charm.
Coin	A coin that bears the year of a leap year is very lucky, as is any coin you happen to find.
Egg	The egg is a powerful fertility charm.
Fish	It's said that a fish brings a large family.
Horseshoe	Hang a horseshoe over your bed for good luck.
Oak	Oak prevents any gossip about you from reaching your ears.
Pig	The pig is a potent bearer of fertility, and the boar protects its owner from the owner's enemies.
Serpent	A serpent brings long life and wisdom.